TOWARD
A HUMANISTIC CURRICULUM

TOWARD
A HUMANISTIC CURRICULUM

Duane Manning
Arizona State University

Harper & Row, Publishers
New York, Evanston, and London

To Mother,
who was my first and finest teacher,
and to my son,
for whom I wish a better world.

Contents

Preface

We are indebted to Russell Baker for his empathic account of
the good things that undone poor Gum.* Gumbacher wanted
to live and tried desperately to do everything just right, but
he was battered to death by the terrifying threats of the American health establishment. Although fried foods were one of
the great joys of his life, he gave them up to avoid fatal heart
seizure. Then he began to lose weight and was alarmed because
that was one of the seven deadly cancer signals. He had doubled
his milk consumption as a result of the suspected link between
brain tumor and tooth decay, but gave it up in the face of
warnings about his high level of cholesterol. He already felt
doomed from smoking two packs of cigarettes a day when he
read that just living in New York and breathing the air was
doubling his toxic intake. He took up jogging to correct the imbalance of a sedentary life, but so many joggers were dropping
dead in Central Park that he switched to swimming and soak-
ing up all that good sunshine and energy. Then the American
Cancer Society announced that exposure to sunshine was one
of the leading causes of skin cancer.

Every hopeful move that he made somehow betrayed him.

* Russell Baker, "The Good Things That Undone Poor Gum" *Life*,
August 15, 1969, p. 16b.

He installed refrigeration and developed air-conditioning syndrome. He was happily embarked upon a diet of increased fruits, vegetables, and fish products when he learned that biological magnification and the half-life of a dangerous pesticide had caused his body to accumulate a hazardous level of DDT.

What could Gumbacher do but die? He spent his last days soundlessly counting off the minutes he was deducting from his life with each egg, cigarette, or glass of milk, and watching the air pollution drift in from New Jersey.

Gumbacher did not die in vain. His case provided evidence that attempts to prolong life may be fatal. But, what of the schools? Will attempts to improve them be fatal, also? The teacher in America is warned by the psychologist that he must nurture the self-concept of youngsters and extricate them from the academic jungle. As he reaches out to perform his rescue mission he is attacked by the subject-matter specialists who see salvation as being inextricably bound up within their respective disciplines.

Some say his teaching is not relevant and that he should be doing something about sex education. Before his committee can even complete its study of what might be done about such a delicate matter, however, he has become the target of an organized torrent of abuse from the John Birch Society.

He is urged to try team teaching, differentiated staffing, and a unit on drug addiction. Then he is soundly denounced for experimenting with the schools. He cannot even withdraw now to the quiet shoals of the status quo without being contemptuously accused of doing nothing. This is one of the unforgivable failings, for as every semiliterate knows today, a person simply cannot remain in a fixed position; he either moves forward or deteriorates.

It is difficult for schools to avoid paralysis under such circumstances, but essential, of course, that they do so. Curriculum development means that one foot is on the ground and the other is going somewhere. It is hoped that the schools will keep surfacing with efforts to change, that they will continue to take their bearings, and that they will move courageously ahead with their many commendable efforts to give children a better tomorrow. A large part of that better tomorrow is to create an environment in which life is more human and authentic for everyone. That is what this book is about . . . *the humanizing of school living.* It plants one foot squarely on the many stable virtues of the schools as we have known them, but the other is going somewhere. It is moving deliberately and realistically toward a humanistic curriculum.

D. M.

There was a child went forth every day,
And the first object he looked upon
    and received with wonder, pity, love,
    or dread, that object he became,
And that object became part of him for the
    day, or a certain part of the day, or for
    many years, or stretching cycles of years.

Walt Whitman

Chapter

Humanistic
Schools

1

Chapter

Humanistic
Schools

1

Humanistic schools may be conceived as being totally different from anything that is currently known. This is an exciting prospect and it is to be hoped that sooner or later someone who has that dream will choose to share it. The conception to be developed here, however, is a more evolutionary one. It is the idea that interwoven in the good schools of the past and present are many commendable humanistic practices that can be gently extricated and shaped into a better place for children to learn. Such a school should constitute more than a mere sanctuary against the forces that tend to depersonalize school living, although that alone would be a very worthy contribution to what has always been regarded as the protective environment of the elementary school. It should be envisioned, additionally, as an instrumentality for helping to counteract those eroding forces and to restore the primacy of the human spirit.

The concept is intended to be a balanced and sensible one. Although the feelings and general well-being of the persons concerned are of central importance, matters relating to the nurture of the mind, as well as the sense of responsibility to others, receive an appropriate emphasis. The characteristics that follow constitute an image of such a school. They seek to interpret rather than to define, and collectively, they reflect a setting which moves realistically toward a humanistic school.

A Continuing Concern for Children

The humanistic school will not abandon its abiding concern for each child in its custody. It will not be deterred by the fact that persuasive voices ridicule the concept of the whole child, for it knows that this is what arrives at school. So, rather than retreat from its efforts to give each youngster a fair role in the total scheme of things, it becomes more resolute in its determination to do so.

Such a concern for children has many ramifications. It means identifying and developing their unique qualities, being responsive to their feelings and aspirations, and helping them to find in the curriculum a place where they can be comfortable, successful, and secure.

In an unbalanced or exaggerated emphasis this concern can lead to serious errors. It can generate unbridled permissiveness and the glorification of individuality over a concern for others. This is unrealistic and damaging. The child's individuality must have a thoughtful and gentle nurture, but it must also find outlet and expression within a society characterized by groups. The same basic concern that causes one to respect and prize individuality requires sensitivity and respect for the feelings and individuality of others as well. The enlightened school avoids this pitfall. It is not like the parent who pampers and spoils his children. It is more like the one who loves and respects them, but holds them accountable.

No school will be humanistic without such a concern, and no school with a claim to leadership will retreat. It will take a militant stand on this issue and it will say by word and by deed to all within the orbit of its influence:

This child is a precious thing. Try to know him well.
Bring him into your classroom as a loved and esteemed
member of the group. Respect him for what he is and
guide him to discover what he can do best. Help him to

*grow in wisdom and skill. Show him that he has within
him a capacity for greatness. Give him the will to touch
the stars. Protect him, and cherish him, and help him to
become his finest self.*

A Continuing Concern for a Democratic Way of Life

Along with a genuine concern for children, the humanistic
school shows an unmistakable concern for our way of life. It
seeks intelligently to reflect the finest elements of democratic
living in the fundamental operations of the school by giving
children a voice, assisting them to experience citizenship at increasing levels of maturity, and helping them as they move
through school to achieve a growing independence of thought
and action that is the hallmark of a free and powerful people.

As a microcosm of democracy it will not tolerate arbitrary
and unreasonable behavior from its administration and faculty
simply because they are adults. It will not stand for any form
of physical or mental brutality in its classrooms. It will not
allow a child to be hurt or to receive an inferior education because of the pigment in his skin. For it is an instrument of society, guided by a basic respect for human dignity, seeking to
reflect and perpetuate all that is best in our way of life. It
opens its doors, it opens its mind, it opens its heart, and it says
proudly:

*Take all of these children—Catholic and Jew, Negro
and white, ragged and rich, handicapped and gifted . . .
and teach them to respect and appreciate one another.
Help them look beyond their individual needs to consider
the common good. Help them to preserve their individ-
ualities, but to grow in their ability to enrich the quality
of group living. Show them a functioning model of justice,
and their role in a way of life which may elevate all
mankind.*

A Versatile Offense

A humanistic school looks at its wealth of human diversity and faces the challenge by bringing into play a selective and powerful array of ideas. Like a successful modern coach it has a versatile offense. In a complex problem such as grouping it is not limited to the single alternative of homogeneity versus heterogeneity for it has an expanded awareness of the concepts and practices which more nearly comprise a balanced approach. It has identified the elements which constitute an excellent system of reporting to parents. Its grasp of the nongraded school has advanced beyond a confused or nebulous view to a formulation of alternative models. It knows multiple approaches to the screening of content and to the teaching of any given area of the program. It knows how to capitalize upon the competencies of its faculty and how to offer a richer spectrum of challenges and opportunities for its gifted youngsters.

It is a school with sufficient resources in ideas that when one does not work it shifts easily and skillfully to another. With its adequate grasp of professional know-how it has the wherewithal to push ideas through to completion.

A Flexible and Enlightened Administration

A humanistic school cannot function without a flexible and enlightened administration that seeks creatively to implement the curriculum rather than to restrain it. It is an administration that properly regards itself as a servant rather than a master, as an arm of the total enterprise rather than a presiding judge. In too many schools the administration still suffers from inflated ego and impoverished insight.

In an age that cries out for relevance in education some administrators do not allow classes to take field trips. With all the scientific knowledge of human potentiality they still equip each room with thirty-five identical texts for each subject. In many schools throughout the nation teachers are exhorted to be creative and concomitantly required to order their supplies a year in advance. By some strange paradox of events the larger and more sophisticated the district becomes, the more it seems to produce written policies that restrict human freedom.

These anachronistic practices may have resulted in part from moving into the elementary principalship individuals who were not qualified for the job. Some communities have placed unsuccessful high school coaches in the principalship. There are many graduate schools where men frustrated in their basic vocational choice are preparing for the elementary school principalship although they lack depth of understanding as well as genuine interest in elementary education. Such factors tragically weaken the school. The principal should be a leader. His personal qualities of leadership should exist *in addition to his intimate understanding of the elementary school.* He can be a leader because of such understanding. How can anyone be a leader of an enterprise that he does not understand?

The school that is being sought simply cannot exist without a flexible and enlightened administration. Like an All-American quarterback, it knows when to gamble for long yardage and when to grind out a first down. Like a skillful expediter it knows how to circumvent and resolve the trifling obstacles that constantly stand in the way of innovation. Like a brilliant wartime commander, it knows how to hedgehop the many unimportant islands of activity and move in on the target. Without such masterminding the resources of the school mill around at cross purposes and never become effectively coordinated. This is no job for a vegetarian, an introverted scholar, an unsuccessful coach, or a "friend" of the school board. It is a job for a sensitive and aggressive humanist, for someone who is eminently successful in his work with children, his relations with adults, and his general professional performance.

Such persons are worth all that the community can pay them. Their salary should be equivalent to that of a United States senator, but there is not a single community in the nation that has had the wisdom to recognize this. When and if communities do wake up to the matter, they may substantially increase the incidence of that healthy breed of emerging young administrator who moves out of his office into the classroom, helping to plan and expedite the ideas of a creative faculty and community.

Personal-Social Goals

As in the case of any effective enterprise the humanistic school is goal-directed. The goals, however, must be those which improve the quality of life and are personally-socially oriented.

In the latter part of 1969, President Nixon decided that the United States should proceed with the development of the giant supersonic transport. Every previous generation of aircraft had been cheaper, safer, and more comfortable than the one before; but the SST as proposed was only faster. In this monstrous craft it was possible for passengers to be hurtled through the air more than twice as fast as before. The cheers for this decision came mainly from the manufacturers and the airlines. The plane as envisioned at the time of decision was known to create a sonic boom over a fifty-mile-wide corridor indiscriminately shattering windows, eardrums, and the serenity of everything within its reach. How did such a decision contribute to the quality of life? Like so many of the decisions of the fifties and sixties it reflected, consciously or unconsciously, a priority of technology over humanity. During those two decades man systematically poisoned and destroyed his environment to an extent that cannot be fully assessed. Lakes, streams, and air were dangerously polluted. Landscape and wildlife were irrevocably damaged and the upsetting of the balance of nature may even at this stage of the devastation prove to be irreversible. No one really knows how much harm has been done.

It is possible that a generation that had been thoughtfully immersed in an education emphasizing human values might not have allowed this blight, uglification, and poisoning of the environment to occur. Such a generation might have harnessed technology in such a way as to cleanse the streams and purify the air, in proper stewardship of two of the most precious gifts of the universe. Technical knowledge could have been utilized to assist rather than frustrate the balance of nature. Technology could have been conceived as being always subordinate to the well-being of the citizenry, and each technological decision might have been thoughtfully weighed in terms of its ultimate contribution to the quality of life. It is of course very late to do that now, but even more critical that it be done. That is one reason why the humanistic school is imperative.

What kind of goals does a school seek if it wishes to promote the good life under discussion? There are five to be interpreted here and each of them makes a distinct contribution to the kind of school sought. Collectively they add up to a concerted emphasis upon and contribution to the humanistic school.

Nurturing Creativity. A few years ago, when the poverty of Appalachia was first receiving national attention, a ten-year-old boy came up with a suggestion that would have cost the government nothing. His idea was that the United States Post Office should deliberately print a small number of flawed stamps which would be sold to the people of Appalachia for the regular price. These fortunate people could then sell the stamps as collector items for inflated prices and enjoy instant affluence. The post office, of course, did not choose to deliberately put such a blemish upon its record; but what a delightful and novel suggestion to a problem. One wishes that such a youngster might in later years make a career of government service and bring his creative thinking to bear upon some of the accumulated bureaucratic mess. In another instance relating to the postal service several citizens have suggested a way to put more zip into the zip code. As the reader perhaps knows, the zip code did not actually zip because the proportion of mail that was so addressed did not reach the percentage required to make it feasible. The citizens mentioned simply suggested differential rates. Letters mailed with the code would go for the regular rates and would presumably move faster. Letters mailed by those who were unwilling to include the zip code would still be processed, but would require a somewhat higher rate. In one simple stroke this suggestion would have increased the revenues for an arm of the government that constantly runs a deficit and would also have provided an incentive for more people to use the code.

These are small matters of course; but utilizing the ingenuity of people in bringing novel or creative solutions to bear upon individual and social problems is not a small matter. Such solutions are desperately needed on the critical problems of society. Poverty, crime, disease, drug addiction, race relations, environmental pollution, and other major concerns of the day will require all of the ingenuity that can be mobilized. The creativity which exists among a people in a free society is probably its most precious national resource. It is related to the survival of the society as well as to the enrichment and the refinement of the quality of life. Few goals would have a higher priority than nurturing this precious commodity with all of the means at a nation's command. Education in general is the best single instrumentality for this gentle nurture. Elementary education, in particular, has a very special role, for it is this segment of the schools that first receives a child and it is at this stage of his life that the twig is as green and susceptible to influence as it will be at any point in the organized program. The nurture of creativity is a priority goal for the humanistic school and will be discussed in greater detail in a subsequent chapter.

Developing Self-direction. America ran scared in its educational programs after Russia's initial space spectacular. Her concern was necessary and probably contributed to the splendid victory of being first to land a man on the moon. In such a dangerous world the nation must remain alert and competitive, but it should compete with its major adversary in the image of the American Eagle instead of the Russian Bear. The care and feeding of an eagle is different from that of a bear and requires a different curriculum. The mistake of imitation renders him inadequate as an eagle and even less adequate as a bear. Imitation is the surest road to tragedy.

Self-direction is the hallmark of a free people. Ideally it receives its initial nurture in the home, is extended and practiced in the schools, and flowers subsequently into enlightened citizenship and government. To what extent is the ideal of self-direction embraced by the schools? How widely is it practiced?

No one knows the answer to the above questions. Observation of schools confirms the belief that, by and large, such a philosophy either is not widely held, or bogs down in implementation. A study at Indiana University attempted to determine how much self-direction was functioning in two markedly contrasting twelve-year schools.[1] One school was identified with a philosophy of self-direction, and the other was not. The study focused upon the social studies portion of the curriculum on the assumption that this would be one of the most logical places within the program to find the philosophy reflected. A technique to determine the ratio of pupil direction to teacher direction was used; the data were obtained for grades two, four, six, eight, ten, and twelve in each of the two schools.

The findings indicated that teacher-directiveness ranged from a ratio of 4 to 1, up to the most highly teacher-directed situation which was directive in the ratio of 90 to 1. The overall emphasis in the twelve situations observed was teacher-directed to the extent of 14 to 1. Perhaps the finding which was of greatest significance to this discussion was the one indicating that the amount of teacher-directiveness reflected in the schools tended to increase at advancing grade levels. In other words, younger children who are presumably less mature and less capable of assuming any significant degree of direction of their own school living reflected more self-direction than older children who are more mature and more capable of assuming that function. This is a most provocative finding and merits careful reflection. How can a society in which self-direction is so significantly imbedded in its way of life, justify educational experiences which seem to progressively limit freedom as the learners move through the program? To whatever extent the

[1] Duane Manning, "An Analysis of the Relative Directiveness of Instruction," Bulletin No. 2 (Bloomington: Indiana University Press, 1950), pp. 81–85.

findings of this study might reflect a general and more wide-spread pattern in schools, it would seem that the pattern should be deliberately reversed. The stakes are high and the need may be greater than is realized.

Helping to Forge Character. There is much ambivalence and confusion today concerning the proper role of the school in shaping character. Some indicate nostalgia for the past and the moral overtones of the McGuffey readers. Others contend that teachers have no right to impose their values upon children and that character education is more properly assigned to the home and the church.

In the first place, it is doubtful that adults can impose their views upon children. As in physics, every action has an equal reaction; and children seem to have a remarkable capacity to sift out and internalize whatever they wish to appropriate from the values and beliefs of adults.

Secondly, it is not the strong or even impassioned expression of beliefs which is wrong. What is wrong is the creation of a climate surrounding the exposition of a belief that discourages or denies disagreement with that belief. Someone who has spent a lifetime of study and reflection on a matter surely has an obligation to the learner to sift from his labors what he believes to be truth and to present it as his *present perception of truth*. If in so doing the teacher has built into the situation a freedom from fear to disagree and has additionally helped learners to know how to test and challenge the very belief that he has presented, then he has appropriately protected the learner and the morality of the situation.

Just as no teacher should feel the restriction of being unable to express any conviction for fear of imposing his views, so also should he be relieved of the ridiculous burden of feeling that he must give equal time to all theories regardless of their validity and value. The scientist, for instance, knows that the earth is not flat as the Australian bushman believes but that it is instead rather pear-shaped. To give equal time to the bushman's theory is surely misguided. It is not misguided to present the theory, nor to encourage in the friendliest type atmosphere any challenge to the pear-shaped theory that has been emphasized. Equal time to the students is desirable, but equal time in the exposition of unequal ideas is an undiscriminating concept that may retard personal development as well as the advancement of knowledge.

With respect to character development the humanistic school as conceived in this document accepts the obligation to help students forge character as being a necessary and vital goal. Schools will influence character whether they wish to do so or not. If they choose not to deal with the matter, they will affect it negatively by omission and default. If they do not even consider the question, their influence is likely to be unconscious and confused. If they enter the arena deliberately, their influence is open and subject to sensitive evaluation and refinement.

Moral values represent the distilled wisdom of a civilization. They constitute a viable and cohesive force in society that enables it to stay alive and to function. They may be wrong and are subject to challenge and change as the civilization matures, but they cannot be neglected. To omit them from the planned education of the young is to court disaster. At a time in which many believe that society is coming apart at the seams it becomes an even more critical matter.

The sincere belief that character education should be undertaken solely by the home and the church seems unrealistic. The church has contact with a very small segment of the young, for perhaps an hour a week. What is reasonable to expect from such minimal contact in an era in which institutionalized religion as the nation has known it may even cease to exist? And what of the homes? With the massive breakdown in communication between parents and their children, with the divorce rate approaching the rate of marriages, and with the tragic phenomenon of widespread drug addiction indicating perhaps a lack of influence in the home . . . what is reasonable to expect from this vital source?

The facts would seem to be that it is going to take all of the resources available to move forward on this front. Many resources are available in the schools that are not available to either the home or the church. There is also a less personal relationship in the school and students may feel free to discuss matters that are important to them with teachers when they cannot do so with their parents. To pass up this opportunity to help children forge moral values is an unwarranted and hazardous omission.

Achieving Intellectuality. Although the schools must generate a creative, self-managed, and moral environment they must strive for intellectual excellence as well. To know, to reason, to apply intelligence to improve the quality of life is self-fulfilling and humanistic in the finest sense of the word, for it benefits not only the individual but humanity as well.

In the past decade there has been a newly awakened interest in intellectuality. The movement has within it a vitality that can improve the metabolism of the schools. Properly directed it can have a healthy impact upon educational practices; improperly directed it can do irreparable harm. How should this worthy goal be sought in the schools of the seventies?

The power of released interest is still a high road in the development of intellectuality in a young child. An incident involving an eight-year-old boy provides a provocative example. He had received as a gift a small pamphlet of the United States presidents. For reasons best known to himself he was quite interested in this and studied it entirely of his own volition, without his parents even being aware of it. Later they were delighted to discover that he could name every president in sequence and give the dates for each. The boy experienced a delight and satisfaction in this self-appropriated learning that seemed to exceed any response to his formal learning in school up to that time. Retention was excellent and years later he still knew what he had learned.

One of the intriguing aspects of life is the fact that one cannot seem to find happiness by pursuing it directly. Happiness is more likely to occur as a by-product of being intensely and constructively involved in some other goal. Could it be that this is the nature of intellectuality as well? Have the schools of the sixties pursued it too directly as though children were vessels to be filled rather than lamps to be lighted? The decade just passed has witnessed a return to fact stuffing, the piling up of senseless tasks to perform, and an accelerated pace that deprives many children of the simple joys of being a child. Will this produce true intellectuality or snuff out the small aspiring flame?

The pursuit of intellectuality for a young child is more of a gentle than a rigorous process, more of a quest than a race, more a loosening than a tamping of the earth, and more an opening of the doors of the mind than the pages of an encyclopedia. Many practices currently used by the schools can have a real impact upon such an approach. Role playing in the social studies, inquiry learning in science, guided discovery in mathematics, the language experience approach to reading, and a host of other enlightened practices can contribute to effective intellectual nurture. Such practices should not be lost to the children of tomorrow. The devoted teachers who used them did so at some personal sacrifice because they had a larger and more splendid vision of their role. They knew that they should be teaching architecture rather than carpentry, and painting rather than color mixing. This is lamplighting . . . and may the tribe increase.

Maintaining a Humane Environment. The interpretation of this vital goal is extracted from the remarks of an earlier address which seemed to capture so well the intended spirit of this manuscript:

> *We are all aware of how we learn best through our own personal experiences. As we become older and move more deeply into life, we may even feel that from the piling-up of those experiences we have been able to extract a central truth. Simply stated, it is that I can feel good about every small act of kindness or compassion which I was able to show for a child, and have lived to regret every single negative act. I did not learn this soon enough, but am grateful to have learned it at all.*
>
> *This is not an easy world for the child any more than it is an easy world for you or for me. There is love in the world, but there is still much hate. There is limited peace in the world which is only another way of saying there is limited and volatile war. In an age of unimaginable overkill we plan for tomorrow with no assurance that we shall ever see it arrive. And so it is an uncertain world*

into which we have brought our children, and it is compounded by the fact that they are surrounded by a generation of insecure and uncertain adults.

We cannot directly change the nature of the world except through our personal reflections of the central truth.
Thus, I can say to myself that I will make a greater effort
to be humane. In a harsh world of too little kindness I
shall be kind. In a world that becomes too hurried and
impersonal, I shall show each child that I care. In a
world that seems riddled with anxiety, I shall find ways
to make my own classroom more secure. I cannot use a
system of grading that requires me to fail a child who has
done his very best, for in the protected environment of
the elementary school a child's best should surely be good
enough. I cannot use a system of grouping that places
children in fixed positions of superior and inferior roles,
for it is not only unnecessary, but grossly damaging to
their sense of personal worth. I will not restrict my program to a maze of verbal learnings at which only a few
can succeed, for this is not only unrealistic, but prevents
all children from becoming the most that they may become.

And I will fight against one of the great tragedies of
our times which is the steady erosion of childhood. So
many people today believe that the child must not waste
any time, and that each of his experiences must stand
the test of factualism and practicality. Garth Blackham,
of Arizona State University, said it best when he observed
that: ". . . Rumpelstiltkskin and Goldilocks are being replaced by Nurse Nancy and Mr. Fixit. Journeys to the
Land of Oz and the World of Pooh are being replaced by
trips to the airport and the sewage plant. The flopping
rag doll which did nothing and yet everything has given
way to the true life model which leaves nothing to the
imagination. And the transparent man with the removable
organs has replaced that ancient lead soldier." [2]
As a parent you may want your three-year old to learn
to read; I would rather have mine playing in his sand

[2] Unpublished remarks in an address to parents at the Payne Laboratory
School (Arizona State University, Tempe, Arizona).

*box. You may want your eight-year old to have his nose
buried in the new math before he turns out his light at
night; I would rather have mine reading* Stuart Little.
*You may want your ten-year old to take the Saturday
morning art class for gifted children; I would rather have
mine scuffling with his neighborhood playmates.*

*For in the mysterious phenomenon of becoming, there
is a time for things to take place. And if they do not take
place when they should, then the organism seems doomed
to reached out hungrily to satisfy that need for as long as
it lives. Real maturity is blocked, and the person who was
not allowed to be a child becomes a childish adult. Childhood is the time to live splendidly as a child, and if it is
denied we shall in the years to come pay a very exacting
price, for one must drink deeply of childhood if he is to
become a man.*[3]

Such is the formulation of the personal-social goals. Each of
them is believed to be highly relevant to the larger task, compatible with one another, specific enough to provide concerted
emphasis toward the school desired, and globular enough to
avoid prescription and rigidity. Thus, the humanistic school
of tomorrow will move quietly forward to achieve a higher
level of true intellectuality because that is the proper business
of the schools. It will be humane because, after all, it is dealing with children and one must be allowed to really be a child
if he is ever to really be a man. It will make a new try for
creativity because, over and above its highly personal contribution to the quality of life, it may in the long run make the essential difference as to whether or not the society even continues to survive. It will nourish self-direction because this is the
chief instrumentality for reflecting and perfecting our way of
life. And it will help young people to forge character because
that makes possible the reflection of a way of life at ascending
levels of morality.

[3] From an unpublished address by the author, "What Is Worth Teaching?" (Elementary Education Conference, University of Wisconsin, River
Falls, Wisconsin, March 1964).

Chapter

Person-Oriented Design

2

Chapter

Person-
Oriented
Design

2

Curriculum design is the *superstructure* of curriculum organization. At its higher levels of quality or potentiality it is a structure that is developed with great sensitivity to internal and environmental needs. It is thus an *external manifestation of internal conditions.* The primary defect of most curriculum design lies in the tendency to reverse this process. In such instances, design is arbitrarily frozen or imposed; teachers and children are required to fit into it as best they can. An imposed or frozen design is an error in conception. *Curriculum design should serve teachers and learners rather than rule them.* It must be able to bend and adjust to internal needs. It should continue to serve a role as an overall type of organization that rightfully exercises controls and gives a quality of cohesiveness to the total school organism; but it must be flexible enough to adjust to those continuing classroom needs which require and merit change. *The problem is one of combining order with flexibility.*

The design of curriculum is regarded by many teachers as a remote consideration which does not relate itself in any important way to the teachers' work. Such an attitude is naive. Curriculum design affects children and teachers in highly important ways. The design may be so vague as to cause teachers to feel insecure in the performance of their job. It may, on the other hand, be so restrictive as to prevent them from providing experiences that are needed by their children. It may, additionally, be so confused that excellent advances at one level are negated at another. And it may be so misguided that it seeks to develop the mind as it brutalizes the spirit. Curriculum design is, therefore, an instrumentality which is intimately related to the purposes and quality of the program.

This discussion of design has two central purposes. One is to provide background for better understanding and perspective with regard to the possible choices of curriculum design. The second is to pull from present understandings some specific ideas that may be particularly desirable and necessary.

Designing Versus Design

Because curriculum design has often restricted teachers and children in a way that is detrimental to effective learning, some curriculum authorities have recently placed the idea of curriculum design in disrepute and have sought to replace it with the concept of designing. This would mean that a teacher would be relatively free from any preconceived curriculum plan and that she could thus sit down with a group of learners and cooperatively develop a learning environment designed to meet their needs. There is, no doubt, a definite advantage to this concept; a wise and skillful teacher might work with children in such a way that the curriculum could be close to their lives and be a genuinely worthwhile experience. The idea of an overall curriculum design, however, need not rule out the significant aspects of such an experience. It might instead actually provide for them. The broad aspects of an overall curriculum design operate as an orderly framework within which individual planning can better occur and also better relate to the efforts of others. Consequently, the cumulative effect of a six- or eight-year curriculum can be stronger. Care must be taken, however, not to make the planning too tight or there is no opportunity to do the fine tuning and adjusting that is a professional necessity for each group.

Subject Designs

Susan was a very intelligent and enlightened first year teacher. She accepted a job with the Mars School District and was well pleased with her salary and the general level of wealth of the community. One day early in September she went in to her principal to clear arrangements for her children to visit the local museum. Her principal, Mr. Black, questioned her sharply about her reasons for visiting the museum and told her he thought she could use her time to much better advantage within the classroom. He reminded her that the content of the curriculum was heavy in fifth grade and that the children would be doing well if they mastered all of their fifth grade texts. Susan thought Mr. Black was testing her. She pointed out that there were a number of items at the museum that were discussed in their unit on the early settlers and that she knew her children would enjoy and profit from seeing them. She added that she thought there were many things that children could learn outside of books. Mr. Black suddenly became cool. He told her not to go to the museum and terminated the conference. Susan was shocked and returned to her classroom. She made an effort that year to fit into and adjust to a philosophy that was foreign to her own. At the end of the year she resigned and became an airline stewardess.

Mr. Black is an extreme conservative in his educational views. He is sometimes known as an essentialist. He tends to spend a great deal of time in his office. His files and records are apt to be very accurate and well organized. He writes memoranda and bulletins to the teachers. He prides himself on being efficient. He keeps the machinery of his school functioning smoothly. He rarely gets into a classroom and knows very few of the children in his school. The children and teachers address him carefully and respectfully as Mr. Black.

Mr. Black's concept of the learning environment reflects what has ordinarily been called the subject curriculum. His views on the curriculum are as follows:

1. A curriculum should be organized into parts called subjects. Thus, children study geography, history, mathematics, etc.
2. The subjects should be arranged logically so that learnings at one level prepare the child for learnings at the next level. The content is largely preplanned by adults who best understand the subject matter.
3. The teacher's job is to cause children to master the subjects. The main focus should be upon the intellectual development of the child.
4. Methods of teaching are built largely around verbal activities. Questions, recitations, and lectures figure prominently in the teacher's direct contacts with children.
5. The teacher is the dominant and controlling figure in the classroom. He controls, directs, initiates, and brings to a close all classroom activities.
6. Books are the chief resource for learning. All children have a copy of the same book.
7. Memorization is the major indication of achievement. Thinking is largely an adult activity. Children should learn and memorize the many fine things that adults have already thought and written in books.
8. Tests are the chief source of information as to what a child has achieved. The results are mysteriously grouped into amounts of achievement and grades are assigned in accordance with the amounts.
9. Achievement is reported via report cards. Multiple types of achievement are jumbled together and reduced to symbols which are relatively meaningless. These symbols are then meticulously conveyed to parents.

Mr. Black represents a potent force in the elementary schools. No one knows how many Mr. Blacks inhabit the schools, but Susan could easily have identified his educational beliefs before she signed her contract if she had visited and observed his school. There are many shades and varieties of Mr. Blacks, and some are more extreme than others. In general, they reflect what educators have called the book-centered school.

The proponents of Mr. Black's school like it because they believe:

1. That subject matter is basic and enduring.
2. Such a curriculum is easily organized and presented.
3. Most teachers and parents understand it and prefer it.

Opponents of the subject curriculum contend that:

1. The learnings are too compartmentalized and fragmentary. There are too many little appendages floating around with no apparent body or relationship to one another.
2. The curriculum is too far from the learner. Ignoring the interests and purposes of the learner results in great loss to the curriculum.
3. The logical arrangement of content is not necessarily logical to the child and, therefore, becomes a relatively useless bundle for learning and use.
4. Subject matter organization is not related sensibly or appropriately to the natural functions of everyday living.
5. Subject curriculums do not develop habits of effective thinking, inasmuch as they reflect a belief that the thinking has already been done and the job of the learner is to memorize it.

Activity Designs

Susan could have had a job with the Fairview District. Fairview had a reputation for being progressive in its school practices. Mr. White, principal of one of the older schools in the district, had taken her through the school in the spring when she was considering the position. Fairview was not a new building, but the rooms were attractive and colorful with their displays of children's work. She remembered that the children brightened perceptibly and seemed pleased when Mr. White came into their room. He seemed to know most of the children by name. He was relaxed and friendly with them and showed a genuine interest in what they were doing.

Mr. White spent more than an hour with Susan that day, carefully showing her through the school He asked her to observe as they went into different rooms to see if she could tell what unit or center of interest was in process. In almost each room she was able to do so, for the reading, language, and creative activity blended together to indicate a major emphasis. She was especially impressed with the children's creative efforts. Their artwork was fresh and individualistic and seemed to reflect a child's world rather than a world of adults. From the appearance of the rooms she could see that the children pursued many different paths in their artwork instead of making thirty-five identical tulips.

Mr. White showed her the school gardens and explained how he felt they contributed to the academic learnings. A bus pulled up and unloaded thirty-five flushed six-year olds. Mr. White said that they had just returned from a trip to the zoo. Several mothers had accompanied them to assist the teacher with the trip.

It was a very pleasant morning for Susan. The teachers were friendly, the children were interested and responsive, and there was a wholesome atmosphere in the school. Susan would have preferred to teach at Fairview, but Mr. Black's district offered her $1000 a year more salary.

Some people call Mr. White a progressive. He does not spend much time in his office and, unlike Mr. Black, there are times when he cannot even find something in his files. He likes to know, however, what is going on in his classrooms. Mr. White believes that a school environment should be a relaxed and happy place where children can find many opportunities for development. His ideas stand in considerable contrast to those of Mr. Black. Mr. White's views of the curriculum may be summarized as follows:

1. A curriculum should be organized into centers of interest selected by children. Thus, children study the fireman, the circus, prehistoric animals, space travel, etc.

2. The centers of interest are arranged psychologically (logically from the point of view of the child). Pupil-purposing and planning today are the proper prerequisites for purposing and planning in the years to come. Information and skills will develop naturally in the process of pursuing one's genuine interests.

3. The teacher's job is to develop children along the broad lines of their present interests. The main focus is upon the total development of the child.

4. Problem-solving is the basic method. Teaching is largely a catalyst activity, functioning in such a manner as to develop in children the problem-solving approach.

5. The children are the dominant figures in the classroom. In growing measure they control, direct, and bring to a close their own learning experiences.

6. Firsthand experiences are the chief resources for learning. Books are used as references. Each child in the classroom might logically have a different book.

7. Creative expression is the major indication of achievement. Memorization is imitative and relatively unimportant. If children can become creative, memorization is inconsequential and will largely take care of itself.

8. Observation is the chief evaluative teachnique and is directed toward evidences of personal growth and change.

9. Achievement is reported in personalized descriptions of the child as a unique individual. Evidences of growth, barriers to growth, and unique strengths and weaknesses are described. The report is generally conveyed by letter or personal conference.

Mr. White is still a visible force in the elementary schools. No one knows how many Mr. Whites inhabit the schools, but there are probably more Mr. Blacks today than Mr. Whites. There are many shades and varieties of Mr. White, and some are more extreme than others. Some, for instance, believe a child should study or undertake only those aspects of the curriculum which he wishes to study. In general, they reflect what may be called the child-centered school.

The proponents of Mr. White's school like it for the following reasons:

1. Children are more interested in what they are doing because the curriculum belongs to them and is close to them.
2. Greater interest inspires more effort and personal growth.
3. Development of the children is along more functional lines such as purposing, thinking, planning, organizing, expediting, culminating, and evaluating.
4. Such a child-development approach results in a better integrated, better developed child, more capable of taking his place in a shifting and dynamic society.

Opponents of the activity curriculum contend that:

1. Such a curriculum has little organization. The neat, expeditious form of subject organization is cast aside with no suitable substitute.
2. There is no continuity of experience. Children flit from a little of this to a little of that, leaving wide and important gaps in their learning.
3. Such a to-do about things of the here and now does not adequately prepare children for the future.
4. The curriculum lacks a conscious social direction.

Core Designs

Mr. Grey is principal of a school employing the core curriculum. Mr. Grey is a somewhat new type. Although he has elements of both Mr. Black and Mr. White in his philosophical orientation, he has a central emphasis which differs from them both. His motivation has a constant and deliberate social direction. Like Mr. White he has a keen interest in children, but he is perhaps more of a sociologist. He does not believe that interests and purposes of children are the sole guides to learning experiences. He believes that they are important and he will try to identify and release them, but he will sift and channel them in such a way that they are directed specifically at the problems, the needs, and the aspirations of the culture. Whereas Mr. Black's school was book centered and Mr. White's school was child centered, Mr. Grey's school is life centered. Mr. Grey sees the curriculum as deliberately reflecting and embodying the major elements of the culture. It is a synthetically created segment of life itself.

Mr. Grey encourages his teachers to use problem-solving as a basic method, but expects the problem-solving to be keyed to and directed at the real social problems that exist. He goes beyond this in his beliefs, however. He sees the school as an instrument of leadership in social change. He would focus the curriculum on refining and improving the society itself. That is why he is often called a social reconstructionist. His school is not a passive and imitative organ like Mr. Black's, nor is it limited to using the community as a laboratory like Mr. White's. He aims to use the community as a laboratory for both discovery and improvement.

The compelling criterion for choices of learning centers or units of work in the pure type of core is whether the problem is socially significant. A second criterion for the selection of units or problems is sometimes added in the form of a question. Can anything be done about the problem by the class if they do study it? If no possible solution or contribution seems possible with respect to this class, then the problem may be reserved for a group that can act upon it.

Core curriculums will emphasize at the learner's level of maturity current social problems such as crime, urban sprawl, environmental pollution, drug addiction, and race relations. Teachers in a core program should ordinarily be well trained in the social studies, for this area of the curriculum often constitutes the core. Core theory generally reflects the following beliefs:

1. A curriculum should be organized around social problems or themes of social living. Thus, children study conservation, safety, production, inventions, etc.
2. The structure is fixed by broad social problems or themes of social living, such as making a living, governing ourselves, producing and distributing goods.

3. The teacher's job is to help children understand, adjust to, and constructively refine and improve their corner of the world.

4. Problem-solving is the basic method, but the problems must be socially oriented. Teaching is largely a catalyst activity functioning in such a manner as to develop in children the problem-solving approach.

5. Society and its needs and aspirations are the dominant consideration. Children and teachers work together cooperatively to help fulfill its needs.

6. Social problems from real life are the chief resources for learning. Books, pamphlets, films, etc., are supplementary. Life is the master text.

7. Improvement of the social problem or aspect of social living is the major indication of achievement. Purpose, attitudes, and effort are blended to achieve this end.

8. Observation is the chief evaluative technique, and is focused on children's constructive participation as members of a team.

9. Achievement is reported in personalized, descriptive statements of the child as a unique contributor to the group and his personal qualities as a socialized human being. Attitudes and performance with respect to qualities such as tolerance, suspended judgment, critical thinking, fair play, etc., may receive special attention.

Proponents of the core curriculum claim the following advantages:

1. The curriculum is more lifelike.

2. Being more lifelike it contributes more directly and significantly to the society it is designed to serve.

3. Its orientation is such that it may actually contribute to the improvement of the society itself.

Criticisms of the core curriculum often include the following:

1. The school is a conservative institution which best serves a society by perpetuating its culture rather than by actively initiating change.

2. Teachers ordinarily are not sufficiently well grounded in an understanding of their own culture to function effectively in this design.
3. The problem of organization and sequence in core design is difficult and has never been adequately resolved.

The Continuum Concept

It is possible to identify a number of alternatives in philosophy and structure of design, and to string them along a continuum from the most rigid form of a compartmentalized subject design to the most open form of an integrative process design, as indicated in Figure 1.

Thus, at the extreme right of the continuum, one would place what has come to be known as the separate-subjects curriculum. This is a very old and very tight form of organization, and is widely conceded to the most rigid form of the subject design. It has a kind of button-shoe image and has taken much ridicule and abuse from liberals who have tried for years to stone it out of existence. Apparently it has also a remarkable longevity and capacity to absorb abuse, for it is very much alive in schools all over the nation. It is true that in its purest form it is of limited value, for it tends to ignore interrelationships in learning. It would be foolish to claim, however, that good things cannot occur in separate subjects design, just as a number of good things undoubtedly occurred in those button shoes. An example of what it may look like in its arrangement of a daily program appears in the subject column of Figure 2.

The correlated curriculum introduces a slight relaxation or modification. The subject divisions remain substantially the same, but there is a conscious effort to develop what may be called limited reciprocal relationships. For instance, in the subject-type column of Figure 2, music follows history. The music teacher might select and teach those songs which were related to the history being studied at that time. In the same column spelling follows mathematics, and the spelling list could be deliberately altered to include some of the mathemat-

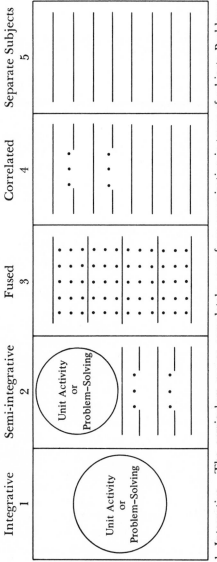

Integrative	Semi-integrative	Fused	Correlated	Separate Subjects
1	2	3	4	5

1. Integrative — The curriculum moves completely away from organization in terms of subjects. Problems or interdisciplinary units of work are studied, and the subjects are pulled into the learning as they are needed.

2. Semi-integrative — One segment freely crosses subject boundaries and establishes relationships among separate disciplines in problem-solving or unit activity. The remainder of the program may be as subject oriented as desired.

3. Fused — Subject boundaries for a broader field are preserved but relationships are stressed within that field or block of the program.

4. Correlated — Compartmentalized with minor natural relationships established between some of the subjects.

5. Separate Subjects — Completely compartmentalized.

Figure 1 A CONTINUUM CONCEPT OF ALTERNATIVES IN CURRICULUM DESIGN

Figure 2 EXAMPLES OF THE INFLUENCE OF TYPES OF CURRICULUM DESIGN ON DAILY PROGRAMS OR SCHEDULES

Subject Type	Block Type	Process Type
8:45–9:00 Opening Activities	8:45–9:15 Planning Period	8:45–9:15 Planning Period
9:00–9:40 Mathematics	9:15–10:25 Language Arts	9:15–11:40 Time Used as Planned
9:40–10:00 Spelling		
10:00–10:15 Recess		
10:15–10:45 Geography	10:25–10:40 Recess	
10:45–11:00 Handwriting	10:40–11:55 Social Studies	
11:00–11:40 History		
11:40–12:00 Music		11:40–12:00 Evaluation Period
12:00–1:00 Lunch	11:55–1:00 Lunch	12:00–1:00 Lunch
1:00–1:20 Current Events	1:00–2:00 Science and Health	1:00–1:15 Plan-Modification Period
1:20–2:00 English		
2:00–2:15 Recess	2:00–3:00 Creative Activities (Art, Music, Construction, Poetry, etc.)	1:45–2:40 Time Used as Planned
2:15–2:35 Health		2:40–3:00 Evaluation and Cleanup Period
2:35–3:00 Reading		

ical terms being used. Correlation of this nature is limited in scope and a relatively simple act to perform. Good teachers have been using correlation in this sense for many years, even if they did not know or apply the terminology to what they were doing. It is merely an effort to sensibly relate one part of the curriculum to another, without the necessity of changing the basic form of either. Insofar as the three pure types are concerned, the correlated curriculum is not a new type. It edges forward on the continuum, but it is only a somewhat less rigid form of the subject design. It is an option that seems to be well within the grasp of almost any professionally prepared person.

The subject-type column of Figure 2 can be substantially rearranged so that more homogeneous groupings appear. In other words spelling, handwriting, reading, and English could be grouped together into a block called the language arts. Geography, history, and civics might be grouped together into another block called the social studies. This pulls together like elements within a broad subject field, and is frequently identified as a fused curriculum. Portions of the curriculum which relate to the same subject field are brought together into a larger segment of the program, and the subparts within that block are deliberately taught in relationship to one another. This has the effect of carving the curriculum up into a smaller number of larger blocks of time and content and is reflected as a daily program in the center column of Figure 2. As in the case of the correlated curriculum, this should not be identified as a new type of curriculum design, for it is simply a more open form of the subject curriculum; it offers considerable latitude for exploring new combinations of content into units of instruction, the teaming of personnel, and the stressing of natural relationships within a given discipline. In terms of the professional competencies of most schools it can represent a fairly sizable step, and may be as far forward on the continuum as most schools are at the moment prepared to go.

Moving to the extreme left of the continuum one may select a form of curriculum organization which completely removes subject matter boundaries or divisions. Ragan calls this the integrative curriculum.[1] The integrative curriculum can be pursued either in terms of the pure type of core or activity designs as they were interpreted in the earlier discussion. There is a fundamental difference in emphasis between the activity and core, as one gives priority to the interests and purposes of children and the other emphasizes deliberate social direction. This distinction may be less basic in an elementary program inasmuch as many of their interests seem to grow out of social processes. Each alternative eliminates subject matter compartmentalization of the program, however, and capitalizes upon the relevance of life, the interests and well-being of the persons involved, and attention to meaningful problems or topics. The design places the person in his social setting first and subordinates knowledge to the role of a rich resource to be drawn upon as it can best serve human ends. Thus its orientation is humanistic.

Although subject matter plays a definitely subordinate role, its function is an important one, for each unit or problem draws naturally and logically upon the related disciplines. It is even conceivable that a curriculum design which deliberately reduces the primary focus upon knowledge might result in better attitudes toward it, as well as mastery of a greater quantitative amount. The manner in which this design is reflected in daily programming is indicated under the process heading of Figure 2.

In a conservative estimate of the current scene one may place the number of teachers who wish to function within the framework of an integrative design as less than 10 percent, and it may be even closer to 1 percent. It is not popular and probably calls for a higher level of professional competency, not only in terms of broadly based knowledge, but also in terms of teaching style. Admittedly, also, one must recognize that there can be too much of a good thing. With this in mind an intermediate point on the continuum of Figure 1 has been designated as a semi-integrative design. In this option teaching in one portion of the day may ignore subject matter boundaries and pursue the interest, the problem, or the unit

[1] William B. Ragan, *Modern Elementary Curriculum* (New York: Holt, Rinehart and Winston, 1966), p. 166.

of work with the same freedom as in the integrative design. In the other segment, one may unabashedly roll up his sleeves and go to work on the subject matter or academic discipline in any form desired, whether it be separate subject, correlated, or fused. These contrasting portions of the design do not need to be equal and may function in any proportion that personal style and circumstances seem to justify. If one hour a day satisfies the need for an integrative approach, then one hour is used. If half of the day is needed it is utilized. If some days require more time and others less, the arrangement should be flexible enough to accommodate varying distributions. Because of the day-by-day flexibility that is implied, the plan cannot function within a school that uses departmental organization. It seems feasible, however, for either self-contained classroom organization or for team teaching. The semi-integrative form may appeal to a considerably larger number of professional personnel than the completely integrative design. It gives free play to the instincts of those who have faith in the value of a discipline or subject and at the same time aids and abets a more limited approach to the integrative form.

Humanistic Factors

The background that has been developed indicates some of the major alternatives in a consideration of theoretical curriculum design. Professional personnel should have an awareness of such alternatives as a prerequisite to formulating their own programs. The discussion which follows is an attempt to identify and highlight some factors which should have special priority in moving toward a humanistic school.

Provision for Teaching Style. The overall framework of a curriculum should be some concrete reflection of the continuum concept. The reason for this is to provide a humanistic setting for the teachers involved. The design cannot be a pure subject, activity, or core simply because it does not fit the very people who must make it work. It is desirable for curriculum authorities to identify and interpret pure types of design and,

when the schools can produce pure types of teachers to man
the positions, the concept may become operational. Until then
the realistic and workable concept is to provide sufficient latitude so that each faculty member can take his place on the
continuum at whatever point he can work with greatest commitment and effectiveness. Furthermore, he should be able to
assume this approach to his job in an administrative climate of
complete respect for his philosophy and approach. If the administration of the school cannot give a teacher this solid basis
of support it should not employ him. The alternative to this
recommendation would seem to be a situation interlaced with
subtle or overt pressures to become something or to do something as a teacher that one may not wish to become or do. De-
ception, hypocrisy, loss of commitment, and frustration in the
development of one's unique teaching style are all by-products
of such a strained setting; children as well as adults lose in the
process.

The essence of this position is that if a teacher is the primary factor in determining the quality of the program, then he
must have the fullest possible opportunity to be effective. The
freedom and encouragement to function in terms of one's true
beliefs is an indispensable factor in that effectiveness. In the recent past, teachers even in rather sophisticated school districts
have been skillfully manipulated to adopt methods and approaches to which they felt unsuited and hostile. This was not
humane, professional, or wise. No form of design or method
of instruction can achieve optimum results without the com-
patibility and cooperation of the teacher involved. Even a less
effective method in the hands of an enthusiastic teacher is
likely to be more productive than a better method employed
by a teacher who does not believe in the approach and uses it
reluctantly.

The recommendation does not exclude the possibility of
clustering together teachers of a like philosophical orientation
into a setting in which a purer type of design is to be implemented. In favorable circumstances this may be a highly desirable choice. In the more typical and realistic setting, however,
diversity of belief and style should flourish and be respected.

Priority Content. Within the continuum framework some pre-determined elements of content should be pinned down for special emphasis and mastery, but the total amount of this would be sharply reduced. The designation "priority content" suggests that it is very selectively derived, and relatively basic for all children to learn.

First-level priority would be accorded those learnings which make the greatest contribution to the well-being of the individual and society. Thus, for example, matters relating to health and safety would transcend in importance a child's knowledge of the new math. The child may live a vital and useful life without learning to compute in bases other than ten; but, if for lack of knowledge he succumbs to a pusher in elementary school, his entire life may be adversely affected.

At a significant, but lesser, level of importance would be those knowledges and skills that have a high degree of relevance to the discipline itself. Thus the recognized subjects within the present scope of elementary programs would continue to be prominent, but the total amount might be radically pruned to its more essential elements. This would have the effect of reducing the content burden felt so keenly by teachers and students and of creating time for more personal learning. One of the major complaints of person-oriented teachers is that the sheer content burden of a curriculum prevents them from identifying and carrying out more legitimate priorities. They cannot continue with "this rich and timely discussion" because they must push on. They cannot indulge the luxury of discovery learning for there is insufficient time. They cannot really listen to children and be responsive to the yearnings of the human heart, for two hundred years of conditioning to the sacredness of content-to-be-learned propels them relentlessly onward. So a blight sets in and children learn to tune out and to regard education as being something that is less personally important to them.

The act of reducing the content burden will not in itself automatically produce these other vital uses of teaching time, but it is a necessary prerequisite in moving toward them. It is important that this be incorporated into any written philoso-

phy of a school with something akin to constitutional importance. Otherwise those who wish to take refuge in the sanctuary of overwhelming content have a license to continue to
do so and the blight remains.

There are two other advantages that may accrue from the
quantitative reduction of required content. One is that the
content which remains has a better chance of being learned
because of its additional significance and emphasis. The other
is related to the articulation of the entire program. The
streamlined curriculum for each grade or level is more com-
prehensible to the entire faculty and has more chance for cumulative emphasis. The primary reason for this recommendation, however, is to create time, room, and general climate for
a sensitive and personal responsiveness to the persons concerned.

Optional Areas of Study. The time saved by reducing required content should be specifically reserved for optional
areas of study by each classroom; this, again, should be stated
within the curriculum guide. These optional areas of study
should be activities or learning experiences that have been
personally appropriated or selected by children and teachers
in the rooms concerned. They should be high in interest value
and should be characterized by a marked degree of freedom
with respect to what children and their teachers do with them
and about them. This builds flexibility into the design and
makes possible a reality and relevance that is particularly vital
in a rapidly changing society.

Within these areas an alert teacher does not need to wait for
the elaborate grinding out of officially approved curriculum
changes by the professional establishment. Presumably he has
been chosen as a faculty member because of his professional
competence. His competence and judgment are respected and
trusted. He is responsible for the end result of his actions, but
he is not placed in the demeaning position of getting several
layers of approval for the day-by-day performance of his role.
Lag factors may be sharply reduced under such an arrangement, creativity and innovation are enhanced, school becomes
a much more interesting slice of a child's life, and there is the

possibility of a much closer relationship between teachers and learners.

Although the nature of the learning experiences selected under such an option may be highly unusual, or even unconventional, one should not overlook the fact that conventional knowledges and wisdoms are in no sense neglected. They receive reasonable emphasis in the provisions for priority content. In fact optional areas of study may quite logically grow out of these conventional segments as enrichment activities or pursuits in depth of more challenging portions. They do not need to emerge in this manner, however, and may depart radically from such material. The essential point is that they be selected personally by the individuals concerned.

The margin of time for this aspect of the curriculum should be flexible, in consonance with the continuum concept and the acceptance of a variety of teaching styles. A creative, flexible, and resourceful teacher might use up to 50 percent of his total contact time on such learning experiences. Another good teacher with less flexibility and experience might use considerably less. Such variations are acceptable and desirable, but the built-in provision for this factor is to be regarded as an essential part of a humanistically conceived design.

Pupil-Teacher Planning. Within the optional areas of study the design should emphasize the desirability of faculty growth in its ability to *plan with children*. The optional areas can function in a somewhat limited fashion without this factor, but their full value and impact can be realized only if genuine pupil involvement is a part of the process.

It may be that one of the richest sources of change for the school of the future lies in the capacity of children to shape their own destiny. This is a factor that lies dormant in most schools, partially because of the pressure of events, but more largely because parents and schools have never really caught the vision of children becoming active and respected partners in their own education. Some seem to believe that planning is a function to be exercised only by the mature, but surely this ignores one of the processes by which one becomes mature. Presumably one becomes more mature by having opportuni-

ties to participate with growing intelligence and skill in functions relating to maturity. The act of planning is such a function. It is a real skill transcending in importance almost any
given school subject and able, when interwoven with it, to improve any given subject.

There is no intent to suggest here that such planning
should take place only in the optional areas of study, but
rather that it should take place at least within these areas.
The curriculum might be further improved by weaving elements of democratic planning throughout many aspects of the
school day, but this recommendation does not require that.
There are limits to the application of student involvement in
the affairs of the school just as there are in other social institutions. It is not desirable, for instance, to apply the principle of
one man, one vote to decisions made in the emergency room
at the hospital. There it is desirable for those who are most
qualified to make the decisions to get on with it. The writer is
willing to accept the assumption that, by and large, decisions
as to what should be taught in the disciplines are the logical
prerogative of those who know most about the disciplines. But
in many other areas of the child's life *he is the specialist*. He
alone may know what he needs, what he seeks, what he wishes
to become. The school must find a place in its program to listen to this, to respect it, and to nurture better than it has ever
done before the child's role in his own creation.

Problem-Solving. The design of a program should provide
ample opportunity for children to solve problems which are of
genuine concern to them as well as to adults. Perhaps it is
overly pretentious to use the term "problem-solving." In its intended sense, however, it does embrace the essential elements,
for it seeks primarily to develop in children a greater ability
to identify problems, collect data, formulate possible courses of
action, test hypotheses, and evaluate the results. Problem-solving is another process concept. Like genuine pupil-teacher
planning, it adds strength to the curriculum by bringing it
closer to the lives of children and by emphasizing another important life skill.

A school's view of problem-solving is likely to be heavily influenced by how it conceives of its central mission. Many schools apparently believe that their central mission is fulfilled by helping youngsters to learn the many fine things that others have thought. If this is indeed the central mission, problem-solving is less necessary and may even be a waste of time. Others believe that in the cognitive realm of the school's mission, the larger purpose is to help children develop the *power to learn*. To people of this persuasion problem-solving weighs in as an indispensable feature of the design.

The rich heritage of what has been thought in the past belongs in the education of the young and should receive its due emphasis in the priority content segment of the program. To restrict the function of the school to this more limited vision, however, is to compromise the future. Yesterday's solutions will not resolve tomorrow's problems. Every aspect of the social structure seems to be undergoing subtle or overt transformation. Marriage, religion, work, welfare, education, and even parenthood are in the process of very basic change. What can be seen is the fact that widespread change is occurring at an accelerated rate, but no one really knows what new forms are going to emerge. Knowledge of the past has much worth. It gives perspective, it reflects values, it provides a basis for deeper understanding of the emerging forms. It is not enough, however, and the young minds being formed in the schools of the seventies need something better than that. They need casting in a crucible that mobilizes all of its resources to make them open, inventive, resourceful, questing, and tough. Problem-solving has a distinct contribution to make to such an educational crucible and constitutes a more balanced preparation for life.

The point is that problem-solving in some form, and to some degree, is an integral part of an effective, modern, and humanistic design. It is a very flexible kind of factor in application. It can function as well within the priority-content segment of the curriculum as in the optional areas. In fact it probably makes a stronger contribution when it deliberately embraces two types: (1) problems that are important to children whether or not they are considered to be important by adults and (2) problems that are important to adults whether or not they are considered to be important by children. Problems of living obviously do not confront people merely on the basis of choice.

Vertical Flexibility. No design of curriculum can be effective or humanistic unless it makes realistic provision for the vertical placement of a child. This factor has greater significance for the knowledges and skills comprising priority content, but it affects other aspects of the child's school living as well and becomes a pervading influence upon the quality of what transpires. Succeeding portions of this book will deal with ways to help resolve the problem. There are, for instance, a number of provocative courses of action possible through grouping of students as well as through changing the organization to one or more of the models of a nongraded school. At this point, therefore, it is sufficient to simply identify a characteristic that must be an integral part of the design.

To clarify the problem in the language of child development one can say that nature in its wonder created children who constitute *infinite variation in a pattern of sameness.* Parents send this splendid mixed package to schools and the schools generally put them with children of their own age. When the teacher receives her bundle of six-year olds no one actually believes that they are all alike, but in most schools they may have the same curriculum. They receive the same books, cover the same terrain, and are expected to meet the same standards of achievement.

It is in the nature of things that differences widen rather than narrow as children progress through the school; and, so, as the children grow older the problem is compounded. Yet, as ten-year olds, they may still each receive the same book, cover the same ground, and be expected to meet comparable standards of achievement. There is an air of fantasy about the entire process. Schools know how markedly different children of the same age may be, they know that the system does not work, and they know how inefficient it is. Yet, they not only perpetuate the practice but feel guilty if they make sensible adjustments and deviations for children who desperately need them. Schools do make such adjustments, but they tend to be half measures taken often very reluctantly without having either the blessing or encouragement of the parents in the action. Thus the school may feel courageous in doing a simple and sensible thing or it may feel martyred that it was required to do so.

This narrow conception of grade level may well miss most of the children, for the number who are not up to a given grade level plus the number who do not need it exceeds the number who are properly placed. No one should underestimate the problem, for it is enormously complicated. By and large it is probably desirable to keep youngsters as much as possible with children of a similar behavior age and make vertical adjustments more commonplace for portions of their school day. The problem for curriculum design is to create a structure that makes this a regular rather than an irregular event and a simple, normal adjustment rather than one which must be achieved at cross purposes with the tone and organization of the school. It is important enough and difficult enough to require the mobilization of many of the resources of the school to achieve that end.

Planned Review and Action Program. The design and functioning of the program should be reviewed by teachers and children at least once a year. This review or evaluation might be appropriately held in the spring while the experiences of the past year are still fresh in everyone's mind. The basic question involved in this review is how the curriculum might be improved from the point of view of the children and teachers in each level or grade. Children should participate freely in this annual review with their teachers in each room prior to the formal airing of ideas. The stage should be set for the review in such a way as to encourage very candid discussion of the issues involved. The discussion should be chaired by an elected member of the group rather than by one of the status leaders of the school. Children should have a panel of discussants to present their views and should receive the same courtesy and respect as the adults. The meeting should be held during released time in surroundings as attractive and comfortable as the school can provide. Key administrative and supervisory personnel should be present as observers and should have an opportunity to react to the suggestions.

Ideas and recommendations from the planned curriculum review should be acted upon. The review cannot be a dynamic factor in the appraisal and improvement of curriculum design unless its ideas and efforts are to bear fruit. Nothing destroys the vitality and general level of morale in curriculum improvement more than the practice of actively soliciting ideas that are later politely ignored.

Acting upon an idea does not necessarily require its adoption throughout the entire system. Many ideas can be given a trial run in some portion of the system as a check on their merits. Such a trial run should be conducted by those who are primarily interested in its success and should be launched in a setting conducive to its success. A change in reporting to parents for example from letter grades to planned parent conferences might be tried as a pilot study in the school having the most interest in making such a change. It might also be limited initially to the parents of the six-year olds inasmuch as they are likely to be the youngest patrons of the school and the most responsive to change.

Action programs are indicative of a healthy learning environment and reveal the presence of a growth edge. Changes in practice are more likely to occur and to be maintained if they are a consequence of inquiry and assessment in which the affected parties are intimately involved. The thoughtful testing of ideas with a sharing of results is one of the more promising and stable paths to an improved curriculum design, and the manner in which it has been presented in this particular recommendation has a potentiality for humanizing the program. It puts the people first who should be first and creates a force which is more likely to produce design that is truly an external manifestation of internal needs.

Articulation. The design of a curriculum, whatever its form, should represent an articulated overall plan through which the learner can move from level to level smoothly, continuously, and with a minimum of institutionalized confusion. Articulation causes the beneficial aspects of curriculum to be cumulative and increases its total possible influence. If the interpretation of smooth, continuous progress is from the point of view of what happens to the learner, rather than the older notion of keeping the administrative machinery spotless, then the interpretation is humanistic.

Articulation is a multicolored cloth and can benefit from a number of different practices. At the content level it may be furthered by careful pruning and streamlining as interpreted in the discussion of priority content. This is additionally heightened by a telescoped review of the preceding year's work before one begins the current year, as well as a capsule view of the following year's work at the end of the year just completed. It is given a boost by continuous student and faculty involvement in assessing and revising the program, by the combination of pupil-teacher planning and optional areas of study which keep the program closer to the learners, and by sensitive vertical placement of youngsters as they experience their unique and uneven patterns of development throughout the program.

In a school that is going to respect diversity of philosophy and teaching style, some will contend that articulation is not a realistic expectation. No doubt there is truth in such a claim and some loss may accrue. Total articulation is never achieved, however, in any program devised. The position taken here is that whatever loss occurs as a result of the presence of diversity will be more than compensated for by the nature of a professional climate in which diversity is respected and secure. For it is the secure person who has within him the capacity and desire to reach out and help others experience the same benefit.

Chapter

Organizational
Flexibility

3

Chapter

Organizational Flexibility

3

One of the most baffling problems in elementary education is that of creating an organization simple enough to administer and yet realistic enough to cope with the wide spectrum of differences that children bring to school. Two of the educators who have done the most to illuminate and resolve the problem come quickly to the crux of the matter in discussing the child and Procrustean standards of the schools:

> Greek mythology tells us of the cruel robber Procrustes (the stretcher). When travelers sought his house for shelter, they were tied onto an iron bedstead. If the traveler was shorter than the bed, Procrustes stretched him out until he was the same length as the bed. If he was longer, his limbs were chopped off to make him fit. Procrustes shaped both short and tall until they were equally long and equally dead.[1]

It is true that many schools have seemed to be trying to make all children of a given age fit the same bed, but in their defense it should be recognized that they were given a rela-

[1] John I. Goodlad and Robert H. Anderson, *The Nongraded Elementary School* (New York: Harcourt, Brace & World, 1963), p. 1.

tively impossible task. Society handed them masses of children along with an implied obligation to provide individualized instruction. Even for capable and dedicated teachers it was an overwhelming burden. They tried valiantly to improvise materials and procedures that would more closely approximate the wide range of needs of their children, but still fell short of the goal.

In retrospect the goal was unrealistic for the era in which it was generated. With the limited resources for learning that were available to them, the less than supportive educational climate of the times, the organizational obstacles, and the sheer weight of numbers of children, it was not an attainable goal.

Today the prognosis is more favorable. Technology has vastly increased the possibilities for individualization of learning, there is in general a more enlightened and supportive educational climate, and the emerging organizational patterns have a better chance to thrive. The goal is still possible only in a relative sense or a matter of increased degree, but nevertheless its moment has more nearly arrived. It now seems feasible to implement flexible schemes of organization on a much wider scale than was envisioned heretofore, and it is still as necessary and desirable to do so. What is the case for organizational flexibility?

The case rests upon certain generalizations that can be rather easily verified by data already within the files of most schools. Authorities who have worked with such data would probably agree with each of the following points:

1. Children entering first grade already differ in mental age (an estimate of the mental capacity to learn) by at least three full years.
2. With exposure to the school's program their actual achievement soon approximates their capacity to learn.
3. The differences in achievement tend to widen as the children progress through school. By the time children complete fourth grade the range of mental age and achievement is approximately the same as the number designating the grade level. For instance, pupils in the

fourth grade may differ by as much as four years in mental age and achievement; in the fifth by five years, and in the sixth by six years.

4. The individual pattern of achievement for a given child in various areas of the program may show an equivalent range. A fifth grade youngster, for example, might range from fourth grade level in his lowest subject to ninth grade level of achievement in the area of study in which he does best.

As indicated in an earlier discussion on the overall design of the program, the current practice of organizing the school by grades may actually miss most of the pupils, as the number who are below level plus the number who are above level exceeds the number correctly placed. It does have the advantage of being simple to administer, but it is unsatisfactory and ineffective in very fundamental ways. The students who are at the bottom of the class in a given subject may be overpressured and even humiliated in their own eyes and those of their classmates. The possible damage to the self-image and to attitudes toward learning is considerable. On the other hand, the students who are at the top of the class in a given subject are insufficiently challenged and may be affected by boredom as well as by inflated and unwholesome notions about themselves. In addition, the system tends to give respectability to the myth that all children in a grade can work profitably on the same tasks and, thus, perpetuates Procrustean practices. Graded school organization continues to retard the progress of the schools and should give way to more flexible forms. These forms seem at the present time to be types that are called nongraded.

The Levels Plan

In theory all models of a nongraded school sweep away the rigid encumbrance of organization by grades and substitute something that is intended to be a more realistic and flexible arrangement. One form is known as the levels plan and is represented by Figure 3.

(9 months)		(9 months)	(9 months)	(9 months)			Level 1
6 months	3 mo | 3 mo	6 months	6 months	3 mo | 3 mo	6 months		through level 6 takes 36 months
Level 1	Level 2	Level 3	Level 4	Level 5	Level 6		

(9 months)	(9 months)	(9 months)	(9 months)	Kindergarten through third grade takes 36 months
Kindergarten	First Grade	Second Grade	Third Grade	

NOTE: A child who is progressing normally will spend 6 months on each level. Some may take more time — some less time depending on the rate of growth. Any level can be lengthened or shortened to meet the needs of the child whose rate of growth deviates from the majority of children. This type of organization prevents failure and repetition. Growth is continuous.

Figure 3 LEVELS COMPARED WITH CONVENTIONAL SCHOOL ORGANIZATION

The lower portion of Figure 3 shows a four-year interval of time divided into the four common segments of a graded school—kindergarten through third grade. Since each grade normally takes one school year and each school year ordinarily consists of nine months, the total time span is thirty-six months. The upper portion of the same figure shows how one of the simplest variations of a levels plan would redistribute the thirty-six months into six levels of six months each.

The plan functions in such a way as to provide several kinds of flexibility. The teacher in each classroom has children representing two levels. If a child assigned to level 1 is mature enough to profit from the somewhat more formal learning of level 2 and does not need the kindergarten experience of level 1, he may be immediately reassigned to level 2. Inasmuch as there are two levels in his room he does not need to change teachers or rooms but is simply reassigned within the same room and does the more advanced work of that level. If, on the other hand, the child is less mature and needs even more than the normal six months of the kindergarten experience provided in level 1, then the level may be extended to nine months to enable him to get off to a better start. The end result of such a plan is to *stretch the concept of what is normal progress.* It allows children who can complete the program without strain in less than four years to do so, and also allows those who need more than the four years, to have the additional time required. The plan seeks to follow the principle of continuous progress so that failure in its more conspicuous form is eliminated. It is true, of course, that some embarrassment to parents, as well as to children, occurs in instances in which children require more than four years to complete the program. The arrangement probably softens this embarrassment by making it somewhat less obvious, but does not eliminate it. Consequently, there is much time devoted to interpreting the program to parents each year and preparing those with children who need the additional time to understand and accept it.

The Primary-Intermediate Plan

A second model of the nongraded school is known as the primary-intermediate plan. This plan also seeks to remove some of the rigidities of the graded school but differs in some basic ways from the levels concept. Grade lines are removed and, in effect, are expanded to two major divisions of the elementary school designated as the primary and the intermediate departments.

When a child enters school at the age of six he is assigned to the primary department with other six-year olds. He is not in first grade, for there is no first grade, and the room to which he is assigned has some neutral designation such as "the six-year olds." The teacher in charge of such a group would be counseled somewhat as follows:

Here are your thirty children. They are all six, but they are all different. Your task is simply to accept them as they are and take them as far as they should go. There are no fixed expectations as to how much they are to accomplish, for this should be determined by the readiness and maturity of the group. Avoid pressuring them to undertake any learnings which seem beyond their present capacity, but allow them full opportunity to work at advanced levels if they have the ability to do so. Do not worry about whether the curriculum which evolves is more or less than is normally achieved by children in this first year of school. The amount of learning desired in this class is the amount that is appropriate for each child in your room.

Freed in this manner from formal expectations of a predetermined and fixed amount of content to be covered, or growth to be achieved, the teacher is in a position to be more responsive to children's needs. She has the opportunity and encouragement to create a learning environment that is just right for her group. The teacher who receives them next year as sevens has the responsibility of taking up where they left off and reflecting the same philosophy. Children are not retained at the end of their first or second year in the program but move on with their age group.

After three years in the primary department the school may set up a sort of check station for determining whether or not the child is ready to go on into the intermediate department. If, in the judgment of the teacher, the child is not considered ready for the more advanced work of that department, he may be held back for one or even two semesters of work in the primary department. There is a careful avoidance of the word failure at this point; the child and his parents are likely to be told that he has not completed his work. Theoretically, the child may advance flexibly into the intermediate department whenever his work has been satisfactorily completed. If it requires two full semesters to do the job, he has spent an additional year in the primary division and would ordinarily then be ten years old. It is, of course, important to anticipate such cases well in advance, and work closely with parents in keeping them informed.

The machinery of the intermediate division operates in the same manner. The child who has spent an extra year in the primary division would be ten, eleven, and twelve during his three years in the intermediate department. A similar check station functions in the third year of the intermediate division, and he might be held up for as much as another full year at this point before being advanced to the junior high school. As indicated in Figure 4, all children would be moved out of the elementary school at the age of thirteen on the assumption that their personality and needs can no longer be adequately provided for in the elementary school.

Five advantages are ordinarily claimed by those who favor the primary-intermediate plan:

1. *It reduces failure.* This seems true in a quantitative sense at least, for it may happen only at two points rather than at six. Obviously, however, removing the language of failure is not the equivalent of removing failure itself.
2. *It promotes continuity in learning.* There is some sup-

Figure 4

	The Graded Plan		The Primary-Intermediate Plan		
CL	Age	P.A.	CL	Age	P.A.
6	11	16–17		Check Station	13
				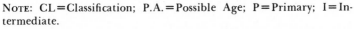	
5	10	14–15		11	12
			I	10	11
4	9	12–13		9	10
3	8	10–11		Check Station	9
2	7	8–9		8	
			P	7	
1	6	6–7		6	
Emphasizes: Standards Continuity of Teaching Minimum Goals			Emphasizes: Growth Patterns Continuity of Learning Child Development		

NOTE: CL=Classification; P.A.=Possible Age; P=Primary; I=Intermediate.

port for this claim in the sense that teachers are freed from the pressure of bringing all their children to a given point. The facts of human differences are more realistically accepted and teachers are thus in a position to adjust the curriculum to the group. There is, of course, no assurance that this will be done.

3. *It promotes pupil security.* This may be true in the sense that a child is not confronted with the yearly threat of being separated from his group. He becomes a member of a group and enjoys the security of remaining a part of it for at least three years.

4. *It is more compatible with known facts of child development.* There is some substance to this claim. Plateaus in learning are common to all children. They may be caused by shock, illness, injury, or simply by the process of catching up with oneself. If a child hits a plateau for a substantial portion of the year, he may be doomed to failure. The wider division of time in the primary-intermedi-

ate plan allows for both the plateau and the growth spurt which follows. This may allow a child to regain the growth which was lost for circumstances over which he had no control and to catch up with his group without ever being retained.

5. *It is more flexible in operation.* There is a definite possibility of more flexibility. As was pointed out earlier, the presence of grades stratifies the organization and tends to make a more rigid structure. The ungraded school has as much freedom of maneuver horizontally and more freedom vertically.

The primary-intermediate plan is provocative and potentially effective. It differs markedly from the levels plan at both the beginning and the end of the program. In the levels plan the program is stretched out in the beginning by extending the length of a level for an immature child. This has the effect of holding him back in the initial stages of his education in order to enrich his background, allow time for additional maturing, and to generally assist him in getting off to a good start. In the primary-intermediate arrangement such a child is moved on with the other members of his group; any holding back that occurs takes place at the conclusion of three full years in the primary department. The models do not necessarily differ in the grades which they encompass and replace. The levels plan can be extended up into the middle grades, and the primary-intermediate plan can be cut back to the primary division only. Either form of reorganization is applicable to the entire elementary school or to any given portion thereof.

The Multiage Plan

The least used, and most promising, of any of the plans in current use is the multiage model. As in the case of those already described, it is applicable to a portion of the older graded organization of the school, or to the entire graded structure. The plan is remarkably simple to initiate and to administer, for it can be implemented with a single teacher in a single school if that is the extent of the resources for change.

The essence of the plan is to put children of different chronological age in the same room with one or more teachers. For example, if one wishes to use the plan in a self-contained classroom with a single teacher the principal would assign her the usual number of children. Instead of thirty six-year olds, however, she would receive ten sixes, ten sevens, and ten eights, as indicated in Figure 5. She would also be assigned multilevel

Figure 5 THE SIMPLEST ARRANGEMENT FOR MULTIAGE GROUPING

(Envisioned as a self-contained classroom with a single teacher)

10 eight-year olds
10 seven-year olds
10 six-year olds

materials and, in an atmosphere of complete curricular freedom, would be encouraged to build a program that fitted the members of her total group.

Two inherent advantages are apparent in this model:

1. It is an excellent and effective way of providing for the variations in achievement that exist *within a given child.* An eight-year-old boy, for instance, who has not learned to read may work with the beginners in reading. He can do this without leaving his room and without being separated from the other children of his own age, except for that limited portion of the program. In other activities he may be participating with his fellow eights. This is a very significant advantage, for the arrangement shows more concern for the feelings of the child and avoids the humiliation of permanent placement with students that are much younger than he.

   Conversely, the child who is very bright and advanced enjoys a similar advantage. As a six-year old, he may

work with the sevens and eights in an area of strength
such as math or reading without physical separation from
other sixes. After all, even though his mental endowments
may place him above his peers, he is still a six-year-old
child and needs the emotional and social satisfactions that
he finds in their companionship. He can have this, plus
intellectual opportunity and nurture, without sacrificing
either.

2. In addition to the academic advantages the arrangement
offers the possibility for richer personal-social relationships. In effect, a youngster under such a plan experiences three sets of psychological relationships. He has
first the experience of being one of the youngest children
in the room. In his second year there are children in the
room who are younger than he, as well as some that are
still older. And, finally, in his third year he may have the
exalted feeling of being one of the senior members of the
group. This increases the opportunity to learn from one
another and adds new dimensions to learning. It offers
all of the advantages of cross-age grouping without administrative inconvenience or the involvement of other
teachers.

The multiage plan may be extended throughout the school
in a very interesting and effective manner by utilizing overlapping age groupings as indicated in Figure 6. In this arrangement one teacher has children with chronological ages of six,
seven, and eight; another has the ages of seven, eight, and
nine; the third has eight, nine, and ten; etc. Such a plan has
added flexibility in terms of optimum placement of a given
child. For instance, in the case of a very bright child who is
placed in the first age span, there is no difficulty in providing
intellectual opportunity in the first year of the experience, as
he may work occasionally with the sevens and eights. Even in
the second year, he still has possible stimulation from working
with the eights. During the second year, however, he may have
taken up the intellectual slack in the situation and need an
adjusted placement. If so, the second group which was initially composed of sevens, eights, and nines may represent a

more appropriate placement for him. Placing him in that second group does not remove him from children of his same chronological age, as the overlapping made provision for this. It does, however, place him again in a setting in which a third of the group is a year older than he and the remaining third is a full two years older. The individual adjustments can be applied to appropriate placement in terms of personality needs as well as intellectual challenge.

Teachers in general will probably be reluctant to undertake an assignment involving a three-year span of ages as interpreted in the multiage plans; if so, *it is unwise to require*

Figure 6 OVERLAPPING GROUPINGS IN A MULTIAGE PLAN

C.A.	T-1	T-2	T-3	T-4	T-5
12					10
11				10	10
10			10	10	10
9		10	10	10	
8	10	10	10		
7	10	10			
6	10				

NOTE: C.A.=Chronological Age of Children; T-1=Teacher 1.

them to do so. There are unusual opportunities for teaching in such a setting, but it cannot and should not be forced. It is the uncommon teacher who sees the possibilities inherent in cross-age relationships and desires to work in such an open and fluid classroom. This is the teacher who should be given a multiage assignment and then also given every possible material and psychological encouragement to make the venture a success. In addition to the multilevel materials that are essential, it seems justifiable, additionally, to reduce the size of the group by three to six students below the average load for the school.

Although no teachers should be required to participate in the plan, there should be some enlightened discussion about it. It is possible that the difficulties of working with a wider age span are grossly exaggerated by teachers. The range of differences even in the same grade are considerable and simply proceeding as though they did not exist creates strain for everyone concerned. It is at least conceivable that the mental hygiene of openly acknowledging and extending the differences, plus preparing to deal with them realistically, might even lighten one's total teaching load. Many educators believe that in some respects the one-room school of the past was the best setting for learning that has ever been conceived. The multiage plan is a miniature model of that one room school.

Middle Schools

Middle school is a fairly recent organizational concept and seems to be emerging as one of the more widely discussed types of change. It is a Humpty Dumpty kind of term and means what the user chooses it to mean. In general, however, it refers to a school that lies between elementary and high school and is thus envisioned as an *alternative to the junior high school.*

An alternative to the junior high school is considered desirable by many educators because of the degree to which it has imitated the sophistication of the senior high as well as its rigidity, its academic orientation, and its general lack of responsiveness to the personality and needs of the students. Murphy reports a description of such a school in Pittsburgh as follows:

> *The Middle School will exist as a school in its own right,*
> *free of the image of the senior high school and free*
> *to serve as an educational laboratory for the early adoles-*
> *cent. It would serve as a transitional phase between the*

paternalism of the neighborhood elementary school and the varied, departmentalized environment of the senior high school. The school would depart fundamentally from elements of the present junior high school which contribute to early sophistication and its undesirable by-products.[2]

Such a school would ordinarily be concerned with the education of children from the ages of ten to fourteen. In terms of graded schools it would serve as a replacement for the present designation of grades five through eight. This creates what is called a four-four-four organizational plan, as contrasted to the more familiar eight-four or six-three-three arrangements. Its basic motivation is to achieve for the middle grades the same flexibility and person-oriented kind of program that was interpreted for the levels, primary-intermediate, and multiage models previously discussed. It is not necessarily, therefore, a new model, for it may assume any of those nongraded forms that have been identified, as well as any unique form which better suits its purposes. What it does seem to add up to, however, is that middle school as an idea *is an upward extension of the basic concepts of the elementary school rather than a downward extension of the basic concepts of the high school.*

Although the nongraded form assumed by the middle school may be similar to the other models, it may be expected to make more extensive use of teaming and differentiated personnel. Teaming can be utilized appropriately in any of the models described, but probably has more justification and natural outlets at the middle and upper levels of the program where children are more mature and academic concepts are more advanced. Although teaming and nongrading are compatible concepts and practices, neither is contingent upon the other. A school may become nongraded with or without teaming, and it may use teaching teams with or without nongrading. This will be examined in more detail in the discussion of faculty utilization.

[2] Judith Murphy, *Middle Schools* (New York: Educational Facilities Laboratories), p. 7.

The Continuing Teacher Plan

In the event that circumstances within a school are such that no organizational revision seems feasible, it is possible to create additional flexibility on a more limited scale within the graded structure. One approach to this is known as the continuing teacher plan. All that is involved in such a plan is for a teacher to continue with her group of children for a second year. The chief advantage to this may be the feeling that one can do what is really best for each individual child in the room without worrying about possible criticism from the next teacher. In such an arrangement the teacher has two full years to carve out a humane and enlightened program for her children, and she will appropriately reduce the pressure upon some and speed others on their way. The plan assumes an excellent teacher who has good relationships, not only with the children, but with their parents as well.

An important dividend that accrues from the extended time with a group is that it allows the teacher to capitalize for another year upon what she already knows about each child. It may take half of a school year to learn what each youngster is like, what he can or cannot do, and how to work with him effectively. This priceless investment of time and energy can pay off much more handsomely by allowing the knowledge to be used for a longer period of time. In fact, some of the South American countries have been known to use the continuing teacher plan throughout the entire elementary program. This seems excessive, but it could under very favorable circumstances be extended to three years, which would mean that for all practical purposes the school had created a one-room ungraded primary department within a traditional graded school. The plan can be geared to the faculty of a given school. If there is more than one teacher who is well qualified for extended contacts with children, the program can be thoughtfully expanded. It should be recognized, also, that such an experience may be very beneficial to the teacher involved. Some fine teachers have taught the same grade level for years, and it is an exciting and valuable form of professional growth for many of them to continue with their group.

Humanistic Factors

The organization of a school must be supportive of its overall goals. To be supportive in a humanistic sense it must have the capacity to be sensitive and responsive to the vast range of abilities and the feelings of the children it serves. The criterion of adequacy for organization would seem to lie in the degree to which it allows each child to be simply and easily placed at the appropriate vertical point in each area of the program. Such a goal is idealistic, of course, and will not be attained completely in any form of organization as presently conceived.

Organizational innovations do help, however, and some of them seem more promising than others. The present graded structure of the schools is surely the least adequate of any of the models discussed. The graded school is not hopeless, however, and enlightened teachers can stretch the concept and philosophy of a "grade" in order to more adequately provide for the youngsters so assigned. Such stretching is against the grain of the administrative structure, however, and creates additional obstacles and strain for a dedicated teacher. The teacher who is so inclined deserves a form of organization that actually supports and facilitates her efforts. Each of the nongraded models seeks to give such support.

Some schools have extended the levels plan to twelve or fourteen specific levels within the first three or four years of the elementary program. Although it is admirable to try to expand the possibilities for vertical placement, there are two inherent dangers in the proliferation. One is that it tends to be based more solely upon reading and, therefore, fails to provide for appropriate placement in areas of the program that differ from reading achievement. The other is that the levels may become crystallized so that, in effect, the system has created multiple grades, or *grades within grades*. If such rigidity occurs, the system has moved backward rather than forward toward greater flexibility.

Goodlad has aptly interpreted the essence of a nongraded school as one which lowers the floor and raises the ceiling for achievement in each classroom. If this is the case, some additional plaudits should be reserved for the multiage model. It has infinite possibilities for flexible response to varying levels of achievement in all areas of the program, and it provides this with *maximum sensitivity and protection of the child's self-esteem*. At this stage of development in organizational plans, it seems to come closest to approximating the ideals and aspirations of the humanistic school.

Chapter

Faculty
Utilization

4

Chapter
Faculty
Utilization
4

The one-room school with its battered desks and potbellied stove has almost disappeared in America. Some mourn its passing, for it was a poignant symbol of life in rural America. There is no way of knowing how well it served. In this era genius flourished as in all eras and the nation experienced its share of moments of greatness. The schools themselves must have played some role in those achievements. There is a tendency, however, for a nation to overcriticize its schools in moments of crisis and to overeulogize them when they have moved on into the nostalgic past. Some of the recipients of that one-room education still bear their emotional scars, but others have generously attributed to it much of the motivation for whatever success they experienced in later years.

The assignment of faculty was a simple matter with each teacher taking over the entire operation. He not only assumed responsibility for teaching all of the subjects to all of the children in all of the grades, but frequently served as janitor as well. Some in later years even did related moonlighting by driving the bus. Faculty utilization was more of a total commitment reaching harshly even into one's personal life as indicated by the following page from the past:

Teachers each day will fill lamps, clean chimneys, and trim wicks. Each teacher will bring a bucket of water and scuttle of coal for the day's session. You may whittle nubs to the individual tastes of the pupil. Men teachers may take one evening each week for courting purposes, or two evenings a week if they go to church regularly. After ten hours of school, the teacher should spend the remaining time reading the Bible or other good books. Women teachers who marry or engage in unseemly conduct will be dismissed. Every teacher should lay aside from each pay, a goodly sum of his earnings for his benefit during his declining years, so that he will not become a burden on society. Any teacher who smokes, uses liquor in any form, frequents pool or public halls, or gets shaved in a barber shop will give good reason to suspect his worth, intentions, integrity, and honesty. The teacher who performs his labors faithfully and without fault for five years will be given an increase of 25 cents per week in his pay, providing the board of education approves.

The teacher of today may feel that there has not been a significant improvement. He has dispensed with his janitorial responsibilities but has picked up a number of other encumbrances so that he is not convinced it was a good trade. Somewhere along the way he began to receive larger numbers of children, as well as an expanding list of intraschool tasks. In addition to his teaching duties (which are always considerable) he may be expected to assume study hall, playground, or lunchroom supervision. He is frequently asked to coach, direct school plays, manage the safety patrol, and handle all manner of clerical duties and money collections. One teacher kept the following list of twenty-seven different collections and involvements in which she had been required to participate:

Book fees	Polio drive
Workbooks	Heart fund
Lunch money	Carnival tickets
Milk money	P.T.A. dinner tickets
School insurance program	Play tickets

Individual pictures	Operetta tickets
Group pictures	Party money
Red Cross	Cancer drive
Junior Red Cross	Muscular Dystrophy
United Fund	Thanksgiving baskets
P.T.A. dues	Christmas baskets
Clothing drive	School newspaper sales
School savings plan	School shows every Friday
T.B. drive	

The involvements above are only a part of the extra assignments that may occur. In addition to those a teacher is frequently called upon to assume many other ill-fitting community tasks which no one else is willing to undertake. He may be asked to conduct community drives, act as cubmaster, or teach church school. Some would welcome an opportunity to return to the potbellied stove and their uncomplicated custodial duties.

Although a teacher is now largely emancipated in a personal sense and his life out of school is his own concern, the unenlightened use of his school time and energies is still one of the stark realities of today. In fact, the misuse of a teacher's time is probably one of the great educational abuses of the century. A new day is emerging, however, and it promises to reduce the unwise exploitation and create a more truly professional use of teaching time.

Current Patterns of Utilization

The chief patterns of faculty utilization of the past fifty years have been known as the self-contained classroom, departmentalization, and team teaching. In the self-contained classroom one teacher assumes the responsibility for all, or almost all, of the program for a given group of children. Children spend their entire day with that teacher unless the school provides specialized instruction for areas such as music, art, physical education, or industrial arts. Even if such instruction is available, however, the self-contained classroom teacher does not have those periods free. He is in most schools required to be present as an observer or assistant and to provide follow-through instruction.

Departmentalization provides for some degree of specialization of the faculty in elementary schools by sending the students to different instructors in different rooms for portions of their school day. One teacher, for instance, might teach all of the math and science for the middle grades, while another would take all of the reading and language arts. Departmentalization does not *require* any cooperative planning among the teachers who work with the total number of children involved, and each faculty member may pursue his segment of the program independently.

Team teaching deliberately shatters the insulation of the teacher and strives to generate a real team effort. It is the result of two or more teachers assuming cooperative responsibility for the instructional program of the same group of children. As in the case of departmentalization, it provides for specialization of the teachers but does so within a cooperative framework which seeks to eliminate fragmented actions by members of the team. Teaming seems to transcend departmentalization, for it absorbs the advantages associated with the opportunity to specialize without the disadvantages of carving up unrelated portions of the school day. It is one of the most widely discussed of the current innovations and has been favorably received by schools and communities throughout the nation. Both teaming and the self-contained classroom will be more carefully examined for their potential contributions to a humanistic school.

The Self-contained Classroom

It became fashionable in the sixties for many members of the professional community to ridicule the self-contained classroom. Thus, one educator, presumably speaking as the voice of the NEA for Project Instruction, made derisive reference to it as the "self-contaminated classroom." Classrooms, of course, can be either illuminated or contaminated from within, as can

the profession, by action of some of its members. Obviously
this is a product of the personal influence of teachers rather
than the form of organization. Self-contamination, for instance, *might occur in multiples with teaming or departmentalization.* On a separate occasion another contemporary
leader spoke of the self-contained unit as "the mother-hen concept" in elementary education. Although it was so intended,
the latter remark is not necessarily derogatory, as mother hens
have a rather distinguished record with baby chicks.

Is the self-contained classroom indeed obsolete as a form of
school organization? Is it as defective and inadequate as it is
portrayed by its critics? The changing conditions of life do result in obsolescence for ways in which institutions have functioned, and reexamination is certainly necessary. What
strengths or advantages, if any, does this older form of faculty
utilization possess? Those who still believe in it would be inclined to defend it upon points similar to the following:

1. It is a more person-oriented arrangement. The teacher
   has one group of children for all or nearly all of the
   school day. Thus, he has an opportunity to observe them
   in a rich variety of situations, and can develop a deeper
   understanding of each. This understanding of each child
   is almost impossible to acquire if one is required to work
   with rotating groups for more limited periods of time.
2. The organizational arrangement provides more flexibility. This is possible because there is only one cook in the
   kitchen. The teacher is in complete charge, and can more
   freely and creatively function in terms of the teachable
   moment. If a given learning situation is rich and exciting, it can be simply and easily extended. If it is relatively unproductive, it can be shortened and delayed
   until a more opportune time. If response and ideas from
   the children point to a completely different use of energies, the leads can be followed. All of this can be done
   without upsetting the plans and lives of one's colleagues,
   for they are not involved. Changes can be immediate because they do not have to filter through committees or
   layers of other personnel. The more people there are in-

volved in day-by-day routine, the more complicated are the conditions for change.

3. There are more genuine opportunities to interrelate learnings and to achieve the advantages of correlation, fusion, or integration. Interrelationships in learnings are frequently so subtle that they cannot occur unless one person who has a grasp of the total program sees the opportunity to help expose and establish a meaningful cross-reference. Frequently, also, perfect timing is necessary to capitalize upon the relationship by utilizing the teachable moment. Both of these conditions are possible within the self-contained situation. Neither of the conditions is as likely to occur in departmentalization or teaming. In the latter arrangements no one has the total grasp and, if the right moment cannot be seized, something vital seems to be lost by the delay.

4. The planning which takes place is the kind that is more necessary and beneficial to the development of children. Planning which takes place within the self-contained unit can be genuine pupil-teacher planning. It can give a prominent role to children in each of the very basic functions of deciding what is to be done, how it is to be done, and how well it was accomplished. These are the kinds of pupil involvement that are intimately related to their progress toward maturity and self-management. There is no guarantee that such planning will take place within this setting, but the point is that it easily can. The planning that takes place in departmentalization and team teaching tends on the other hand to be logistical. The dominant considerations are who will do what, when, with what youngsters, in what space, and with what materials. The role of the youngsters in the planning is visibly reduced.

5. Self-contained classrooms provide the basis for a more satisfactory parent conferences. In a planned parent conference, which involves only one teacher, he is in a position to answer questions about the child's work in any of the significant areas of the program, because he works with the child in those areas. This is comforting to

the teacher and even more so to the parents. In multiple-instructor plans, however, the entire teaching team cannot sit down with each parent and the responsibility is divided. This means that questions may be raised that cannot be answered by the teacher conducting the conference. Referrals must be made, new conferences arranged, and time and additional trips are necessary. It is not an economical arrangement but, more significantly, the conference cannot fulfill its intent. The possibility of having the entire team made available for each conference is inordinately burdensome and time-consuming, and simply cannot be accomplished under present work loads of teachers. Perhaps other forms of reporting may be devised, but the planned parent conference, properly conducted, is one of the most effective single school practices of the past decades. It is most appropriate and compatible with the single-teacher plan.

6. The self-contained classroom is the best vehicle for expression of values that have always been regarded as central to elementary education. Some of these have already been interpreted. The closeness, the special opportunity for a single mind to observe and know a child in a variety of situuations over an extended period of time, the easy flexibility, the unique opportunity to interrelate learnings, and the rich accumulation of insights to record and report in meaningful form, are all dividends that accrue naturally from the situation. In addition, there seems to be a possibility for the achievement of wholeness and continuity in the single-teacher classroom that may not be as possible in other plans. There are certainly other worthwhile values that pertain to arrangements utilizing multiple instructors, but one should recognize that the particular values indicated have consistently ranked among those that are the most cherished in the education of young children.

From this perspective it would appear that the single classroom teacher with the appropriate personality and professional skill has a potential for cumulative impact upon a

(modestly sized) group that has no easy equivalent. The aban-
donment of a setting in which this teacher can best bestow his
gifts is justifiable only if there is impressive evidence of a superior way.

Team Teaching

The Lexington Team Teaching Program was launched in
1957 at Franklin School in Lexington, Massachusetts. It was
one of the earliest projects involving cooperative teaching and
became one of the most highly developed.[1] The personnel of
the Lexington schools, with the vital assistance of the Harvard
Graduate School of Education, did more than any other group
to make the term "team teaching" famous. The leadership of
Robert Anderson in that project has caused him to be widely
regarded as the father of team teaching.

It is a rather phenomenal achievement to attain in such a
relatively short period of time the degree of acceptance that
has been accorded team teaching. By the end of the sixties it
was not only one of the most prominently discussed innovations, but one of the most widely implemented as well. For
better or for worse, it has shaken up the profession and drastically altered patterns of faculty utilization. As a result of this
influence it deserves a very thoughtful assessment. Although it
is now a well-known education term, there are enough variations in form to require some additional clarification.

By definition, team teaching is the result of two or more
teachers cooperatively assuming responsibility for a significant
portion of the instructional program of the same group. The
teams can be horizontally selected as in the case of teachers
working with combined sections of the same grade or vertically formed by teachers working with combined sections of
different grades. The teams may function with informal leadership, in which case the assumption of a given responsibility
or role evolves according to the decisions of the group, or it

---

[1] Medill Bair and Richard G. Woodward, *Team Teaching in Action* (Boston: Houghton Mifflin, 1964), p. 15.

may be a formal type of hierarchical organization. In the latter there are status positions that are assigned to each team member. For instance, a team might be composed of the following in descending order of responsibility and importance:

A Team Leader
A Senior Teacher
A Regular Teacher
An Intern
A Teacher Aide

In addition, teams may vary considerably in size, as well as the manner in which they are formed. With respect to size, the smallest possible team would involve two teachers with responsibility for forty to sixty students. The team might be as large as eight or ten teachers working with as many as two to three hundred students. In forming teams within a school the decisions are frequently made by the administrative or supervisory personnel on the basis of complementing strengths and compatible personality factors. In other cases, teachers are allowed to form their own teams on the basis of their personal preferences, but also with consideration to pulling together complementing strengths. Schools may build their teams in almost any form desired, which is as it should be. The concept of teaming would seem to be maintained if the cooperative planning and utilization of teaching strengths is applied to the combined group. The following is an attempt to identify and personally assess some of the advantages that are claimed for this form of faculty utilization.

1. Team teaching is a more professionally stimulating endeavor for professional personnel. The basis for this claim is the idea that working in the presence of one's colleagues is more interesting and challenging than working with children only, as in a self-contained classroom. One has an opportunity to observe and learn from colleagues as they make their contributions in terms of their special teaching strengths; conversely, one tends to heighten his own preparation and efforts in order to do

well in the presence of his peers. There is surely some substance to this claim, but in analysis it provokes some interesting thoughts. Is it to be assumed that a teacher does not grow, does not do his best, and is not professionally stimulated unless he is being observed by other adults? Surely such an assumption suffers from some exaggeration. In addition, is it really true that team teaching provides this much opportunity for one person to do his thing, while others are free to relax and learn from his performance? If so, then too much time is being allocated to large group instruction; too much reliance is being placed upon telling, explaining, and showing; and too little use is being made of the teaching strengths of other members of the team and of the advantages of smaller group instruction.

2. Team teaching allows for the special teaching strengths of individuals to be spread over a larger segment of the student population. This assumes that any given teacher may have special gifts or forms of competence and that there are other aspects of his total performance in which he cannot do nearly as well. This is a valid and significant assumption, but it is diminished somewhat by differences in the ability to project. For instance, there are teachers at all levels from kindergarten to university who are very effective in a classroom situation with perhaps thirty students, but remarkably ineffective with large audiences. For some reason they simply do not come through or project as well. The essence of the advantage that is submitted, however, is an important one and schools will be improved in some proportion *to the degree to which they can bestow the sum of their teaching gifts upon the sum of the student population.*

3. Team teaching reduces the impact of the weak and ineffective teacher. This is a natural corollary to the point just made; for, to whatever extent the teaching strengths are more utilized, the weaknesses are proportionately diminished. It is a very important factor because in a self-contained classroom the exposure to a teacher is for the full school year. If the teacher is simply weak and

inept the results may be a lost year; if the teacher is hostile and ill, however, the damage may be incalculable. It is absolutely ridiculous to pretend that the profession has no incompetence or mental illness among its members. There are incompetent and disturbed lawyers, scientists, physicians, engineers, and teachers. These failings know no professional boundaries. It is more serious in teaching, however, for the exposures are mandatory, of prolonged duration, and occur at highly impressionable ages. It is unthinkable to expose children as a captive audience to an adult carrying an infectious disease and it should be equally unthinkable to expose them to someone who is mentally ill. The profession has defaulted in its obligation to its clientele in this sense, and it is a major factor in the impact of the schools. To whatever extent the schools fail to cleanse themselves in this regard, this claimed advantage for teaming remains one of the most persuasive.

4. Team teaching offers a better opportunity for children to identify with an adult. The thinking on this point is that: (1) it is important for a child to be able to identify with and respond to his teacher, (2) he is not able to do this with just any teacher to whom he might be assigned, and (3) an arrangement that exposes him to additional instructors multiplies his chances of success. Again, one can say that there is merit to the idea, but that it requires closer scrutiny. There is probably no hard evidence indicating that children are unable to learn from teachers with whom they cannot relate, but it is reasonable to assume that liking and responding to one's teacher heightens learning. It should be recognized, however, that a single-teacher classroom also has latitude in this regard. *If the school is willing to acknowledge and accept personality factors as being important in placement,* children can be assigned and reassigned in pursuit of a more acceptable environment for each youngster in the school. The official attitude toward this matter probably exceeds in importance the differences in organizational form.

5. Team teaching results in a more economical and effective use of instructional time. Instead of having to make the

same presentation to eight different groups, on eight different occasions, a single presentation can be made to the total combined group by a team member most qualified to do so. Time and energies that are saved by this format can then be devoted to small group instruction. This is one of the most interesting claims made by advocates of multiple instruction and merits several reactions.

a. Is it really true that a presentation to three hundred students is as effective as one that is made to thirty? Questions by students are sharply reduced or eliminated. The running dialogue and interaction between the teacher and students is less possible. The blown-up picture of the magnet which is thrown on the screen is surely inferior to the experience of handling and using one in the group of thirty. Such a presentation, as was indicated earlier, also reflects a belief in the value of telling, explaining, showing, or demonstrating—even though most educators attach a secondary importance to such forms of teaching.

b. Is it really true that all of the students are that much in need of the same thing? The adjustment of teaching to individual needs has been one of the major goals of the schools. Do the advocates of large group instruction believe there is sufficient commonality of need to justify such forms of mass instruction? If so, there may be no psychological reason for limiting the groups to three hundred, for dialogue, interaction, and group dynamics are nonexistent anyway. The consequences of extending this reasoning are provocative. If a group of three hundred is educationally sound for the reasons that are ordinarily advanced, then perhaps groups of three thousand or three million are even more so. As the audience gets larger, the selectivity and resources that can go into the presentation get richer. Physical groupings as such could be eliminated, and the presentation might take the form of a television spectacular beamed at every child of a given level of maturity in America. Each child might receive this portion of his education simultaneously whether he lived in a tree, a cave, the ghetto, or deep in the reservation. The savings in personnel could be enormous. Dealing in multiples of thirty, an audience of three million eliminates the need for one hundred thousand presentations per topic.

c. Is it really true that teaming saves teachers' precious teaching time? All of the team teachers who have discussed this with the writer have indicated that they seem to have less time. Bair and Woodward report the same reaction from the Lexington teachers who found the arrangement to be time-consuming and demanding.[2] Time is used differently, but it is doubtful if much is saved. There is more of what resembles committee work in the collaborative effort, and if one enjoys this then his satisfactions should be greatly enhanced. One of the well-known but meaningful jokes about such activity is that a camel is a horse designed by a committee. In teaching this can be detrimental, particularly if an individual's ideas must be continuously compromised so that his expression as a person and teacher cannot emerge in uniquely personal form.

Differentiated Staffing

One of the most revolutionary concepts under consideration today is the idea of differentiated staffing. It is not an essential corollary to team teaching in all of its forms, but would be a highly compatible and natural extension of the hierarchical model. It breaks sharply with the traditional belief that teachers can do all things and with the idea of a single salary schedule as well. It offers a way of emancipating teachers by changing and enlarging their roles, increasing their autonomy and decision-making power, and offering career advancement *within the classroom* itself.[3]

[2] *Ibid.*, p. 194.

[3] M. John Rand and Fenwick English, "Towards A Differentiated Teaching Staff," *Phi Delta Kappan*, January 1968, pp. 264–268.

Differentiation is at least three-dimensional, involving role, responsibility, and salary. The patterns vary from one plan to another, but they will ordinarily delineate at least four different roles and levels of responsibility as indicated in Figure 7. There is a distinction in salaries at each level, but the proponents of the plan do not concede that it is merit pay in disguise. Their reasoning is that upper levels have higher salaries because they carry heavier responsibilities. Inasmuch as one presumably rises to higher levels or responsibility on the basis of perceived merit, the distinction is somewhat blurred and is often a point of controversy.

Figure 7 DIFFERENTIATED TEACHER HIERARCHY

| $18,000 to $24,000 | CURRICULUM ASSOCIATE
Doctorate
twelve-month contract
nontenure position
minimum teaching responsibility 50% | 1/10 of staff |

| $12,000 to $18,000 | SENIOR TEACHER
M.A. typical
eleven-month contract
nontenure position
minimum teaching responsibility 80% | 1/5 of staff |

| $6,000 to $12,000 | STAFF TEACHER
B.A. typical
ten-month contract
tenure position[a]
full-time teaching responsibility | 7/10 of staff |

| | PARAPROFESSIONAL AIDES
nontenure position
responsibilities as assigned | |

[a]Tenure after satisfactory completion of probationary period.

The top level is regarded as the apex of professional advancement and is achieved by a relatively small proportion of the total personnel. It is identified in Figure 7 as the curriculum associate and requires very significant competencies and responsibilities. The role is interpreted as the *self-renewal unit* of the organization, with primary responsibility for introducing new concepts and ideas. Personnel selected for this level would be likely to have special strengths in human relations, as well as a grasp of curriculum and research. They would maintain sensitivity to the felt needs of the practitioners within the school and would translate research into practical instructional probes. The position functions within the total organizational structure as that of a classroom teacher with possible salaries rising above $20,000.

The senior teacher is a master practitioner and highly skilled diagnostician of the learning process. Depending upon the organizational features of the school, he would either head a subject group or be a team leader if team teaching is being utilized. He works closely with the principal in selection of personnel and in evaluating teaching performance. He is primarily responsible *for the application of educational innovations to the classroom* and spends approximately half of his day with students. His contract would probably extend beyond the regular school year to a total of ten or eleven months, and the top of his possible salary would approach the beginning salary of the curriculum associate.

The staff teacher is the professional who spends his full day as a teacher and performs the usual functions, except for one substantial change. He is relieved of the responsibility for non-teaching tasks which are taken over by various types of aides. He is employed for the regular school year, and the upper level of his salary is likely to be approximately 50 percent of the top salary of the curriculum associate. The staff teacher is in every sense a full professional, but one who simply may not care to assume responsibilities that go beyond that of being an excellent classroom teacher.

At the lower end of the hierarchy are the paraprofessionals who function as academic or technical assistants. Academic assistants might do limited teaching, grade papers, and supervise

activity or study centers. The educational technician types, du-
plicates materials, keep records, operates audio-visual equipment, and assumes other time-consuming clerical or technical
duties. The technician, however, has no teaching responsibilities. All of the paraprofessionals assume duties that are necessary, but somewhat peripheral to the central mission of teaching. Thus they make a significant contribution to the
preservation of teaching time for major teaching tasks. The
nature of their function is such that they do not have to be
full-fledged certificated personnel and do not have to be full-
time employees. This makes possible a very rich pool of valuable prospective aides. They can be drawn from the ranks of
mature seasoned housewives who have the interest and the
available time. The college population is a rich resource from
which to draw, and it is a valuable experience for the college
students as well. In addition to considerations of competencies
and skills, aides can be selected on the basis of cultural and
ethnic factors which help to round out the strengths of the
staff.

It is, of course, an understatement to say that differential
staffing is a provocative idea. The aspect of giving more autonomy and decision making to the teaching faculty is attractive. The various levels of administrative approval through
which ideas must presently filter in order to effect change is a
definite impediment to change. Administrators do not have
the time and sometimes also lack the kind of understanding
and style which enables them to be effective contributors to
the initiating of new concepts and ideas. This would be altered and improved by bringing this function clearly within
the authority and responsibility of the teaching staff.

Such emancipation is desirable and should make a marked
contribution to the climate for change. The breakthrough in
salaries is also highly commendable. Many good teachers have
abandoned the classroom and moved into administration even
though it did not reflect their first professional choice. It was
necessary to do so in order to advance in the profession and to
reach higher salary levels. In some instances, however, they
were excellent teachers who became rather ordinary administrators, for the competencies are not synonymous. Differentiated

staffing removes the necessity for doing this. It is surely true that differential salaries are justified, and the rationale of placing this on a level of responsibility basis rather than merit is a more feasible approach. There will be much dissent regarding this matter, and upon the hierarchical aspect as well. Nevertheless, the idea should be kept alive and tried out as a worthy probe.

Teacher Aides

Teacher aides were partially interpreted in discussing the paraprofessional level of differentiated staffing. The future of differentiated staffing is cloudy, but the case for aides is not a matter of controversy and can be considered independently of any particular form of faculty utilization. The Bay City Program, initiated by Superintendent Charles B. Park, was launched because of a shortage of classrooms and teachers. Their solution was to bring nonprofessional local people into the schools to assist the teachers.[4]

Prior to doing this, Bay City conducted a stopwatch survey to determine how much time the 137 teachers were actually spending on nonteaching tasks. The survey revealed that a teacher's priceless gift of ability to teach was being squandered on routine chores such as cleaning boards, monitoring lunchrooms and playgrounds, collecting numerous funds, and performing miscellaneous clerical duties. The total time spent on such daily activity ranged from an hour and fifteen minutes to an amazing four hours and nine minutes of the teacher's teaching day. There was an overall average loss of 26 percent which did not count nearly twelve hours a week of overtime work outside the classroom that was devoted to nonteaching chores.

The aides utilized at Bay City were the kind that could be found in almost any community, but the school officials were amazed at the number of excellent prospects that were interested and available. Eight of them were carefully selected on

[4] Arthur D. Morse, *Schools of Tomorrow—Today* (Garden City, New York: Doubleday, 1960), pp. 61–78.

the basis of interviews and those chosen were wholesome, enthusiastic people who had at least a high school education. Park preferred an enthusiastic high school graduate to a junior college graduate who had mildewed. No former teacher or trainee was considered.

Each aide was assigned to function as a definite subordinate to the teacher and to assist in the performance of peripheral tasks. Paramount in the project was the central purpose of freeing the teacher to teach. Some of the reported results were as follows: [5]

1. 48 percent less time was spent on nonprofessional chores.
2. 20 percent more time was spent on making assignments.
3. 100 percent more time was spent on lesson plans.
4. 27 percent more time was spent on individual help.
5. A full hour a day was added to recitations.
6. More time was spent on personal counseling.
7. A 20 percent sampling of parent attitudes toward the aide plan indicated that:
   a. 100 percent thought the children enjoyed school more.
   b. 83 percent thought the children had learned more.
   c. 100 percent voted for a continuation of the plan.
8. A survey of the attitudes of all of the sixth graders involved in the project indicated additionally that:
   a. All of them liked the idea.
   b. 94 percent thought that the teacher had helped them more.
   c. 83 percent believed that they had learned more.

The use of teacher aides seems to be increasing nationwide. There is a cost factor involved, of course, and the aides do increase total expenditures for the school unless it is deliberately offset by an increase in the number of pupils that are assigned to the teachers concerned. If one considers the value of aides in terms of the logic of the situation, there is no question about their worth. For what is involved is the idea of better utilization of the higher levels of teaching competence. In other words, using the figures from the Bay City experiment,

[5] *Ibid.*, pp. 75–76.

one is paying for 100 percent of the teachers' competency but is placing the person in the kind of situation where the average return can only be 74 percent. This is neither good management nor good economics. The school is paying for time at professional salary levels and receiving clerical and housekeeping performance in return. More significantly, however, it is the kind of factor which retards the development of the profession. Good teachers are lost each year because of the subprofessional duties they must assume, and excellent potential members of the profession are discouraged from becoming teachers. It is, in this sense, a critical matter that far transcends economic considerations, for it involves a kind of loss which is incalculable.

Humanistic Factors

This chapter has examined some of the principal forms of utilizing teachers in today's schools. A special look has been taken at the self-contained classroom, team teaching, differentiated staffing, and teacher aides. Obviously, many courses of action are open to the schools of this decade. What action should they take? What are the humanistic factors? The suggestions that follow can be categorized as an attempt at sensitive speculation about the matter. This speculation is based on the total circumstances as they are presently perceived and, of course, also upon the perspective and limitations of the observer. They are presented not as truth, but as ideas for the decision makers in any given school to consider.

The first suggestion is that some of the nation's educational leaders are in too big a hurry to bury the self-contained classroom. They have taken what seem to be small bits of scattered logic and woven them into an indictment that somehow seems to miss the truth. To this observer, the facts seem to be that some teachers are very adequate to the challenges and opportunities of being a generalist and that such teachers have done a magnificent job.

Critics of this older form of organization like to point out the hardship and impossibility of a teacher performing all of the roles required in the self-contained classroom. Yet, at the same time, they contend that greater challenge is one of the factors which will attract more promising members to the profession. Challenges according to this curious reasoning are apparently all right only if they are the ones proposed by the critics. Why not each to his own challenge? Why not accept and respect basic differences in teaching personality? Why not match teacher preferences and style with the patterns of organization through which they can make their best contributions. All educators are likely to have had the good fortune to witness at first hand the kind of teacher who can function splendidly in this setting and *wishes to continue to do so*. To deny this wish, to fail to respect it, to want to throw all of this away, is incredibly short sighted. The profession should have great pride in members who have taken such a difficult assignment and performed so well. It should encourage them to try teaming for a semester, but if a teacher is miscast in the new format and wishes to return to the old, that request should be honored.

The great resting place of overrated and expired educational ideas is full of practices that were once defended as ardently as teaming is defended by its illustrious advocates today. Thus, it is rather puzzling that in a relatively enlightened day so many competent people reflect the conviction that teaming is *the way*. One of the well-known advocates of team teaching, speaking at a national conference, said that a teacher who was not suited to teaming was "unfit to teach." This is an example of contemporary "nonthink." Some teachers by personality and style can make their best contribution in the setting of the self-contained classroom; others can make it as a member of a team. This difference does not make either of them superior to the other. The humanistic school should have enough imagination and diversity to allow and encourage both to function simultaneously.

A second humanistic recommendation is that the self-contained classroom be given a better chance for optimum performance by a significant increase in the use of aides. More money is going to be spent on schools no matter what changes are invoked, and this is an expenditure that can pay handsome returns. Paraprofessional aides can fit easily into the existing structure without major dislocations or loss of stability in the present ongoing enterprise. They can provide emancipation from the accumulated trivia that has been borne too long by an abused profession. It is a splendid investment also in the holding and recruiting of even more able members to the profession.

The cost of providing aides is comparatively reasonable. Teaming, for instance, generally increases a school's expenditures by about 10 percent. For this same amount of money a school can provide approximately three hours of clerical or technical assistance to each self-contained classroom each working day. The aides are long overdue and simply must come in order to create enlightened conditions of work, as well as to avoid the very formidable possibility of revolt from within.

The third suggestion has to do with teaming. This is a deserving option which has been good for education, and it should be encouraged. It should be encouraged, however, as *one of the desirable forms of change within a school, rather than as a sole form of faculty utilization.* Teaming probably does not have equal relevance at all levels of the program; as one moves up the educational ladder its contribution becomes more essential and valuable. In other words, its contribution is viewed here as being more appropriate in middle than in primary grades and even more appropriate in upper than middle. This is due in part to the relative difficulty of finding teachers who are sophisticated in all areas of the program as the academic difficulty increases at advancing levels; but it is also based upon the maturity and needs of the child. As suggested earlier, the mother hen concept *is more applicable to the young child.*

Teaming may have something in common with marriage, with perhaps less intensity and a somewhat comparable incidence of success. When it really works out and the members are harmoniously complementing one another, it seems to approach a quality of school living that is of great worth. If it does not work out and the situation deteriorates, it must be restructured or abandoned. The continued exploration of the dynamics in this approach should seek better answers to the basic question of who may best team with whom? Progress on this point seems to have been minimal. Until better answers are found the system that is used should be careful to avoid conditions in which members may be locked in. Easy withdrawal must be discouraged, but withdrawal must also remain possible.

The final suggestion is made somewhat reluctantly, for it is a predictably stormy course, but *differentiated staffing deserves an open mind*. It should be carefully explored in as unemotional a setting as possible. It is surely not true that teachers are all of the same value. Some selflessly give to their students all that they have to give, while others are merely present at the scene. Some reach deeply into their students' lives and cause them to aspire to be more than they would otherwise have wished to become, and others drive youngsters to a decision to quit school. Some are brilliant performers and others are relatively inept.

It is true that assessment is grossly imperfect and that efforts to relate it to salary have frequently produced end results that were detrimental to almost everyone concerned. The concept of a single salary schedule, however, was never basically sound. It is a lock-step arrangement for adults, and it has proved detrimental by giving protective sanctuary to mediocre performance and faint praise to its most distinguished members. Differentiated staffing will attempt to alleviate this in the context of levels of responsibility, rather than a merit which is so difficult to define. The approach deserves a very good try. If it can get started and established, it should be able to win increasing acceptance. Launching it should be attempted only from within the ranks of the teaching staff. It must evolve from them and be acceptable to them, for its success is completely dependent upon their attitudes and willingness to make it work. It is a doorway to greater emancipation and growth of the profession. The path may be so rocky and torturous that it must be abandoned, but it is worth the try.

Chapter

Internal
Organization
and
Management

5

Internal
Organization
and
Management

Even if one envisions a marked reduction in the present number of roles played by the teacher, those that remain must be organized and conducted in one manner or another. Such functions are interpreted here as internal management and three are selected for special scrutiny. They involve decisions relating to daily programming, unit teaching, and classroom guidance or discipline. There are so many possible points of emphasis to be developed in each of these functions that they must be deliberately screened and reduced. An attempt has been made, therefore, to pull out for consideration only those that are believed to be of more central importance to the humanistic concepts.

Criteria of Daily Programming

The basic curricular goal of daily programming is maximum utilization of time. This does not mean keeping the child constantly busy, for this would reduce general effectiveness as well as the quality of school living. One simply cannot pull on the oar all of the time nor should he do so. The pause between pulls is necessary and even improves the pull itself. Maximum utilization of time involves an enlightened and judicious look at the child's entire day to help insure realistic and wise use of time with concern for the well-being of everyone concerned. What are some of the guides to this aspect of the program? The following are believed to lie well within the context of an effective and humanistic school.

1. The Criterion of Targets. This criterion has to do with the process of involving students in the identification of special targets or tasks for the day. It is the idea of pulling out for particular attention any matters that were not completed the day before or any which seem to have shifted in their degree of importance so as to require a higher priority. Nancy may need to complete the time line, Mark may need to finish editing the class paper, Sally's group may need to make its appointment with the principal, and the class must finish its recommendations for changing the student council. The targets that are identified may be academic or nonacademic, but they are important enough to be pulled out for more immediate attention, and the students are significantly involved in the process. This idea probably serves at least two important functions in addition to the more selective utilization of the time. One is the idea of giving greater visibility to the school's goals, and the other is the act of making this a shared process.

2. The Criterion of Flexibility. Flexibility was provided for in the conception of overall curriculum design, and this is a specific application of that concept to the operation of the school day. Some carefully laid plans do not go well and are relatively ineffective at the moment of execution. This is inevitable and simply cannot be avoided. What can be avoided, however, is doggedly carrying on in spite of the lack of productivity. The common-sense response is simply to shorten or phase out the plan and wait for a more propitious time. By the same token, it is impossible to know in advance which activities are going to go so well that they may be logically extended and what rich new leads will develop spontaneously that can be profitably followed. The criterion of flexibility is reflected by showing sensitivity to such factors and making the daily adjustments that capitalize upon what is actually taking place. In a qualitative sense this criterion can make a considerable contribution to the goal of maximum utilization of time.

3. The Criterion of Variation. This is the criterion that is concerned with deliberately varying the rhythm of work and play, the use of large and small muscle activity, and the change from one kind of learning to another. The purpose is to keep energy levels high and fatigue low so that a more optimum use of energies can be achieved. In the old-fashioned school with screwed-down desks, teachers used to have youngsters stand in the aisles and do simple calisthenics at odd intervals during the day. The teacher did this when students seemed to need a change of pace that was not being provided for by the nature of the program. This criterion of daily programming seeks to provide for the idea *within the program itself.* Coming in from a rousing session on the playground is a relatively poor time to practice handwriting, but may be an appropriate occasion to hold a discussion or listen to a story. The criterion of variation is sensitive to mood and nuance and seeks imaginatively to sustain interest throughout the school day.

4. The Criterion of Balance. The criterion of balance has two meanings. One of the meanings is commonly recognized and accepted; the other is less recognized and is inclined to be used unconsciously if at all. The common interpretation is that of carving up the program in order to achieve balance by giving each area its designated portion of time. Thus, language arts may receive 50 percent of the day in the primary grades and be reduced to 35 percent in the middle grades. Math may receive only 10 percent of the time in primary grades and 20 percent in middle grades. Each part of the program receives a predetermined amount of time and emphasis; and this is a useful approach to balance. The uncommon meaning is designed to supplement and strengthen it. If, for instance, a given class of children had a teacher in third grade who was very creative but poor in math, the teacher may have unconsciously reflected this in her use of time. Thus, she may have done a great deal of fine work with creativity but have neglected math. The program for those children became unbalanced and the teacher who receives them next year should help restore the balance by providing additional time and emphasis for the neglected area. The criterion of balance is more realistic and effective when both meanings are consciously accepted and applied.

5. The Criterion of Routine. This is not ordinarily identified as a criterion and is somewhat more difficult to interpret. In order to make good use of their time and energies, children need to have a great deal of understanding about what comes next and how it operates. This enables them to fit into the process more intelligently and increases satisfaction in learning. Establishing a reasonable amount of sensible routine seems to facilitate this. In addition, it reduces the waste generated by some teachers in constantly explaining and presiding over matters that could be organized so simply and so well that they would function as routine. One first grade teacher spent time in the first few days of school helping her students understand all of the acceptable activities that were available to them during their free time. After the understandings were developed, the activities were identified on a large chart that also included each child's name. The functioning of the plan was admirably simple. As the teacher worked with a reading group, children might complete their seat work and be entitled to choose one of the indicated activities. In doing so, it was not necessary for them to get approval or interrupt their teacher. Each child simply went to the large chart, make a check mark after his name under the selected activity, and proceeded to paint at the easel, work at the science corner, or engage in any of the nine legitimate uses of his time. Even with six-year olds the plan functioned smoothly and well with savings in time, energies, and satisfactions to all concerned.

6. The Criterion of Self-direction. This criterion is closely related to the one above and builds upon it to effect an even greater contribution to the humanistic concept. The purpose is increased self-management and direction of children's school living. In the example given above, one small segment of the program has been organized by the teacher so effectively that it can be self-functioning. This is a start which needs to be systematically enlarged throughout the school year. After such a start has been made, a teacher can then select a second aspect of daily school living and attempt to organize it, also, in such a manner as to become ultimately self-functioning. As the year progresses each additional segment that can be shifted to self-management provides real experience and seasoning in an aspect of personal development, which is one of the central goals in a humanistic school. This element deserves to be consciously and systematically extended and is a logical factor to include in appraising one's own success in teaching. In other words, how much daily school living is self-managed by children at the end of a year as compared to the amount functioning at the beginning of the year?

7. The Criterion of Accomplishment. The application of this concept relates to the first criterion of targets. At the end of the day many modern teachers will take time to look back and make an inventory of accomplishments. Was the paper edited, the mural completed, the appointment made, and the council report readied? What were the achievements of the day? Such an assessment of special accomplishments has many advantages. It reflects continuity of purpose and feeds naturally into the identification of targets for the next day. It helps to keep children appropriately involved in the class proceedings, and it also carries a hidden dividend. All over America children may go home to the question from interested parents: "What did you learn in school today?" On too many occasions the question draws an unsatisfactory response. Children may not have sorted out things so that they have any informative reply or they may colorfully describe a playground fight or frothy incident which in no way accurately or justly depicts the events of the day. If the accomplishments have been brought to the surface, however, just before the youngsters go home, there is an excellent chance that some kind of accurate reporting will take place. Many parents really want to know what is going on in schools, and this is one of the ways in which communication can be improved. Enlightened schools have known for years that their best goodwill ambassadors are the children themselves. Here is an opportunity to improve the ambassador concept.

8. The Criterion of Satisfaction. Mary was a brilliant, humanistic teacher of a second grade. Her children had gone home for the day, and she was sitting at her desk thoughtfully looking over the room as though they were still there. The principal dropped in for a chat and, in spite of the erosions of inflation, offered "a penny for your thoughts." What she had been doing was silently reviewing the events of the day with respect to whether each child in her room had experienced some kind of satisfaction. If not, that became one of her special goals for tomorrow. This was a responsibility that she had conceived for herself, and it was built into her daily approach. Mary was a teacher in a million and her criterion of satisfaction for each child is an enormously difficult burden. Her thought, however, is beautiful and has great power. Teachers like Mary could almost single-handedly move the curriculum toward a humanistic school by applying this criterion.

In recent times the term "modular scheduling" has received attention and emphasis, particularly in high schools, junior high, and middle schools. Modular scheduling takes a standard unit of time called a module and allows teachers or teams of teachers to use any multiples of that unit in order to provide the amount of time needed for the activity that is under way. It is a way of achieving at upper, more rigid levels of education the same expression of flexibility that has been commonly accepted for the elementary program. Some schools have experimented, also, with letting students make out their own daily schedules, arranging modules for the day in whatever way seems beneficial to them. Such movements are highly desirable attempts to achieve greater flexibility, as well as experiences in self-management at upper, more rigid levels of the program. Their purpose is similar to the motivations for the

criteria of targets, flexibility, and self-direction commonly used
in the elementary schools and do not, therefore, require separate identification as additional concepts.

Supportive Unit Concepts

Unit teaching was once defended as staunchly and passion-
ately as some of its partisans defend team teaching today. A
teacher was either a believer or an unbeliever, and was either
in or out, depending upon his allegiance to the notion that
this was *the way*. Fortunately this fever has passed, and the
concept can be viewed more objectively. Stripped of its exaggerated pretensions it still weighs in, however, as a valuable
educational concept and practice.

The dictionary of educational terms defines a unit as an organization of various activities, experiences, and types of learning around a central problem or purpose developed cooperatively by a group of pupils under teacher leadership.[1] This
definition expresses some wishful thinking and is not necessarily true. It is still a unit whether or not it is developed cooperatively with the pupils; some kinds of units do not require this element at all. Definitions of units tend to be
somewhat wordy. The unit is a large learning situation and
can be adequately interpreted as the organization of learning
around a central idea or problem. Four terms may provide additional clarification:

1. *Subject-matter unit.* This is the kind of unit that brings
    together a predetermined segment of content in a prede-
    termined form and is generally prepared in advance.
    Pupil planning is considered to be unnecessary.
2. *Process unit.* This unit is not prepared in advance. It
    evolves or takes shape in a cooperative setting through
    pupil-teacher planning which determines its direction,
    its substance, and the manner of arriving at its goals. Pro-
    cess units and subject-matter units are antithetical con-
    cepts.

[1] Carter V. Good, *Dictionary of Education* (New York: McGraw-Hill, 1959),
p. 587.

3. *Resource units.* This unit brings together under a common theme a rich variety of ideas, materials, and suggested activities that is much broader and more extensive than any one would be expected to use. It is, as the name implies, a resource from which a teacher and students may draw whatever they choose. In effect it allows one teaching group to stand on the shoulders of what another has already done.
4. *Teaching unit.* This is what actually transpires in terms of what is selected or carried out from the total compilation of ideas in the resource unit above.

There are five rather basic ideas associated with unit teaching that have special relevance to the concepts and practices interpreted up to this point. Each of these ideas is regarded as being compatible and beneficial to the central theme, and they are cast in the form of the following suggestions:

1. The units should be based as much as possible upon practical themes or problems so that learnings have more relevance to the world as it is perceived by the students.
2. The learners should, to whatever extent is feasible, be actively and honestly involved in the development of the units. They should play an important role in selecting them, deciding what will be included in them, and how best to proceed.
3. The units should cut freely across subject-matter boundaries so that there is a greater opportunity to see how separate knowledges converge and interrelate.
4. The range of activities and general pursuits included within any unit should be as varied as possible, in order to more closely approximate the range of interests and competencies of the students involved.
5. The time factor should be adjusted to the unit functions that are to be served in two ways:
   a. By allowing for more or less time daily in terms of need.
   b. By altering programming to achieve more suitable blocks of time. For instance it is unnecessary, and

somewhat self-defeating, to teach a unit in science and a unit in social studies concomitantly. Instead of teaching each of the units for a six-week interval of time, the situation could be improved by doubling the time spent on the social studies unit for three weeks, and to follow that by a doubled budget of time for a three-week unit on science. Neither unit is deprived of its legitimate proportion of time, but the larger block that is available is better suited to the type of learnings sought in unit teaching.

Figure 8 is intended to summarize much of the above thinking. As indicated by the dotted lines, the teaching unit is arrived at by moving through the process portion of the figure at whatever degree of latitude or student involvement the teacher feels he can most effectively manage. In this sense it is compatible with the spirit of freedom of choice that was interpreted in the continuum concept of curriculum design.

Provocative Factors in Discipline

If a parent or teacher is confused about discipline today he is simply showing signs of normalcy. One would have to be alarmingly detached or insensitive to complacently assimilate the conflicting claims and testimony on this important topic. On the one hand, there are harsh voices urging a policy of get tough, use power, and conquer or else. On the other hand, one hears gentle voices pleading for more love and understanding and saying that there is no such thing as problem children—there are only children with problems. The hapless individual may meditate on the matter; and, being basically a humanitarian, he develops a feeling of great compassion for these youngsters with problems. Then one night they mug him in the park, or desecrate his home, or club his invalid grandmother, and shatter his illusions about the innate goodness that is said to reside in all youth.

It is still necessary to reflect love and understanding today even though it is more difficult to do so. As this is being writ-

Figure 8 UNIT TERMS AND CONCEPTS

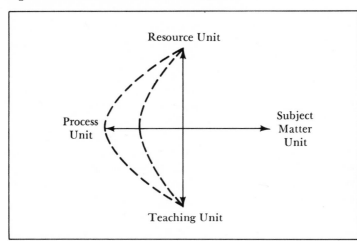

ten one of the weekly news magazines carries the following items: [2]

1. An assistant principal has his throat slashed at a school dance by a former student who came to make trouble.
2. A sixth grade teacher was stabbed by a twelve-year-old boy who had been spanked for attacking the teacher with a broken bottle.
3. Teachers in one system have become so terrified that three out of four are carrying guns to class.
4. Assaults against teachers are rising rapidly as indicated by the following:
   a. The teachers in one large system were attacked 1065 times last year—an eightfold increase in five years.
   b. In another large city assaults increased by 500 percent during the same period.
   c. Elementary students in a third city attacked their teachers eighty-three times in a five-month period.

The problems have been accentuated by desegregation, which in many instances has brought volatile ghetto students

[2] *Time,* November 14, 1969, p. 49.

into more decorous communities that did not know how to
cope with the situation. It is also one of the tragic ramifications of widespread drug addiction. Rousseau's dream of the
noble savage rightfully appealed to many who favored the relaxation of discipline and authority. As one looks realistically
at some of the juvenile gangsters and addicts today, however,
it is obvious that the concept is not applicable. Many of these
young people are not savage; they are depraved. When the
London police finally evicted a group of hippies from a building that had been brazenly occupied they found undescribable
litter, stench, and filth. The interior had been destroyed and
the walls were covered with the foulest possible obscenities.
And this element is one of the voices that cry out against what
they call a sick society proclaiming its intention to reform it.
Society does indeed have much sickness, but nothing makes it
look better than comparing it with the standards of some of
the would-be reformers. The world has not yet reached the
abysmal condition where its most rational alternative is to
turn the institutions over to the inmates.

Such elements have taken advantage of society and become
a malignancy. At this advanced stage of the cancer it is too
late for gentle voices to be effective. The application of soft-
ness to hardened young criminals may be as inadequate as the
hypothesis of the philosophical cat that roamed the jungle eat-
ing birds in order to become more birdlike. Naturally he did
not become more birdlike, but merely became a larger cat.

Some in a half-serious vein have suggested that teachers
should receive combat pay and it is conceivable that in some
areas this may come to pass. In general, however, teachers by
temperament and motivation are not well suited for such endeavor. Should society require them to perform their services
in a hostile and threatening environment? Can they reasonably be expected to do so? The intensification of factors that
may always have been present to some degree creates an entirely different setting for discipline today. Steps that were
philosophically untenable a decade ago may now have to be
taken.

In the meantime, there is a continuing responsibility for
conceptualizing and managing the task at hand. In the discussion which follows, discipline is viewed as the quality of

human relationships one is able to create in the classroom. Most teachers, of course, know a great deal about discipline, but even those who are richly experienced need to take their bearings frequently and refine their views. To that end the ideas which follow may be helpful. They bring to the deliberation of everyday matters some special considerations that may be of interest to all who are concerned with a humanistic school.

1. The Teachable Environment. It is a societal obligation to provide a safe environment for regular classroom teachers and to assign to the teacher children who are relatively educable. A child may be less well endowed intellectually and still be relatively educable as interpreted here. If, however, he is hostile and sick, the regular classroom teacher will probably be unable to provide the kind of situation that is required and attempts to do so may be detrimental to everyone involved.

A teacher is not an enforcement agent and does not wish to be one. In fact, such a role may represent the antithesis of true teaching. In the past, teachers have labored under the burden of taking anyone assigned to them by the administration. The student might be incorrigible, or even psychotic, but for the teacher there was little possibility of adjustment or appeal. In fact, the teacher has been deliberately made to feel inadequate if he did not believe he could handle such a child.

This is wrong and the situation is no longer defensible. There is no moral or educational justification for endangering a teacher and students by placing them in an environment that is hazardous because of the behavior of some of the members. What is at issue here is not the youthful pranks and occasional sass of yesterday, but the filth, the obscenities, and the violence of today. No system should tolerate this in its regular classrooms where teachers are equipped to do a very competent job of teaching but not to handle complex behavior disorders.

The ramifications of this suggestion are as follows:

1. A teacher has the professional obligation to try to reach all of the youngsters assigned to him and to make a reasonable effort to do so. If he cannot do so with any of the

children and those children endanger the safety or seriously disrupt the learning of others in the room, then they must be reassigned. Such reassignment is made upon the request of the teacher.

2. Upon such a request the principal will attempt to make a parallel assignment to another regular teacher, if he feels this has a possibility of success. If, on the other hand, he is convinced that the child concerned requires a specially tailored situation, he will then move to phase two of the process. Phase two involves placing the student in a therapeutic classroom within the school. The therapeutic classroom has a teacher who is equipped by interest and professional background to work with troubled students and elects to do so.

3. In the event that the therapeutic environment is not able to help the youngster, he is officially removed from the school and placed in the best clinical situation that the community is able to provide.

The suggestion as made lies within the context of a theory of differentiated staffing but constitutes a somewhat different application. In addition to structuring a more teachable situation for the regular faculty member, it has two other advantages. One is that it salvages the teaching-learning situation for the larger segment of the student population in any school who are there to learn; the other is that it provides a better focus and plan of rehabilitation for those who need more help than can be provided for them by teachers in a regular classroom. If such advantages can prevail, it is then humanistic in the very important sense of more effectively ministering to the well-being of all concerned.

2. The Role of Permissiveness. The healthy approach to discipline in a school will continue to allow students considerable individual freedom. One of the most provocative pieces of educational research was the four-year study of permissiveness carried out by the Columbia University Council for Research in the Social Sciences. This important study attempted to answer the question of whether it is better to grow up in a permissive or a strict home.[3]

A strict home had reference to the kind in which parents would feed babies on a regular schedule, insist on clean hands and good table manners, toilet train babies early, make children keep their possessions orderly, etc. The strict parent was interpreted as one who believed:

You should make your children form good habits and teach them definitely what is expected of them; good behavior should be approved and bad behavior punished.

A permissive home had reference to the kind in which parents would follow self-demand schedules with babies and later let children eat largely whenever and whatever they pleased. Toilet training was delayed until the child himself wanted it, and children were allowed to keep their toys as messy or as orderly as they wished. The permissive parent was interpreted as one who believed:

Children can well make most of their decisions for themselves, and parents should respect the child's developing inner self-direction. Children need freedom and their experience will tell them what works out well and what does not. They will naturally model themselves after their parents if they love them. Scolding and spanking do more harm than good.

In other words, the homes involved in the study were selected with the specific idea in mind of being in marked contrast to one another so far as permissiveness itself was concerned. Otherwise, the homes, whether strict or permissive, were good homes where children were wanted and received plenty of love. Care was taken not to confuse permissiveness with carelessness or strictness with harshness or cruelty. The study reports that it proved much easier to find very strict

[3] Goodwin Watson, "The Spoiled Child," *McCall's*, May 1958, pp. 33, 170, 172.

homes than very permissive ones. Finally, thirty-eight permissive homes were found to be acceptable and a matching number of strict homes were used.

The children were then turned over to psychologists for observation and study. The psychologists, of course, did not know which children were from which type of home. The following results were reported:

1. Children from the permissive homes were more creative than children from strict homes by a ratio of 7 to 1.
2. Children from permissive homes were found to be more independent and self-reliant by a ratio of 6 to 1.
3. The most socialized, cooperative, and best accepted youngsters came from permissive homes by a ratio of 3 to 1.
4. With respect to problem-solving, children from strict homes tended to quit prematurely on a difficult task or else to keep trying the same thing over and over again beyond the point of intelligence. By contrast, the children from permissive homes worked at a difficult task a reasonable length of time and then gave up. They were less likely to give up quickly and less likely to keep trying beyond the point of intelligence. They would try varied approaches until they had exhausted their repertoire and then give up instead of repeating moves that would not work.

How should a school interpret this research? It presents permissiveness in a most favorable light; for, if one were to deliberately set out to identify qualities more vital to our way of life than creativity, self-reliance, cooperation, and problem-solving, it would be difficult to come up with a more impressive list. Yet, permissiveness is widely maligned in almost every circle and every walk of life. Along with "togetherness" and "life-adjustment," it has been ridiculed and pilloried as one of the archvillains of the times.

Is permissiveness part of the rich, black soil that children need in order to grow? Is it, like sunshine, a basic ingredient that is necessary for one to become his best self? Many schools have already thrown permissiveness out of their curriculum, and others are preparing to do so. Perhaps they should take a second and more thoughtful look at the matter. The present reaction has created a mood in which there is danger of throwing out the baby with the bath. In a humanistic approach to discipline the sunlight of an enlightened permissiveness will continue to play a vital role.

3. Play Therapy. The humanistic school will use play therapy as an integral part of its total approach to discipline. This will be accomplished in two ways. It will function as an actual process in the therapeutic environment discussed in the first recommendation. In addition to this, however, the spirit and intent of the concept will be reflected in the regular classroom.

Play therapy is an arrangement which places a child in a specially planned setting where he can be more free. In this special environment of freedom he can be obscene, he can have tantrums and hurl himself on the floor, he can pull the head off a doll which resembles his baby sister, or take a dummy of his stepfather and beat it until it is limp. It is a deliberately created situation within which a disturbed youngster can externalize the feelings that have piled up inside of him. There are definite things that he cannot do. He cannot strike the therapist, or break windows, or abuse another child. But the boundaries of permissiveness are greatly extended in this special setting, and he is given as much latitude as it is possible to provide.

Such a process is a controlled form of permissiveness, for the deliberate extension of what the child may do takes place only in a particular place and at a prearranged time. Early experiences with play therapy indicated that a child who could externalize his feelings in such a session had less need to do so then in the remaining portions of his day. The direction of this kind of behavior would logically require professional competency in child guidance rather than in instructional fields, and the teacher of the therapeutic environment would be so prepared.

There is a second significant outlet, however, quite aside from play therapy as such. If one really understands the spirit and intent of the concept he can provide for it within the reg-

ular classroom without the need for special facilities. For the
curriculum itself has abundant opportunities for the expression of feelings if the teacher will use them. The outlets exist
in role playing, creative writing and play, puppetry, dramat-
ics, music, art, and dance. The opportunities need only to be
brought alive by a thoughtful and discerning teacher who
knows what it is all about. To the extent that this is done, it
should make a distinct contribution to the wholesome development of all children and perhaps even reduce the number
of those who need to be assigned to a therapeutic environment.

4. Faculty Interpersonal Exploration Experiences. The school
system should encourage and facilitate interpersonal exploration experiences for its faculty. It is highly unlikely that the
prior suggestions relating to freedom and expression of feelings for children can be implemented by faculty members who
are psychologically locked in. For many adults life represents
some degree of isolation and even alienation. They have
learned to conceal or disguise feelings and to act out a socially
acceptable role in life. In somewhat harsher terms they are a
role interacting with other roles or a mask meeting other
masks. Rogers points out that man is becoming aware for the
first time that this is not a necessary tragedy of life and that
one does not have to live out his days in this fashion. He is
reaching out to crack this shell and modify his existential
loneliness. The intensive group experience is one of the ways
of doing this, and Rogers regards it as perhaps the most significant social invention of the century.[4]

Several objections to involving faculty in such activity can
be anticipated. One of the most important concerns has to do
with whether the participants might become mentally disturbed. Serious stress and mental disturbance is very difficult
to measure, but the NTL Institute records suggest that fewer
than 1 percent of the participants develop significant problems
during training under the institute's auspices.[5] In almost all

---

[4] Carl R. Rogers, "U.S.A. 2000" (Paper presented at a symposium spon-
sored by the Esalen Institute, San Francisco, California, January 10, 1968).

[5] "News and Reports on Sensitivity Training" (NTL Institute, NEA,
1969).

such cases the individuals have had a history of serious prior disturbances. Interpersonal exploration experiences are not intended or practiced as a means of correcting serious psychological difficulties and persons needing psychotherapy should not participate.

A second objection has to do with the time involved. One has to evaluate time that is to be used in terms of the possible benefits that may be derived and these are potentially vital kinds of returns. Improving the ability to communicate and to externalize and accept the feelings of self and others is surely basic to sensitive teaching. It is also part of becoming more of a person. In addition, one must also weigh possible benefits against those of other time-consuming school activities such as faculty meetings and various forms of curriculum development. Such assessment may lead one to conclude that time for interpersonal exploration should be accorded a very high priority in the total scheduling of events.

5. Self-control and Self-rule. A humanistic school will continue to nurture and enlarge a healthy form of self-control and self-rule. In Jersild's study of the search for self, he found that many young people listed a lack of self-control as one of the characteristics which they disliked about themselves. He believed that they were showing the influence of a training designed to persuade them not to be emotional and that they were playing up to the ideal of being a strong, silent, dispassionate, and Spartan-like personality.[6]

In its best meaning, self-control is healthy and constructive —best if it means the ability to respond in a way that is appropriate and that one has at his command a good store of feeling for self and others. What is not generally recognized, however, is that *the more a person possesses such capacities for response the less need he has to control himself.*

Jersild believes that the idea of control in the form it often takes is false and morbid. One will keep a stiff upper lip, he will not give way, he will suffer in silence, he will not lose his temper. If he possesses this false notion of control he will not allow himself to weep in sorrow, or cry out in rage, or tremble

[6] Arthur T. Jersild, *In Search of Self* (New York: Bureau of Publications, Columbia University, 1952).

with fear, or shout with joy. If he is on the brink of an experience so charged with emotion that he could both laugh and
cry, he will catch himself and do neither. He must at all cost
put up a good front, always reply "fine" when someone asks
how he is, and always keep smiling.

To Jersild such a concept of emotional maturity is thread-
bare and pernicious. Maturity and control are not the same.
What passes for control of emotion is instead the absence of
emotion. Such a person has never grown up or matured in his
ability to relate himself wholeheartedly to others. One who
has curtailed his development in this manner has surrendered
to a stereotype and is taking part in a masquerade. He leads a
life so barren that he cannot weep with compassion, for he
feels none. He cannot rise in righteous anger in the face of
abuse, for he has surrendered his right to be angry.

Many teachers and parents seem to perpetuate this false and
unhealthy concept of control. The humanistic school will not
subject children to such an emotionally deprived setting. Instead, it will nourish self-control through the expression and
strengthening of appropriate emotional response. Emotionality
is a richly human trait that adds considerable meaning to
one's existence. Its expression should take place on an enlarged rather than a decreased portion of the spectrum. Of
course, the school will help children grow in their capacity to
exercise restraints; but it will not do so by an image that dries
up their emotional response.

The more common meaning of self-control as it applies to
schools is the idea of self-rule. Self-control in this sense is practiced in many good elementary schools by allowing children to
assume a more active role in developing their own rules of
conduct, as well as in making the rules work. In the hands of
an adequate teacher this is an effective approach. It is good
for children to have such involvement and experience in managing their own affairs, for it is in consonance with their way
of life. The school that can successfully involve children in
such self-rule is making a significant contribution to a person-
oriented school.

6. Authority. A new concept of authority is necessary in the
schools. If this is a world of permissiveness at home, play ther-

apy at school, and self-control in the classroom, where is the provision for the essential authority that is necessary to hold things together? How can parents or teachers control a situation so that the house will be livable, the trip to the museum orderly, and the schoolroom a place in which studying can be done? What can give to the adult voice the note of authority that produces attentive response, the indication that the person will be listened to and if necessary obeyed? This note of authority, says Margaret Mead, is absent from the nagging voice of the Cockney mother, and from the voice of the "enlightened" American father as well. Is it necessary to return to the old authoritarian, fear-enforced, hell and damnation type of control in order to get back the note of authority? Mead says it is not. The note of authority can come back, she says, with a difference. The adult voice can now say implicitly:

> *I am the person in charge of this situation, the person who will be held responsible if anything goes wrong, the person with the experience, the knowledge (or perhaps just the time) to take charge. I promise not to abuse my authority. But if you are to take part in this situation—at the dinner table, school expedition, picnic—you must obey those orders which I find it necessary to give.*[7]

Mead would have the individual say this without apology and with full recognition on the part of the adult that obedience is asked not in terms of the divine right of adults, but simply because "I am in charge." And, because it is the nature of situations involving children that someone in charge is needed, the person can speak clearly and without hesitation as a good policeman at a street corner, or a fireman at a fire, or the nurse in the doctor's office who says, "Come this way please." But the other side of the coin, the promise not to abuse the authority, is just as imperative. Policemen do not interrupt the crossing to demand that you take your fingers out of your mouth. The nurse does not interrupt your visit to request that you not hum under your breath. And the fireman

---

[7] Margaret Mead, "A New Kind of Discipline," *Parents' Magazine*, September 1959, p. 86.

does not criticize one's taste in art as he strips the paintings from the wall.

Mead believes that along with our rejection of fear and punishment as part of the adult authority system has also gone a rejection of the all-embracing kind of interference with life which many parents thought was their right.

> . . . to put a stop to fidgeting whenever and wherever they found it; to demand attention at every moment no matter how dull their conversation and how exquisite the day-dream on which the child's inner eye was fixed; to invade the child's life under a thousand small pretexts. The new authority note does not go one inch beyond the appropriate situation, . . . but in this one is only extending into the home what has always been an American attitude towards authority in the army and at work—a deep resentment of its exercise outside the proper limits. The revolution in child care in the last twenty-five years has been an attempt to state the limits and the tone of voice appropriate for teacher and parent.[8]

This is Margaret Mead's view of authority, beautifully expressed throughout and as sensible as umbrellas on a rainy day. It blows like a breath of fresh air through the psychological fallout that has clouded the thinking of many adults. The interpretation carves out a respectable and vital role for the mature experienced adult but does so without abusing or curtailing the development of the child. It is a sensitive and enlightened delineation of the appropriate disciplinary relationship that is sought in a humanistic school.

7. Creative Discipline. The school should encourage the use of more creative approaches to individual problems of discipline. Freddy was a wholesome and mischievous sixth-grade boy. He was a red-blooded, all-American type who fortunately grace elementary schools with their presence. The schools are infinitely richer because of the Freddies that roam the world,

---

[8] *Ibid.,* p. 87.

even though they make it much more difficult for the class-room to remain in the state of tranquility that many prefer. Freddy had an explosive temperment, and occasionally when tranquility had rested on his shoulders for too prolonged a pe-riod of time something would have to give.

Freddy's teacher understood his disposition and the two of them enjoyed a sturdy sort of relationship. He had taught the boy a great deal about athletics and seemed to appreciate the youngster's fine qualities as well as to realistically accept those that caused difficulty. He tried to be aware of when the pres-sures were building up so that he might release or head them off.

One day the class was having an excellent discussion when the teacher glanced over at Freddy and saw that he was about to erupt. His dilemma was that he did not want to do any-thing to interrupt the discussion, but it was necessary to avert the disturbance before it occurred. On an impulse he walked over to his desk and quickly wrote the following note:

Dear Freddy,
    Please do not cause me to come to grips with you today.
                                        Sincerely,
                                        Mr. Moore

He then quietly placed the note on Freddy's desk. Freddy un-folded and read the note. He smiled, then shifted unobtru-sively into the discussion and helped to move it along. A minor crisis was resolved and the discussion was a success.

The incident above may indicate one of the hallmarks of ex-cellent discipline. The approach that was used was *tailor-made to the circumstances, to the kind of boy that was involved, and to the kind of relationship that existed between the child and his teacher.* The technique could probably never be used again in quite the same manner with quite the same results, for it was creatively derived from the factors present in that particular situation. No teacher could achieve a constant state of discipline this individualized, but he can implement the de-gree which he is able to provide. It is a characteristic in disci-pline that reflects maturity as well as resourcefulness, and it is present to some degree in the discipline of any effective school.

8. Rules of Conduct. One of the significant measures of a humane school is the degree to which it can reduce the number of rules. If mankind were perfect, no rules or laws would be necessary. Inasmuch as man has not approached this state, there are rules for children as well as regulations and laws for adults. Rules are necessary, but they are frequently overdone. Movies have vividly portrayed the iron-willed captain of the ship with his impossible standards and his arbitrary domination of the crew. Each misdemeanor received its full measure of punishment, and if there was no regulation which adequately provided for the situation a new one was immediately invoked. By the time the ship approached its destination there were so many rules that the crew could hardly function at a human level of performance. It had been placed in a psychological kind of strait jacket and was almost incapacitated. Some classrooms reflect a similar climate and degree of incapacitation.

Rules exist in a given situation to the extent that enlightened behavior does not prevail, but they are a poor substitute for understanding itself. It is surely true that all schools and teachers might replace some of the rules that prevail in classrooms by helping children develop a better understanding of life, of relationships with others, and of the conditions which made a particular rule necessary.

A teacher might start with a base line of whatever rules currently exist and then work cooperatively with students to see which ones might be eliminated. The emphasis should be placed upon the best possible understanding of the circumstances leading to the rule and the kinds of behavior that are sought in order to discard it. Each qualitative improvement in classroom living that leads to the elimination of a rule should be regarded as a vital form of social development and a real triumph. Bit by bit and brick by brick, such a process contributes to the maturing and humanizing of both the child and the environment. Lao Tze captures some of this in the following provocative remarks:

After Nature was lost, one talked of character:
After character was lost, one talked of kindness:

After kindness was lost, one talked of righteousness:
After righteousness was lost, one talked of rules of conduct:
Now rules of conduct indicate the thinning out of the
   innate honesty of man.

Chapter
Improving
Content

6

Chapter

Improving
Content

6

A great deal of the student's time in school is taken up by exposure to different kinds of content. When one considers the material that is included in elementary social studies, science, mathematics, English, reading, spelling, and health, it adds up to a major portion of his school life. The content of subjects as represented by texts is selected from the vast store of facts, skills, ideas, and values that man has accumulated from all of his collective and specialized endeavors. As such it contains much that is worth while.

Schools have frequently exhibited a very interesting and humble attitude toward the content of texts, and it is one that can have a marked effect on the program. The attitude is one of uncritical acceptance of the entire material. This apparently reflects a belief that the content embodies some sort of perfection and that when the texts are chosen the task of content selection is completed. If such an attitude was ever justified because of the level of preparation of teachers, it is not justified today. The point of view is restrictive and narrow; in no sense of the word is it professionally conceived.

The Teacher's Professional Role

Texts are prepared by scholars who have some degree of competence in their special fields and may reflect their best efforts to sort out and present content that is of value. Any given text, however, represents a selection of material from all that man knows about the subject, and the finished product is a result of the personal judgment of the author. In actuality the material may range from excellent to poor and from relevance to irrelevance for a given individual or group. It is the legitimate and proper function of an enlightened teacher to sort it out and improve it.

Placing this function in the hands of the teacher improves the professional role. The author and the teacher are both professionals, and each may bring a different perspective to the task. The author of the material performs an important service in his initial screening and judgment. The teacher may appropriately regard this as a resource and point of departure. His personal judgment about the needs of his students and the community are sufficiently important to justify a very selective use of the material. He may refine, distill, delay, delete, or add to what the author has produced; it is entirely proper that he do so. In fact, it is improper if he does not. Straight teaching of a text without the exercise of one's personal judgment is a demeaning and lackey kind of role which does not fulfill the standards for a member of the profession.

Teachers will occasionally contend that in a given school they do not have the freedom to perform such a function; this is rarely true. It is true that there are marked differences in the amount of latitude provided by different schools. Ranging from most retrictive to most free, there are generally four levels of latitude in the schools as indicated:

1. *Text level.* At this level the teacher is given his texts and told in effect to teach them.
2. *Prescribed units level.* At this level certain units are prescribed for the students concerned, but there is some

additional freedom in the sense that what goes into each
of the units is regarded as the prerogative of the teacher.
3. *Optional units level.* This level accords a greater measure
of freedom by allowing choices in the units to be taught.
For instance, there may be nine possible units in science
from which the instructor may select any six.
4. *Areas level.* At this level of latitude one is simply assigned
an area of emphasis, such as community helpers, and is
permitted to choose from this area any units that he may
wish.

Even assuming that one is unfortunate enough to teach in a
school that reflects the rigidity of level one, he still has freedom to improve content as well as an obligation to do so.
This is due to the fact that the texts themselves need shaking
out. No group of children will learn all of a text, and the
most important elements of the material should be sifted out
for special emphasis. An optimistic estimate of the amount of
retention of a typical text by a typical group of children
would be less than 50 percent. This surely gives a teacher
room to maneuver within the text itself, in order to apply criteria of content improvement.

Criteria of Content Selection

The following discussion presents a way of performing this
professional function. Nine different criteria of content selection are interpreted. Each criterion constitutes a different basis
for judging whether or not a given item of content has value
for children. In their entirety, the nine criteria form a screening device composed of interrelated ideas which should be
helpful in taking a more thoughtful look at the content in any
area of the school program. The screening device is not envisioned as one in which a particular item must satisfy the requirements of each of the nine criteria. It seems reasonable,
however, to suggest that any given item to be included in the
program should make a demonstrable contribution to one or
more of the nine basic ideas.

1. The Criterion of Utility. The utility criterion has to do with usage; and, the more widely a given item of content is used in everyday living, the better the case for its inclusion in the curriculum. The selection of spelling words provides a good example of the application of this criterion. The many studies that have been made on word usage indicate that some words appear more frequently in the written expression of both children and adults. Thus, a relatively small number of words may constitute a relatively high proportion of the total number used. Horn's work with a basic writing vocabulary, for instance, indicated the following: [1]

1. The one hundred most frequently used words constitute approximately 60 percent of all normal usage.
2. The five hundred most frequently used words constitute approximately 82 percent of all normal usage.
3. The one thousand most frequently used words constitute approximately 90 percent of all normal usage.
4. The two thousand most frequently used words comprise about 95 percent of all normal usage.

Obviously this is one of the important avenues for improving curriculum content. When a given item occurs more frequently than others, it does so because it is serving a need. Providing an appropriate degree of emphasis for such content helps to make the curriculum more practical and more relevant. Spelling seems to have an advantage over other areas of the program in the degree to which research has delineated the need, but the approach is applicable to curriculum content in general.

The application of this criterion, as in the case of applying any good idea, needs to reflect awareness of other factors. For instance, seven fractions may account for more than 90 percent of the everyday use of fractions, but this does not mean that they should be the only ones taught in the elementary school. The teaching of some that are less widely used may in fact contribute to a better understanding of the seven that are.

[1] Ernest Horn, *A Basic Writing Vocabulary*, Monograph No. 4 (Iowa City: University of Iowa, 1926).

In addition, there are many instances in which going beyond the basic need serves to enlarge horizons and enrich the quality of life. What is involved in the matter is not a case for exclusive teaching of such content, but a case for judicious emphasis and priority.

2. The Criterion of Universality. Universality is interpreted as a geographical scope factor. If a given item of content is important in San Clemente, Phoenix, Denver, Indianapolis, Chappaquiddick, and Martins Ferry, it is more essential than if it were important only in Phoenix. The ability to read and to successfully perform the fundamental operations with whole numbers are types of learnings which know no particular geographical boundaries.

In general, such content seems to involve much of what is encompassed in simple literacy. The more that one goes beyond this, the more likely he is to run into regional and cultural differences which must be accommodated. In a larger sense, however, the concept is applicable to the entire planet. Knowledge relating to the nature of man, government, law, survival, and protection of the natural environment may also reflect the criterion of universality. Ten years from now the concept may have a much more vital significance than it has today, for the central thrust of man's affairs is toward greater intertwining and interdependence. It is not that mankind necessarily wishes this to be so, but simply that it is built into the rising crescendo of events. Overpopulation, for example, will be a world problem rather than a local or national one; and the present right to parenthood may become a privilege granted by the state. Conservation of the universe will likely become a world concern and crisis, as will poverty and disease. More and more of what have always been regarded as strictly local concerns will assume national and international importance. Man may have to relinquish some of his cherished freedoms in order that life and freedom may be maintained. It is a concept which individuals and nations will understandably attempt to resist, but one that is not likely to go away.

3. The Criterion of Maximum Return. This criterion has to do with placing a given item of content at a point in the program where the learning may best occur. One of the early studies in mathematics made an effort to determine whether topics were appropriately placed in this sense.[2] The study took topics as they were assigned to grade levels and had them taught in the same manner to thousands of children in more than a hundred cities. The same topics were also taught in the grade level above and the grade below what was ordinarily assigned for purposes of comparison. After teaching and a delay of six weeks, the students were tested for mastery. Placement of the topic was considered to be satisfactory if the testing indicated that $3/4$ of the children could show 80 percent mastery of the topic in the grade level to which it had been assigned. If this degree of mastery did not prevail at the assigned grade level but was reached at the grade level above, then the topic was considered to be prematurely taught. If, on the other hand, adequate mastery of the topic was indicated not only at the assigned level but also at the grade level below, then the topic was considered suitable for earlier placement in the sequence.

This study provides an excellent example of a criterion which seeks to achieve the best possible return from an investment of teaching time and energies. An interesting hypothetical question may be posed, however, to point up one of the limitations in applying the concept. Should an idea which requires five hours of instructional time for a six-year old and only five minutes for a ten-year old be taught at all to the child of six? The answer is influenced by the nature of the idea. If it were a matter that related to the safety and well-being of the six-year old, then it should be taught even though efficiency of teaching-learning time is violated. It should probably be taught, also, if it is the type of learning which is a necessary key to unlocking other learnings, as in the case of reading. The criterion of maximum return is concerned with efficiency of teaching-learning and is of value, but it must be utilized with sensitivity to other factors which may in the last analysis supersede it in importance.

[2] C. W. Washburne, "Work of the Committee of Seven on Grade Placement in Arithmetic," *Child Development and the Curriculum*, Thirty-eighth Yearbook, Part I, National Society for the Study of Education (Bloomington, Illinois: Public School Publishing Company, 1939), p. 642.

The other limiting factor has to do with how an item is taught. In the study interpreted, all classes were taught a mathematics topic in the same manner. Other ways of teaching might achieve the desired measure of adequacy at an even earlier age. Even though it is subject to the influence of methodology, however, the concept of sensible and appropriate placement in terms of the maturity of children is a useful concept. It helps to avoid over- or underpressuring youngsters in a school that unilaterally presents its curriculum by grade levels, and it contributes to a better overall return for the school's investment of instructional energies and time.

4. The Criterion of Shortage. At any given time in the development of an open and changing society there is likely to be a shortage of some form of competency vital to its continued development. This is particularly true during periods of crisis or periods of very rapid change. During war the shortages will probably be felt most keenly in the technologies that must be mobilized to organize and sustain the war effort. During peace the shortages appear in different forms, and competencies must be redirected and refined. If, for instance, the shortages appear in the areas of science and mathematics, then the first level of curriculum change takes place in the colleges and universities as they move to provide additional emphasis where it is needed. This is reflected then in changing emphases in the secondary schools which eventually affect the elementary curriculum as well.

This relationship seems to be a proper one, for the society protects and makes the schools possible and the schools in turn should help protect and improve the society. It is important in the relationship, however, to guard against possible exploitation of children, as well as overreaction to social crisis or social need.

In the late fifties the Rickover breed of critic blamed U.S. education weaknesses for Russia's early lead in the space race; Rickover saw Sputnik as a triumph of Russian education. The *Phi Delta Kappan* editors queried two hundred key figures in America's space effort, however, and reported that there was no basis for the claim that post-Sputnik improvements were responsible for the present U.S. lead.[3] Knowledgeable Americans, they report, now recognize that Rickover was wrong in much of what he said and that the race to the moon was little affected by the hard line in education advocated by the admiral and the Council for Basic Education. The scientists and engineers who put Apollo 11 astronauts on the moon were young, but not that young. Michael Collins at thirty-nine was two years older than the average astronaut, all fifty-three of whom had finished high school by 1958. For the wealthiest and most technologically advanced nation in the world, success in space was simply a matter of adjusting national priorities. All that was required was the national will to mount a giant effort. The situation was ripe for overreaction and misguided accusations.

Such overreaction can lead to exploitation of children and serious imbalances in the program. There is a tendency to "pour it on," as though the child had some kind of direct relationship to the crisis. Child development concepts are frequently violated, and the young learner is treated as though he were a miniature adult. The hard line may then crowd out fragile aspects of gentle, creative nurture and erode efforts to humanize the school. This is not to say that the criterion is dangerous or unsound; only that it must be applied with wisdom and restraint.

5. The Criterion of Difficulty. Other things being equal, it would seem appropriate for the curriculum of the school to focus upon matters that are too difficult to be learned at home. A child may learn table manners, phone courtesy, and traffic safety at home; but he is not likely to learn photosynthesis, azimuthal projections, or the Pythagorean theorem. The criterion represents an effort to create a sensible division of responsibilities for the education of the young and is a useful one even though it becomes complicated by the fact that other things rarely are equal.

What often happens is that many matters which can and

---

[3] "The Schools Behind Masters of the Moon," *Phi Delta Kappan,* September 1969, pp. 2–3.

should be taught in the home are not and a dilemma is created for the schools. They can either ignore the situation, which seems callous, or they can assume the additional burden, which thins out and dilutes their total efforts. A humanistic school cannot ignore the basic human needs of children that are not being provided for by the parents. It must do what it can even if it detracts from its efforts in other areas which are traditionally regarded as more legitimate concerns. Schools have made a splendid effort to feed children who come to school hungry and they were right in doing so. Is a hunger of the mind or the spirit unworthy of the school's concern? Who can say with good conscience and authority that academic needs really merit priority? It is quite likely that in many instances the reverse is true.

The resolution of this dilemma is a matter of priorities, and the enlightened school must possess the capacity and resourcefulness to move on both fronts. By establishing the priority content interpreted in the discussion of curriculum design, a school creates time to deal with more personal needs. Personal needs may also fall into some degree of priorities, however, and those that cry out for immediate attention take precedence over business as usual. Some such matters can be interwoven into the regular fabric of the curriculum and may enrich it and add to its general relevance and practicality. If not, however, other things must move over so that they can assume their proper place. It is reasonable to postulate that more difficult learnings are logically the concern of the school; but it is just as logical to recognize that this concept can embrace matters of the human heart.

6. The Criterion of Survival. Danny lived in the inner city and attended fourth grade. He had a bright smile, a sunny disposition, and an innate sense of justice that made him one of the most beloved youngsters in the school. One morning before daylight he was out passing his morning papers. A light snow had covered the streets with a treacherous film of ice. Danny's bike slipped on that film of ice and he was crushed beneath the wheels of a truck. In its anguish, the faculty wondered over and over again what they might have done at school that could have prevented this tragedy, but for Danny it was too late.

This criterion is concerned with the survival of human life and is, therefore, the most important criterion of them all. All accidents cannot be eliminated. Even under the most favorable circumstances they will continue to occur because of human frailty and mechanical imperfection. They can, however, be reduced and maximum possible reduction is the goal of the concept. The principal who carefully checks the building, equipment, and grounds before children start the school year is contributing to such a goal. The primary teacher who begins her year with a unit on safety is putting first things first. The instructors who involve their children in a reenactment and analysis of school accidents to determine cause and effect are developing attitudes and habits of thought related to the maintenance and preservation of life. One of the regrettable aspects of this criterion is the fact that it seems to be truly meaningful only to those who have had some tragedy touch their lives. To others it is more of an intellectualized generalization that somehow fails to permeate their thoughts. The deeply compassionate teacher may be able to feel the generalization enough to be influenced by it. The intellectual person can, by an act of sheer will, make it an important part of his thoughts. All professional personnel should attempt to do so because of what is at stake.

7. The Criterion of Appropriateness. Paul grew up in the heartland of rural America. He completed his education at one of the large midwestern universities and began his teaching in a fifth grade. One morning one of his students began to cry and became hysterical. She was experiencing her first menstrual period. No one had prepared her for this and she did not know what was happening to her. Discretion was not one of Paul's greatest gifts. He took her out into the hall and "told it like it was." By late afternoon stories were being circulated in the community that Paul was molesting the girls. By the following morning the stories had reached such proportions that he was asked to resign.

Paul was extremely naive, but it is doubtful that he had

done anything morally wrong. What he did do, however, was to make a gross error in judgment. He could have called a nurse who would have appropriately and effectively taken care of the situation. He paid a heavy professional price for his mistake. If one gives him the full benefit of the doubt, it can be said that he was a compassionate teacher reaching beyond the call of duty to help a child in distress. Such action, however, must in such personal matters be tempered with discretion and good taste. He blundered and violated this vital criterion of professional behavior.

Politics, religion, and sex are three of the most sensitive areas within which the criterion of appropriateness functions, and the nature of community mores is such that in some schools it may spill over into additional aspects of life as well. Even with the present relaxed and blurred standards the concept still has considerable importance. One of the humanistic elements which is involved is that it imposes upon a teacher restrictions which he may not be willing to accept. Some schools forbid a teacher to perform even simple first aid such as the application of Merthiolate. A teacher may choose deliberately to violate the concept of what is regarded as acceptable professional behavior in a given situation, because the well-being of a child leaves him no decent alternative. But he should do this knowingly, rather than unknowingly, and he should be sure that a decent alternative does not in fact exist. The meaning and spirit of a humanistic school is such that this must occasionally be done. It must be done thoughtfully and for good and sufficient cause, but it must be done. Any grinding, mechanistic, demeaning standard of conduct which mitigates against the well-being of the persons it is designed to serve deserves to be challenged and changed.

8. The Criterion of Quality. Mrs. Hiatt was a very dedicated teacher who worked diligently at whatever she undertook. Nothing was too much trouble for her to do for youngsters if she believed it was worthwhile. One day in talking with her class she discovered that none of her children had ever seen a table set with linen, crystal, and silver. This bothered her and she wanted to do something about it. The next day she talked to her principal and asked if she might bring her own things from home so that she could provide such an experience for the girls in her room. She and the girls then held a tea for the faculty of the school. It was a pleasant experience and one that she thought was very good for the children about whom she had been concerned.

The next day one of the teachers in the upper grades also went in to see the principal. The principal was surprised to find that this teacher was quite indignant about the tea and the motivation for holding it. She said that the girls from this disadvantaged area would never live in homes where they would need to know anything about such matters and that the entire episode was like giving Cadillac training to Ford mechanics.

The quality criterion is concerned with deliberately weaving into the lives of learners some of the finest elements of the culture. The first teacher's gesture was understanding, compassionate, and humanistic. It was a feeling response to what she perceived to be a personal need and was arranged constructively into an intellectual context.

The critical teacher's reaction was neither rational nor humanistic. No one can know by looking at a given child what kind of home he will create as an adult, nor what kind of person he will become. One of the inspiring aspects of our way of life is that the individual has access. He can aspire to a better life, and he can make those hopes come true. The humanistic teacher will share those dreams and will help children realistically aspire to become more than they might have wished to become. This is the motor of progress in a society and one of the genuinely exciting aspects of being a teacher.

It is not the intention of this interpretation to represent linen, crystal, and silver as being vital elements of the culture. In discussing this incident, a student who was working her way through college expressed a beautiful thought. She said that one could sit down at a table with paper plates and napkins and reflect the finest elements of life through the simple expression of graciousness and love. Her thought brings to the interpretation of the criterion the intended meaning.

9. The Criterion of Interest. Barney Barnard lived on the B Bar B Ranch in what he described as the "majestic shadow of the Superstition Mountain." He was a cowboy, a rancher, and one of the most colorful of the men who held a passionate belief in the legend of the fabled Lost Dutchman Mine.

With Barney it was not a belief based merely on hearsay, or wild tales concocted by the campfire. He devoted much of his life to researching the legend and interviewing those who had known the wily finder of the mine, Jacob Walzer. From his home on the B Bar B, he had seen the Apaches converge and camp on the slopes near his ranch. He had watched as the braves disappeared into the mountains and had seen them return a few days later to load something into their pickup trucks and leave as suddenly as they had arrived. After such treks he claimed to have verified their shipments of gold.

Barney became convinced that the legend of the lost mine was true. He believed that it was actually a ledge of raw, virgin gold so rich that it did not require smelting or processing and that it was guarded constantly by a roving band of Apaches to whom the mountain was sacred. He contended that the area was safe for those who were out merely to enjoy the wilderness, but that the many prospectors who had met violent death were those who had come too close to the secret.

Most people continue to regard the legend as an artful fabrication. The writer brought Barney to the university campus on several occasions to talk to his classes. He held the students entranced for ninety minutes; his persuasive details made it difficult for them to disbelieve. The Apaches, he said, have now buried the mine and the vastness of the region is such that it will be almost impossible to find. The full truth may never be known. The mountain is there with its brooding air of mystery, but it has kept its secret well. It rises out of the desert with an awesome kind of grandeur that casts a spell upon the visitor. The closer one gets the more he senses a special presence and as he stands under that spell he may feel, as did the warlike Apache, that it is indeed sacred.

All over the world there are legends that are fascinating to all ages. In the Northwest there are many eyewitness reports of Sasquatch, a huge manlike creature that has not only been seen but photographed as well. Nessie continues to elude her trackers in the murky depths of Loch Ness, but recent developments of more sophisticated sonar equipment gives support to the belief that she is there. Hillary's last expedition to the Himalayas cast doubt on the existence of the Abominable Snowman, but the legend persists. Perhaps the most interesting of all current stories, however, is the phenomenon of the UFOs. These accounts have persisted since biblical times and simply will not go away. Reputable reports from all over the world indicate flying objects with a performance that defies explanation by the technology of this planet. The U.S. government has lost much respect by its role in these fascinating and significant sightings.

The point to this discussion is simply that content of rich interest value should be an important segment of the curriculum. It involves children in more intense reading, researching, and practical weighing of conflicting accounts. The wider the spectrum of this kind of content, the more responsive the school can be to individual interests. The content does not have to be directly related to traditional curriculum topics. It has a respectability of its own, for the skills involved in the pursuit of such interests are fundamental forms of development. In addition, it may help many children find a more satisfying niche in the program and give a boost to their progress in other areas of learning as well.

Winston Churchill failed Latin in the grammar grades. In later years when he entered politics he became aware of how impressive it was to stud his political speeches with Latin phrases. He is reported to have gone home and learned his entire Latin book in one evening. Somehow a vital interest in any given topic seems to exert a change in the chemistry of the situation and *to enlarge one's capacity to learn*. This simple criterion is the most powerful of them all.

The criteria which have been interpreted constitute a relatively comprehensive basis for sorting out and improving the content of a program. In application they must frequently be weighed in conjunction with one another, as in the case of the concepts of survival and maximum return. It is a rare teacher who could consciously apply all of them to his ongoing appraisal of the program, but it is a better and more humanistic teacher who gives it a try.

Life Content

It was the last year of teaching before retirement for Miss
Powell and she was not content to coast; she wanted her last
year to be one of her best. It was therefore a keen disappoint-
ment to her that she had not been able to generate any enthu-
siasm from the children for their unit on France. She went to
the principal and told him her problem. She had never been
to France and did not even know anyone who had. She asked
if he knew someone that might come in and talk to her class.

The principal was a resourceful expediter who could not
turn down a colleague in distress. He went to the local college
campus and returned with a lovely, vivacious French girl.
There were other people that he could have brought, but he
cared enough to bring the very best. It was a most fortunate
choice. The girl was delighted to come talk with the children
about her homeland. She was homesick, and as she told of her
country she spoke from the heart.

The effect was almost electrifying. The children hung on
every word, the teacher was radiant, and even the principal
seemed stirred. Midway through her remarks one of the students who knew a little of the language spontaneously said,
"Voulez-vous me baiser?" The charming visitor immediately
went back and kissed her. The boys then experienced their
first pangs of regret for not having learned even the most basic
rudiments of the language. The visitor completely transformed
the situation. It was like a breath of spring blowing through
the curriculum. Forgotten was the intransigence of de Gaulle,
French hoarding of gold, and their failure to pay their war
debts. France became the students' favorite unit. *Viva la France.*

The students will probably never forget that morning with
their enchanting visitor, and their attitudes may have been
forever altered. Of the approximately one thousand other days
that they spent in elementary school, how many will they remember? Life content that is appropriately selected can make
a significant difference in the quality and effectiveness of the
program. Students sometimes ask why this is so. This is not
the kind of question that needs to be answered by five

hundred pieces of research. Why should one be surprised that life responds best to other life?

It is possible, of course, to exaggerate the importance of this kind of content or experience, and one needs to place it in proper perspective. This can be accomplished by hypothetically reversing the situation. Suppose, for instance, that schools had no sequenced verbal-visual materials and were entirely dependent upon direct experience such as the apprenticeship. Surely under such circumstances much that is presently valuable would be lost, and the effect would amount simply to a reverse imbalance. One of the reasons that life content seems so vital in many classrooms today is that it is so infrequently used. If that were all that was used, however, a similar hunger might develop for some of the packaged forms of education that are prevalent today. The curriculum of a school needs both; they enrich and supplement one another.

Dale's concept of a "cone of experience" is useful here. The base of the cone represents direct reality as it is experienced firsthand. He describes it as the bedrock of all education and as an unabridged version of life itself. Each succeeding band of the cone moves in the order of decreasing directness and increasing abstraction. The order of the bands is as follows: [4]

Verbal Symbols
Visual Symbols
Recordings
Motion Pictures
Television
Exhibits
Field Trips
Demonstrations
Dramatized Experiences
Contrived Experiences
Direct Experiences

The cone is not interpreted as a hierarchy or rank order of learning processes, but it does reinforce a concept of the importance of life content.

[4] Edgar Dale, *Audio Visual Methods* (New York: Dryden Press, 1954), p. 43.

Another highly significant form of life content that may tend to be overlooked is that of the resources that lie within the children themselves. The experience approach to reading capitalizes upon such content, and this is one of its compelling strengths. The child entering school may have known loneliness, thirst, and vast reaches of space; or he may have known crowding, littered streets, and patrol cars moving ominously through his neighborhood. He may be primarily conversant with happiness or unhappiness, security or insecurity, tender nurture or abuse. Whatever he has known and lived, however, he brings to school. And what he knows best can be a base and transitional point for further learning. To disregard his prior experiences as though they were unimportant or did not exist is tragically unreal. It is an omission which may produce an artificial schism in his life that is later very difficult to bridge.

The experiences that lie within the children themselves have relevance to all areas of the program. Concept building in the social studies, in science, and in mathematics are all furthered by establishing a vital link between what is going on at school and what they have known. Early educational theory enunciated the important principle that learning takes place on the threshold between the known and the unknown. In practice this principle seems to have been applied primarily to academic learnings, but its usefulness and validity extend into almost every facet of a child's life. The explorations and structure given to the language experience approach are highly commendable. Similar probes in other curricular areas are equally desirable and should be carefully explored.

There is a story about a shy mountaineer woman who walked some distance to a school to enroll her handicapped boy. Her description of her seven-year-old son to the teacher was touching and memorable: "He can't see out of but one eye and he can't hear, but he can lean against himself." What a protective, insightful, and helpful thing to say! Who among the more educated could have expressed it so well? It is good to learn to lean on oneself; life requires it, and maturity is built upon it. One likes to think, however, that the school gave that precious boy many opportunities to lean on others as well; and that, in so doing, he received a richly human response. In many classrooms today, he would; and may there be more of them tomorrow. Knowing and caring what a child is like inside, what he brings to school, and how this may fit into the curriculum for him is such a good way to run a school.

Simulation Content

Content can be improved through more selective screening of the verbal material which occupies such a prominent place in children's educational experiences and through the special vitality of life content. Each of these factors has a large role to play in achieving a more humanized environment; but some learnings require a different medium and approach.

A space center with its complex structures sprawling over several acres of ground may be baffling and difficult to grasp. If it is reduced to a model, however, it becomes easier to comprehend. The model simplifies and reveals what is too large to be perceived directly. This amounts to what one might call an editing of reality. Adults as well as children need this. An area of the city presented through models vastly improves the understanding of those who without such an aid simply could not conceptualize the matter under consideration. It helps to make it seeable.

The model is equally applicable when the reality is not seeable because it is too minute. A model, for instance, of a cell would facilitate understanding beyond what can be accomplished by viewing one through a microscope. The materials can greatly surpass this, however. Located in the nucleus, or innermost portion of the cell, and arranged in single file along the threadlike chromosomes, are the mysterious genes. Although chromosomes can be seen with a microscope, genes cannot. Science and technology can combine their collective genius, however, to project a model of the structure of a gene. Such a model of the very minute may be only an extrapolation, but it adds new dimensions to human understanding that were not available in the education of yesterday. For the education of tomorrow, however, they bring the promise of new excitement, wonder, and a grasp of human knowledge that surpasses most of what the curriculum makers have dared to conceive.

Schools have wisely used simulated content in the past. The kindergartners' sand map of their neighborhood with streets and crude buildings is an excellent example of such curriculum content. The physical models of different map projections and the conceptual and manipulative devices used in mathematics are valuable additions to the content segment of the program. Simulation is blended with the resources that lie within children themselves when the school uses role playing as an important part of the curriculum.

All such forms of content are desirable and necessary. They enable children who have difficulty with symbols to understand; but they enrich and deepen the learning of all students. They make education more fun, more real, and more possible. What has been done with genes may in the future be accomplished with concepts that have heretofore been too baffling to comprehend. It is possible to conceive of a physical model of a decision, morality, or thinking. Today the structure of the gene—tomorrow a physical conceptualization of character or human thought. Who knows? Perhaps some child who learned to "lean against himself" already has it under way.

Chapter
Multidimensional
Grouping
7

Chapter

Multidimensional Grouping

7

Grouping is a matter of continuing controversy and many segments of the profession are in honest disagreement about how it should be performed. One reason for this is that the problem has been grossly underestimated. It is just as difficult to approach perfection in grouping children for maximum learning as it is to approach perfection in science or any other area of the curriculum. This complexity is rarely recognized, however, and much less time is devoted to improving the system than to improving some segment such as the reading program. Yet grouping is a pervading curriculum matter which reaches across subject matter boundaries and influences success in reading, science, and many other aspects of the program. Grouping cannot be lightly regarded in a school that aspires to excellence and humanism, nor can it be resolved by some of the naive questions that have been so heatedly debated. The question of which is better, homogeneous or heterogeneous grouping, is not an answerable question. It is like asking whether a dentist is better than an obstetrician. The problem is multidimensional.

The curricular function of grouping is *to place a child in the human environment in which he can learn best and learn most*. Such a problem has three principal phases. The first phase is the initial assigning of a group of children to a teacher. This is an administrative function which is usually referred to as classification. In the second phase the teacher groups children within her room in an effort to individualize the learning. This is known as internal grouping. In the third phase, at the end of a given period of time, children are traditionally regrouped or reassigned for the next year's work. This is called promotion. All three phases are a part of the concept of grouping, for children are grouped in classifying them, grouped within the room for purposes of instruction, and grouped again for continuation of learning. Learning may be influenced by the decisions that are made in any of the three phases, and the central task is that of placing and maintaining a child in that group in which his growth may take place most effectively.

The following discussion indicates some of the larger dimensions of the problem and suggests seven aspects in which the process can be improved. There are many additional ways to effect improvement, but a school which can successfully implement the seven ideas will have taken highly significant steps toward humanizing this portion of the program. Not a single one of the seven ideas is easily accomplished, nor can any of them be implemented and then forgotten. Grouping, like discipline, is a dynamic matter that requires continuing attention and adjustment. It calls for the kind of alertness, analysis, and manipulation that one observes in a superbly coached team. The function cannot be successfully mechanized or properly bottled and shelved. Mastering such a challenge is an achievement of which a school might be justly proud.

Flexible Admissions

One of the first points at which a school can demonstrate quality in its grouping practices is in its admission policy. This policy should be more flexibly adjusted to allow maturity to be a factor in admission in addition to chronological age. At the present time, in almost all school districts throughout the United States, children are admitted to school on the

basis of chronological age. Thus, a child may enter first grade
if he is six years of age on or before a specified date. The date
is usually set by the school district itself. If a child in a given
district is allowed to enter first grade by virtue of being six
years of age on or before December 1, he might begin his first
grade experience at the calendar or chronological age of five
years and nine months. The specified date is sometimes later
than December 1, in which case the child is allowed to enter
at an even earlier age than five years and nine months. If the
date is earlier than December 1, the effect is to cause him to
enroll at an age correspondingly later than the five years and
nine months.

Chronological age is an uncomplicated and useful admission
device and is typically regarded as the most important single
criterion for grouping. It becomes questionable as a practice
when it is used as the only criterion for admission, for it cannot adequately do the job alone. This becomes obvious when
one considers the following:

*School X allows children who will be six years old on
or before December 1 to enter first grade in September.
Child A is relatively immature and has a birthday November 30. In terms of total growth or organismic age, Child
A in September approximates the level of development
which is typical of an average five year old. Child A,
however, by application of a single criterion of chronological age will be admitted to first grade. Research at the
Gesell Institute reveals that at least one child in three may
be overplaced, and struggling with school tasks that are
beyond him.*[1]

*Child B has a birthday on December 2. In terms of
total growth, Child B is advanced in many aspects of his
development and roughly approximates the maturity level
of an average six-year-old child. Chronologically he is
three days younger than Child A, but with respect to
maturity he is a year more advanced. Child B is ready*

[1] Louise Bates Ames, *Is Your Child in the Wrong Grade?* (New York: Harper & Row, 1966), p. 3.

to profit from a first grade experience, but under the
application of a single criterion of admission such as
chronological age, he would not be allowed to enter school.

A flexible admission policy would allow the level of maturity of a child to become a factor in the decision as to when he might enter school. It would not replace the criterion of chronological age, but would supplement it and realistically improve the conditions for entering school. Some observers say such a practice is not administratively feasible. This has never been demonstrated and is an evasion of the problem. If the practice is worthwhile, creative administrators will find ways to implement it. The function of administration is to serve and facilitate the growth of desirable curriculum practices rather than to prevent them from taking place. The resourceful school will find ways to introduce this kind of flexibility into its admission policy and will allow the maturity of the child to become a factor in whatever decision is to be made.

Planned Diversity

The vision of a strong, new nation as a vast melting pot was part of the Great American Dream. This vision can function in a small way in every classroom in the country. It is fostered by deliberately building certain kinds of differences into the composition of each class. Such differences are then the product of design rather than of accident.

Building this element of quality into the school's grouping practices operates in the following manner. The principal and the teachers who are to receive the children sit around a table together. Using their combined information about the children, they form groups that contain the kinds of differences they wish to include. Thus, each teacher will receive her share of the rich and the poor, the aggressive and the shy, the boys and the girls, the leaders and the followers. The inclusion of such differences in the composition of each classroom is not left to chance as is done in most schools. Each room, instead, is deliberately shaped in the image of the great original dream.

The forming of such heterogeneous groups, however, can be simultaneously controlled with respect to the vertical spread or levels of achievement and ability. Achievement levels in a typical classroom often span six or more grades. Most teachers feel that this unnecessarily complicates their job and that the spread is an important factor in teacher load. Rightly or wrongly, teachers feel they can work more easily and effectively with a group of children which spans three grade levels of achievement than with one which spans six.

The vertical spread of achievement can be a conscious part of the formation of each group. At the same time that sociological heterogeneity is being built into the groups, vertical levels of achievement or ability can be reduced. For example, 150 fifth graders might typically represent a spread of achievement from first grade to ninth. No teacher, however, needs to have the complete range of achievement in his room in order to have the kinds of differences that are desired. The composition of any given class can be deliberately formed with respect to controlling this range. Each teacher's group can be restricted to any three contiguous levels of ability or achievement in order to be sensitive to the factor of teaching load.

Such a proposal is in sharp contrast to the debate of homogeneous versus heterogeneous grouping, for some kinds of difference in the classrooms are obviously desirable and others may need to be controlled. This is a way to draw from the intrinsic strengths of both homogeneity and heterogeneity. It is a concept and a procedure which can help to reconcile divergent views, for in a significant way it is sensitive to the merits of each. Classification on such a basis seems to increase the possibilities of learning from one another and applies a major democratic concept as well.

Balanced Internal Grouping

The discussion up to this point has been concerned with the improvement of grouping through more realistic admission practices and a more carefully diversified composition of the class each teacher is to receive. At this stage the teacher ordinarily arranges some kind of internal groupings in his own room in order to further individualize the instruction. The most common example of such internal groupings is in the reading program. Here, the teacher traditionally forms the best, middle, and slowest groups in a sincere attempt to adjust the program to each child.

Balanced internal grouping is a humanistic factor which should be invoked if a practice such as the three reading groups is used in a given classroom. Such a practice, however, may cause children in the lower groups to get farther and farther behind and more and more discouraged. This is of major significance because it tampers with the child's self-concept. It is vital for every child to believe that he is a worthy self, and the school should consciously reinforce this view.

Mann's study of 102 fifth grade children offered clues to how such grouping affects self-concepts.[2] She used a group questionnaire to elicit self-reports from the children on how they felt about being in the group they were in. There were no negative expressions about themselves in the responses from the top two groups. Negative responses began to appear in the third group, however, and nothing but negative responses about themselves emerged from group four. One child wrote, "I am in the fift Grade I am to dom."

A teacher who uses such status groupings in his classroom would seem to have an obligation at the same time to provide the antidote. This is accomplished by arranging groupings in other parts of the curriculum in which a child who has been cast in an inferior role in one aspect of the program may have a chance to lead or excel in another. This is a simple compensating factor and an act of justice which helps to soften the influence of ability groups. Such groupings do not need to be balanced on a one-to-one basis. The point is that it is highly detrimental for anyone to be cast constantly in an inferior role, and an occasional situation in which he can achieve recognition and respect may be all that is necessary. Every child

[2] Maxine Mann, "What Does Ability Grouping Do to the Self Concept?" *Childhood Education*, April 1960, pp. 357–360.

has something that he can do well; to identify it and give it a place of respectability within the program is a first order achievement.

Team Learning

Almost everyone in professional education has some awareness of team teaching. An idea which may be more powerful and exciting, however, seems somehow to have been overlooked. This is the concept of team learning.

Pupil-team learning consists of the practice of combining children into very small groups such as twos or threes for mutual aid in learning. The idea capitalizes upon whatever natural tendencies children have to work together. It is brought into play whenever the nature of the activity is such that it can increase the amount or quality of learning; it should not be used under circumstances in which it seems to diminish either.

In Klugman's study children who were solving math problems alone were compared to those who were solving the same problems by working in pairs.[3] The results could not be described as spectacular; however, those working in pairs did average seven rights compared to the six of those working alone. Although the amount was greater, the more significant benefits were probably in the category of the quality of what transpired. The pairs generated more alternative approaches to the problem, engaged in more analytical sifting of the possible procedures, and experienced meaningful and purposeful interaction with one another. The work of pairs required 183 seconds more time but this is of little importance when interpreted in light of the qualitative manner in which the time was used.

Durrell reported a novel feature of the evaluation of an extensive team learning project in Dedham, Massachusetts.[4] This

[3] Samuel F. Klugman, "Cooperative Versus Individual Efficiency in Problem-Solving," *Journal of Educational Psychology*, XXXV (January 1944): 91–100.

[4] Donald D. Durrell, "Implementing and Evaluating Pupil-Team Learning Plans," *Changes and Innovation in Elementary School Organization* (New York: Holt, Rinehart and Winston, 1965), pp. 236–243.

feature was called a "subject service analysis" and was based upon an interview with each teacher. In this interview the evaluation was focused upon the degree to which the project had affected such key factors as provision for levels of ability, learning rates, special pupil needs, self-direction, social learning, and enrichment. Each of the items was evaluated on a four-point scale, which was seeking to determine the amount of actual change in instructional services to pupils. The maximum possible rating on the scale was 92.

The results were encouraging, for the average rating of teacher service to pupils jumped from 29.6 in the control year to 63.5 in the experimental year. Many experiments show improvement on paper but not in the classroom. This one seemed to indicate benefits where it counts most. The effect of the project on separate subjects was rated from most to least as follows: reading, spelling, arithmetic, social studies, and language arts.

Some may question the desirability of using such small groupings in team learning. Each additional child that is added to the group, however, reduces the amount of interaction that is possible for each member. Also, there is a most provocative factor involved in the total size which many teachers have not recognized. This has to do with the total number of interpersonal relationships that are possible in groups of varying size. In a group of three, three such relationships are possible. In a group of five, ten interpersonal relationships are possible, however; and if the size of the group is increased to only eight there are twenty-eight possible interpersonal relationships. Bossard indicates the mathematical formula for computing this.[5] If X equals the total possible number of interpersonal relationships, and Y equals the number of members in the group, the formula is $X = (Y^2 - Y)/2$. As the size of the group increases arithmetically, the number of relationships increases geometrically. The difficulties posed for meaningful interaction of youngsters in larger groups is thus enormously compounded. This is summarized in Figure 9.

Durrell aptly identifies one of the weaknesses of present-day

---

[5] James H. Bossard, *The Sociology of Child Development* (New York: Harper & Row, 1948), p. 146.

Figure 9 POSSIBLE NUMBER OF INTERPERSONAL RELA-
TIONSHIPS IN GROUPS OF VARYING SIZE

A	2	3	5	8	12	15	35
B	1	3	10	28	66	105	595

NOTE: A=number in group; B=number of personal relationships.

teaching when he says that so much school activity is based upon the theory that every lesson is a test of achievement rather than a practice in learning.[6] Each mathematics paper and each written product is marked as though it were a terminal examination rather than a single small step in the learning process. This is unwholesome and can be detrimental to children's attitudes toward learning. Pupil-team learning reverses this and places the situation in proper perspective. It assumes that most school activity is practice toward achievement, and that mutual aid in this practice may be desirable. During such practice learning pupils may compare and correct answers, exchange ideas and approaches, and assist one another at points of difficulty.

Team learning can add considerable richness to the internal grouping that is used within a classroom. There is room for much exploration and imagination in the forming of pupil teams. Instead of forming them only on the basis of intellectual or achievement factors such as putting three gifted youngsters together for a given task, teams can be created in terms of possible positive influences upon personality. For instance, two shy children who rarely talk could be paired on an assignment which can only be accomplished by verbal interaction with each other. With the right kind of a task the children might talk more and open up more in that experience than would ordinarily occur in an entire semester. There are almost unlimited opportunities for exciting team formations if one utilizes them for such added dimensions as personality or the concept of supplementing strengths. Pupil-team learning seems right on target for a school that is humanistically conceived.

[6] Durrell, *op. cit.*, p. 237.

Cross-Age Relationships

The major responsibility for helping children acquire those skills, attitudes, and values needed to function successfully as adults has been placed in the hands of parents and educators. This model of a few adults being responsible for such a complex learning program seems, at first glance, to be eminently sensible. In actuality, however, the model reveals serious difficulties and indefensible omissions. The amount of individual attention that can be provided under such an arrangement is limited and inadequate, the teacher's potentiality is exaggerated, and the possible role of children as teachers has been underestimated and inadequately explored. Cross-age relationships is designed to shore up some of these deficiencies.

The children within a school constitute a very powerful educational resource which can be channeled into a program of helping relationships. This is accomplished by having selected children in the school work under the general guidance of an adult to assist younger children. The idea is based upon some general assumptions such as the following:

1. Younger children use the behavior and attitudes of older children as models for their own behavior.
2. The older child as a model enjoys some important natural advantages. He can communicate with the younger child more effectively than adults, he is less likely to be identified as an authority figure, and he provides a more realistic level of aspiration.
3. Almost everyone who is involved benefits significantly. The teacher receives additional assistance, the younger child receives additional attention and teaching, and the helping child solidifies his own learnings, bolsters his ego, and becomes more highly motivated in his own education.

In the Lippitt and Lohman project, sixth graders were involved as academic assistants for the first, second, third, and fourth grades. Their success was the result of several carefully planned steps which would be helpful to others launching a similar project. Some of these steps were as follows: [7]

1. Orienting the teachers and holding frank discussions of the difficulties and possible benefits
2. Interpreting the project to the sixth grade classes in such a manner as to develop their interest and cooperation
3. Selecting children who were held in high regard by their peers to undertake the initial helping roles
4. Providing training for the helping role. This training emphasized such significant matters as what expectations were realistic for the children they were to help, the correction of errors in encouraging ways, giving praise without lowering standards of performance, and methods of taking children from the levels at which they were successful to higher levels.

Benefits from this constructive program of cross-age interaction seem to have lived up to expectations in many of the schools that have tried it. Holmes School in Mesa, Arizona, has used it extensively and calls it the "Big Friend" technique. More than two hundred children were involved in its program, and they employed it sensitively to build up the morale of some of their helping students who desperately needed such a boost.

Cross-age relationships seem to be an effective and practical educational resource that is available to every school regardless of the scarcity or abundance of material advantages in the community. In addition to the benefits that have been interpreted, there is an associated concept that is exciting and powerful. It is the idea of *the multiplication of teaching potentiality*. Authoritative teaching emanating from some central figure that conceives, implements, and controls all of the important functions alone is a most limited concept. Opening up the

[7] Peggy Lippitt and John E. Lohman, "Cross-Age Relationships—An Education Resource," *Children*, XII (May–June 1965): 113–117.

teaching role to utilize in appropriate ways the vast untapped resources of the older children is a greatly enlarged concept. It not only multiplies teaching potentiality, but contributes to the desired humanizing process as well.

Personal Needs Grouping

Martha was a physically unattractive fifth grade girl who seemed always to be on the outside of life looking in. She was a poor student, had a rather bumptious kind of personality, and a singularly irritating voice. If it is true, as some believe, that there is a pecking order among people, she was at the very bottom of the scale. No one would associate with her and in any kind of activity in which the children selected teams she was the last one to be chosen. She was shunned in committee work, ignored on the playground, and even had to walk to and from school alone. She was very hungry for friends and tried in every way that she knew to be a part of other children's lives, but no one would let her in.

Her teacher was aware of Martha's deep hunger for acceptance and companionship and made discreet efforts of his own to include her in the affairs of the class. Three months of the school year had passed, however, and her situation was as miserable as when the year began. One day she had an extremely unkind hurt and was strangely quiet for the rest of the afternoon. Perhaps, for the first time, a feeling of hopelessness had begun to engulf her. Always before she had kept struggling for some measure of esteem. Now he thought that he could sense her feeling of futility as well as grief.

After school that day he asked three of the most popular members of the class to stay and laid the problem in their laps. He talked with them about how very lonely Martha was, how she longed to have friends and be included in children's lives, and how he had been personally unable to help her become an accepted member of the group. He asked if they had ideas about what might be done.

The children rose splendidly to the situation and said all of the right things. They could help and they wanted to do so! They would see that she was chosen for committees. They would see that she was included in their games, and they would see that she did not ever have to walk home from school alone again. Even parents got constructively into the act, and Martha's life took a more fortunate turn.

There are many Marthas in the elementary school who seem always to be on the outside of life looking in. They have a deep hunger for responsiveness and human companionship. If that hunger is not alleviated in some way, their lives will become further twisted; for them as well as for the world in which they are to live, the consequences are tragic.

Personal needs grouping is a concept which recognizes the psychological hungers of children and seeks to respond to them. It contrives arrangements in which isolates can be with stars. Perhaps the activity which is used to bring them together is a simple and transitory one, but the circumstances under which they are brought together should be as favorable as possible to the have-not child. One can take the position that personal needs grouping is beyond the call of duty, that a teacher has no responsibility for carrying such a burden. And this may well be true, for everyone except those who believe in a humanistic school.

Flexible Regrouping

Stanley's father brought the family out of the hills of Kentucky and moved to a city in eastern Indiana. The next morning Stanley went over to enroll in school. He was ten years old, but had never been to school a day in his life. He strode eagerly into the principal's office to find out where he was to go, and the principal looked at him in frank wonderment. He was barefoot, his clean but frayed trousers hung just below his knees, and he was absolutely delighted to be embarking upon his education. The principal had never seen anyone like this —he was like a young Abraham Lincoln.

Puzzling over an appropriate placement for the boy, he

called in his primary teachers and asked for their suggestions. They too were perplexed and were unable to make a recommendation. Still in a quandary over the matter, the principal brought the boy back into the office. Stanley must have heard the discussion about him for he looked hopefully at the principal and said this splendid thing, "Mr. Moore, I don't care where you place me . . . I just want to learn to read."

The school involved was graded, but Mr. Moore was so impressed with the youngster that he proposed a special arrangement for him. Stanley was to go to the first grade until he had learned to read. When this was accomplished he would be moved to the second grade, and when he had mastered that he would be advanced to the third. He could move as rapidly as he was able to master the program. The principal explained the plan to Stanley and asked how he would feel about being in first grade. Stanley said that he liked the idea and that he would "help the teacher."

Stanley liked the idea so much that he arrived at school the next morning at 6:30. No one was there but the custodian. He walked around looking at the empty halls and classrooms and finally asked the custodian, "Where are all the scholars?"

When the others arrived at 8:30, he took his place with the six-year olds. He towered over them like a giant sequoia, but he was helpful to everyone and learned very rapidly. In a few weeks he mastered the work and was ready to move on to the second grade. The school was small and informal, and this was such a happy event that they had a special promotion ceremony for him. He completed second grade in six weeks and moved into the third. By the end of the semester, he was in fourth grade with the oldest children in the school. He was the most respected and beloved boy in school. All of them knew him, for he had been in every room except the kindergarten.

In the spring of the year, Stanley's father suddenly moved the family back to the hills of Kentucky. They left so quickly he did not even have time to say goodbye. Every adult in the school who had worked with him wept unashamedly. It would be pleasant to think that someday one might have a chance to vote for that boy for President of the United States. He has had several votes silently pledged to him since his first year in school.

As indicated in earlier remarks, the essential purpose of grouping is to place a child in the human environment in which he can learn best and learn most. Flexible regrouping is a concept that is necessary in order to keep abreast of the process. Sometimes a child experiences a surge of growth that places him too far beyond his classmates, and suddenly he does not fit there anymore. He has outgrown them just as Stanley had outgrown his trousers. Such development does not constrain or relate itself to the school calendar. When, because of such a forward thrust, a child has outstripped the environment in which he was placed, regrouping is in order at that moment instead of waiting for some predetermined point in the school year. Such an adjustment poses no unusual difficulties in a multiage model of the nongraded school. In a graded organization it is possible to provide for some change through the internal groupings within the room. The concept of flexible grouping, however, requires opening the door for the crossing of grade lines also, whenever the case warrants doing so. Grade lines, after all, are not sacred. They can be crossed at will whenever an imaginative and resourceful school wishes to bridge them.

Open Doors

The parents of a primary child had made her feel uncomfortable about being in the low reading group. She went to her teacher one morning and said, "Miss Harriet, I don't want to be in Janet's reading group anymore. I want to be in Sally's." Her teacher was wise. She simply smiled and said, "Fine, get a book and go over and join Sally's group." A few days later the child came back and asked if she might return to Janet's group.

The hard-line critic of education would be inclined to scoff at the understanding response of Miss Harriet. He would probably feel that she had wasted time, catered to the whim of a child, and that things were now right back where they had started. Things are not at all "back where they started." There is now a completely different factor present in the situation. How the child perceives and feels about being in her reading group has undergone a significant transformation which will positively affect her learning. This points up one of the vast differences between the professional and the critic who thinks that he too is a specialist because he was once a child.

During the war a classification psychologist called in a young aviation cadet to give him some disappointing news. The young man wanted to be a pilot, but the test battery indicated otherwise. The psychologist told him that according to the results of the tests he had only one chance in twenty of being successful as a pilot and he was therefore being classified as a navigator. The young man was silent for a moment as he internalized the blow. Then looking squarely at the officer he said quietly, "But sir, I will be that one in twenty." What a magnificent response! The psychologist had a moment of greatness. He realized that what had just transpired completely eclipsed the importance of his tests. The young man was assigned to flight training and won his wings.

Some schools function as though their mission was to close doors on children. They not only close the door but seal off the escape hatch. Such schools have missed the reason for their existence. The curriculum should open doors for its youngsters, and that is what both Miss Harriet and the psychologist did. They rose above the mechanistic performance of their roles and gave two people a chance. One recipient walked boldly through his door to experience success. The other tried her wings and then softly closed the door on herself. Each of them grew from the experience; and each of the adults who helped them provided, for the less knowing, a passing glimpse of the humanistic school.

Chapter
Approaches
to
Giftedness
8

Chapter
Approaches
to
Giftedness

One of the clichés that enjoyed wide currency in the recent past was the notion that talent will out. This apparently meant that if one really had ability it would be recognized and rewarded. The yeast of an open society should work in such a manner, and many able people in America have emerged from obscure circumstances. Many others have not, however; and, regrettably, many who should have remained in greater obscurity did not do so.

Does anyone believe, for instance, that in the recent national elections the major parties have really offered the country two of the men most qualified to be president of the United States? Does anyone believe that the U.S. Congress contains the men and women with the most wisdom and ability to legislate or that the Supreme Court represents nine of the best legal minds in the land? Democracy will rise or fall in some direct relationship to its ability to sift out its greatest human talent and not only identify but attempt to insure its nurture. The schools play a vital role in this process of sifting and nurture.

Interpretations of Giftedness. The most common designation of giftedness in schools is by IQ or intelligence quotient. Although there is no universal agreement on what constitutes potential genius, it seems more generally to be identified as someone with an IQ of 140 or above. This score may represent the upper 3 percent of the school population in a superior socioeconomic community and less than 1 percent of the students in an average or disadvantaged area. Intelligence tests may fail to identify creative children and may contain cultural bias or excessive verbal weighting which cause them to overlook gifted children who are less advantaged. In spite of being admittedly imperfect tools, however, they have value in the search for youngsters with high intellectual potential. If a school uses them extensively, it should be aware of the fact that 140 is not always 140, as indicated in the interesting data summarized by Gallagher in Figure 10.[1] A fourteen-year old could not even score 140 on the California Test of Mental Maturity (elementary) which has a high of 136, whereas 167 is possible on a Stanford-Binet.

The concept of *multiple IQs* may be even more valuable to schools than the globular concept represented by a single score. Doll says there are in reality four IQs which he interprets as follows: [2]

1. The *intelligence quotient* which is a measure of intellectual potential or brightness—not of capacity or maturity level.
2. The *inner quest* which is made up of aspirations and values that are not always in the conscious mind.
3. The *ideal qualities* which are traits of personality that monitor and maintain a balance between the inner quest and the intelligence quotient.
4. The *innate quirks* which are the obstacles that lie between the individual and his desired fulfillment. Some of these are in the person and some are environmental.

[1] James J. Gallagher, *The Gifted Child in the Classroom* (Washington, D.C.: American Educational Research Association of NEA, 1963), p. 6.
[2] From an address by Edgar A. Doll delivered at the Southwestern Regional Conference of the International Council for Exceptional Children (Arizona State University, Tempe, Arizona, March 1958).

Figure 10 MAXIMUM OBTAINABLE IQ SCORES ON TESTS
OF INTELLECTUAL ABILITY AT TWO DIFFERENT AGE
LEVELS

Intelligence tests	Maximum IQ	
	12 yrs old	14 yrs old
Stanford-Binet	190	167
Wechsler Intelligence Scale for Children	154[a]	154[a]
Otis Quick Scoring Test of Mental Ability (Beta)	153	143
California Test of Mental Maturity (Elementary)	157	136
Lorge-Thorndike Intelligence Test (Verbal Battery)	147	150[a]

[a] Highest score given in norm tables.

A concept of multiple IQs broadens the base for giftedness
and embraces more of the student population. It is attractive
in many ways. For instance, the notion of ideal qualities
amounts to what might be considered social intelligence. Some
people seem to have a rare gift for saying and doing the right
thing in the right way at the right time. This kind of gift
makes a contribution to a humanistic world that is just as
vital as the more commonly extolled intellectual component.
It, too, is intellectual in nature but presents another of the
many faces of intellect. Doll's interpretation is also adequate
to explain the discrepancies between actual performance and
the more narrowly construed concept of intelligence. Some
children with undistinguished intelligence quotients simply
outperform youngsters with higher scores. Such children may
be more highly motivated, or even so superbly organized phys-
iologically that they can function with greater ease at maximal
levels of performance. Many of the world's eminent figures
may fall in this category and would not necessarily show up
well on psychological scores.

The concept of "talent" refers to an unusual capacity or
ability in a special field. Such natural aptitude is capable of

high performance under nurture but does not necessarily imply a high degree of general intelligence. One might have a talent in music, art, athletics, or auto mechanics. Talents encompass a wide spectrum of human potentialities and thus have considerable importance to a school which is seeking to nurture giftedness.

The Basic View

A concept of giftedness, then, can be relatively narrow as in the case of an intellectual component cast in the form of an IQ. It can be broadened by the recognition of different kinds of IQ as reflected by high performance or intelligent behavior in multiple facets of living, and it can be even more encompassing by extending the concept to include the broad range of capacities known as talents. The broadest interpretation is the one to which this view is inclined. Many thoughtful educators and laymen believe that gifted children are one of the nation's most precious resources. They are, indeed; but there is a resource that is infinitely more precious, more realistic, more democratically conceived, and more vital to the culture. *It is the total store of giftedness that resides in all of the children.* This is the humanistic concept—not a mysterious entity of a small number of students who are sorted out and labeled as gifted students but a more pervasive, embracing, powerful idea of *giftedness within children.*

Eric Hoffer is thinking in a similar context when he speaks of the accepted view that talent and genius are rare exceptions or flukes of nature. In contrast to that notion he sees the masses as being like a mine that is rich with all conceivable capacities, waiting for chance and circumstances to wash nuggets out of the hidden veins and bring them to the surface.[3]

To flush out such nuggets from hidden veins is certainly a first magnitude accomplishment. A school that can increase its effectiveness in this manner is making an incalculable contribution to the individual and to society. Though few children

[3] Eric Hoffer, "Talent, Genius, No Rare Items," *Arizona Republic,* October 20, 1969.

are potential geniuses, all children possess gifts which may become their special distinction; and someone must help in early years to search out and foster such natural endowments. These gifts must be enticed out again and again and protected against the annihilating effect of social condemnation. The fair-minded boy may be called "soft" by his classmates, the gracious girl may be accused of posing for adult favors, the budding scholar may be scarred by an epithet such as "bookworm," and the young humorist may be suppressed and branded as an "attention seeker."

Schools must avoid the encouragement of too limited a range of traits believed to be essential to success, to the detriment of the vast range of gifts which children possess. For it is often one of these broader spectrum gifts which is most useful in life. The ability to communicate confidence may at times serve a doctor better than his medical skill. A boy's passionate love of justice that is discouraged in school as an irritant may contribute more to his success as a lawyer than his ability to prepare a brief. The remaining discussion will focus upon some common and uncommon approaches used to enrich and develop giftedness in today's schools, but they will be scrutinized in terms of the larger goal of seeking to discover and nourish a greater proportion of the total gifts that America's children possess.

The Woodring Plan

Woodring believes that the present organization of our school system is totally inconsistent with the American philosophy of education and with the facts of child growth and intellectual maturing. His plan calls for a drastic reorganization from kindergarten through the Ph.D.[4] Although his proposal deals with the entire student population, his basic concern is with the education of the upper third who are distinctly above the average in their general capacity for learning. These are the children who develop good vocabularies at an early age, read

[4] Paul Woodring, *A Fourth of a Nation* (New York: McGraw-Hill, 1957), p. 143.

widely, grasp new ideas easily, and ask intelligent questions. They are also, he says, the ones who will become our leaders. It is from this group that the nation will get its statesmen, scientists, writers, lawyers, ministers, and teachers. Such children are found in all kinds of homes and at all social levels, but they are not in his judgment receiving an adequate education.

Part of the thinking behind this plan is that elementary education does not require eight years, the junior high school is a rather useless appendage, secondary education can begin at twelve as logically as at fourteen, and postponement of college until eighteen is wasteful and unnecessary. The belief is expressed that required attendance until the age of eighteen keeps many students in school who cannot legitimately complete a high school education, do not want it, and cannot profit from it. Furthermore, their presence in school interferes with the work of more able and better motivated students. If, on the other hand, a student is allowed to drop out of school either upon reaching sixteen or completing eighth grade, the result is that some bright students drop out at fourteen while dullards must remain until they are sixteen. This, he believes, is exactly the opposite of what it should be.

His proposal for a sweeping reorganization is indicated in Figure 11.[5] The proposal is provocative and controversial but contains many interesting and thoughtful features. The model of an ungraded primary school, for instance, seems very realistic. It combines kindergarten with what is ordinarily known as first and second grade to comprise an integral first phase of schooling. Within that segment a child moves entirely in terms of his own maturity and rate. If he is an exceptional youngster he may spend only one year in that division and then move on into the middle or elementary school. If he is an average child he would remain there for at least two years before moving on, and if he is experiencing a great deal of difficulty he might remain in the ungraded portion for as long as four years. The intent is to flexibly prepare and move children into the somewhat more formal atmosphere of the third grade of the elementary division entirely upon the basis of their abil-

[5] *Ibid.*, p. 147.

ity to make such a progression. The gifted youngsters are in effect accelerated and fed into the situation much more quickly because of their general maturity and readiness to take the next step. More normal children take the usual amount of time, but those who are less well endowed can have as much time as they need. The effect of such individual pacing should help to get all children off to a better start. The plan attempts to accomplish the very significant goal of *stretching the concept of what is normal progress for the child in his initial curricular experiences.*

The elementary portion of the proposal is envisioned as an environment that would provide a rich range of experiences. Major emphasis, however, would be placed upon skills of reading, writing, spelling, and mathematics. Because entrance was achieved on the basis of maturity, the children at this phase of the plan would almost all be expected to move through the program in four years. In this connection, the hope is expressed that there will be little, if any, failure. Junior high schools which ordinarily follow the elementary program would simply be eliminated. They are regarded as a professional accident and thought to be repetitious and unnecessary.

As shown in Figure 11, the average child, while under this plan, would enter high school at about twelve years of age. Because of the adjustments made earlier for maturation some would be younger and some older, but the group would be somewhat more homogeneous with respect to its readiness for high school. All students in the high school would have some experiences in common, and each grade would be grouped together for social purposes and aspects of the cirruculum that do not make rigorous demands on intellectual capacity. In studies such as mathematics, science, history, or literature, however, they would be regrouped on the basis of demonstrated ability in each subject.

The three levels contemplated for academic offerings in the high school vary markedly in terms of rigor and expectations. The lower-level courses for below average students would emphasize practicality and attempt to prepare students to do better what they are going to do anyway. Their curriculum

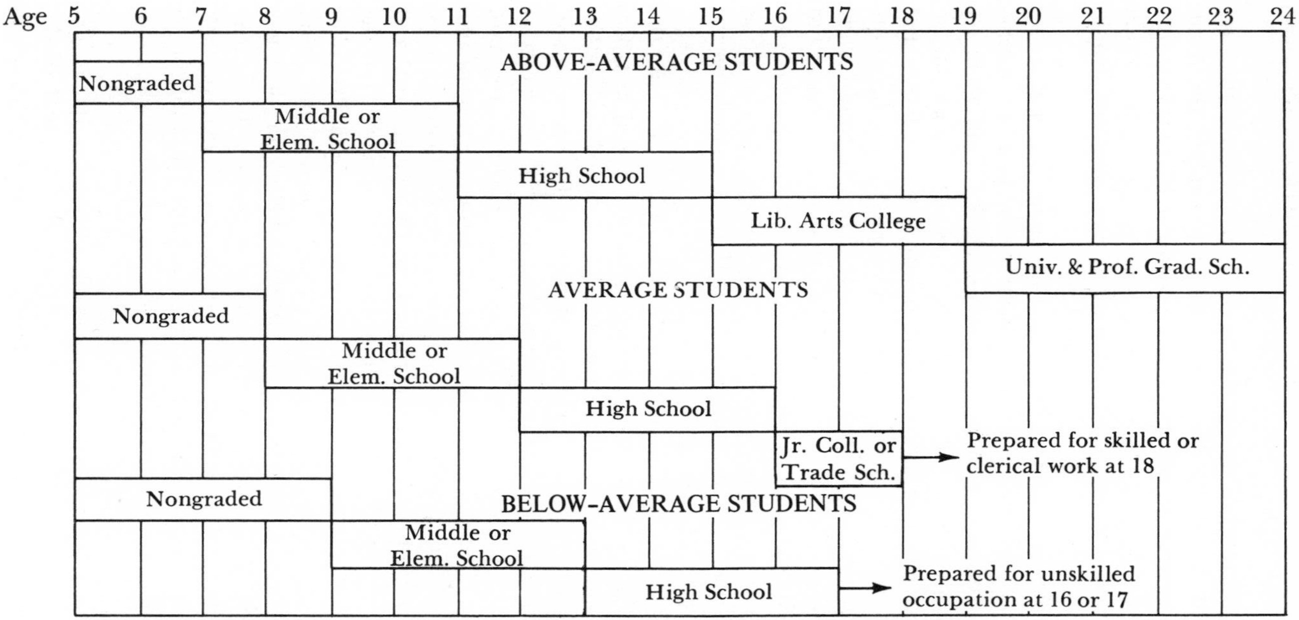

Figure 11 AN INTERPRETATION OF WOODRING'S REORGANIZATION PLAN

would emphasize such matters as learning to compute accurately and to read the newspapers and, for example, the *Reader's Digest* with understanding. They might also make a limited study of occupations. Their formal education would terminate at the completion of high school, and they would then enter the unskilled labor market.

The average student would have a curriculum with more intellectual substance. His group would study practical mathematics with applications of arithmetic, algebra, and geometry to problems of life. He would learn how to compute an income tax return in half the time required by his father and how to determine whether the new car loan is really being obtained for the rate claimed by the salesman. He would study the less serious works of literature and the kind of science and social studies that contribute to effective living and good citizenship. His education would continue into junior college or trade school, at which time he should be prepared for the skilled trades or clerical work.

The above-average student would enter college at about the age of fifteen or sixteen and complete a full liberal arts program with no specialized training. Professional education would follow the full four-year degree in liberal arts and would launch the student upon preparation for his career at about the same age that he begins under current programs. He would then undertake his study of engineering, medicine, law, or teaching with a substantial undergraduate girding.

Woodring's proposal seems to have an European flavor and is not likely to receive an enthusiastic endorsement from the American public. Many college students to whom this plan has been interpreted have reacted strongly against the notion of someone else determining for them whether or not they shall enter the professions. They want to know who is wise enough, perceptive enough, and sufficiently skilled in such matters to play God with someone else's life. In addition to this hazard, they are concerned over the plight of the "late bloomer" who moves with a completely undistinguished record through high school and suddenly blossoms later in life.

From a humanistic point of view the first segment of the plan is attractive and comes effectively to grips with the desired goal of flexible admissions. It allows children who need to move ahead more quickly to do so with a minimum of organizational difficulties; by expanding the concept of what normal progress is, it adjusts the expectations in such a manner as to more nearly fit everyone. The middle school format, also, seems advantageous. It is conceived in such a way that overlapping chronological ages are built into the structure, and it is philosophically hospitable to enrichment as well as a sensible emphasis of priority content. The elimination of the junior high school is most provocative. There is much repetition involved at this level and many children feel that they are marking time; and some even seem to regress academically. Although the plan is described as radical, the provisions applying to the elementary segment of the plan seem eminently sensible. In fact, they have already been interpreted and endorsed in somewhat different form in the prior discussions of flexible admission, of levels and multiage models of the nongraded school, and of cross-age grouping. The Woodring interpretation simply arranges them into a total reorganizational plan.

The Kiva Plan

The Kiva plan was an exploratory curriculum probe initiated by an enterprising principal to serve a single school. It took place in a relatively affluent community and involved about thirty children.[6] Although the Woodring plan was conceived as a total sweeping proposal for reorganization, this one is an example of what was accomplished without reorganizing and with only the resources existing within the school.

Kiva had a rather high incidence of able learners who were believed to be insufficiently challenged by the existing program. The principal discussed this with his faculty and parents and indicated his willingness to hold special sessions with

[6] Most of this interpretation is from remarks by the principal to the author. A full account of subsequent developments may be found in the report by Richard E. Bullington, "Experimental Curriculum for More Able Students," *Journal of Experimental Education*, XXXI (Spring 1963): 291–296.

these youngsters as a form of enrichment entirely different from their regular curriculum. He wished to explore the possibility of motivating and extending them through the introduction of some unusual forms of subject matter.

Children in grades five through eight were involved in the probe. Each child was selected by his classroom teacher as being in the upper 10 percent of the class. The selection by the teacher reflected his personal judgment, but took into consideration actual student performance as well as test scores. The children met with the principal one hour a day in what was designated as X Room. The scheduling was planned in such a manner that students missed portions of their regular program which they could easily make up. In general they were taken out of their classes in spelling, reading, and literature.

The problem for the principal was threefold. He had to select content that (a) really differed from the regular program, (b) was relatively interesting and challenging, and (c) constituted something he personally was capable of presenting to such gifted youngsters. He chose for the initial experience a unit on dead reckoning navigation. The unit included such aspects as magnetic variation, compass deviation, wind drift, true heading, the basic wind triangle, radius of action problems, relative motion, and interception. Experiences with primary elements of celestial navigation were provided, and the students were taught how to use the Weems Plotter and E6-B computer.

As a culminating activity for the first unit the students visited a local U.S. Air Force base. In making the arrangements for this visit, he mentioned to the officer that the base should be prepared for some rather good questions, as these were very bright youngsters. The officer laughed. That officer may never again ignore such an admonition. The group was given the red carpet treatment and were taken right out to the flight line for briefing. The first member of the briefing team, however, had just begun his remarks when up went a hand. In a very polite manner the youngster challenged the officer on an item of fact. The officer was somewhat shaken, but paused momentarily and conceded the child was correct. He then proceeded much more cautiously through his remaining remarks, as did all of the personnel who followed him.

X Room's next unit was on elementary statistics. As in the case of the first one, it utilized a heavy incidence of the problem-centered approach. Emphasis was placed upon interpretation and the group was taught how to calculate and interpret the mean, median, mode, quartiles, standard deviation, Pearson's product moment coefficient of correlation, measures of error, t-test for determining significance of differences, and the normal curve of probability. Stress was placed on the transfer of their previously learned mathematics, plus the development of proficiency in manipulating related algebraic formulas. They not only grasped the content, but enjoyed it.

In later sessions they were exposed to lectures in sociology and anthropology and took up a consideration of group dynamics. In addition, the principal taught a fourth grade teacher's class in order to free her to teach the youngsters French. Motivation throughout seemed high. One parent said that prior to X Room her eighth grade son was so bored he had wanted to drop school; after becoming involved in the project he became so stimulated that he experienced difficulty in going to sleep at night.

The reactions to this change in program for able learners was very good. Parents and teachers all felt that the students were stimulated and challenged. They thought that student achievements were amazing and that the experiences seemed to increase their interest in the regular classroom as well. The principal initially had some concern about having such a wide spread of chronological age and wondered if the fifth graders would be accepted by those in the seventh and eighth grades. In this project there were no problems of that nature indicated; in fact, the most gifted child in the group was a fifth grade boy. The success on this score supports the earlier endorsement that was made of the multiage model of the nongraded school.

As a result of insights derived from working with the program the principal had some recommendations for anyone considering a similar venture. He thought it important to use subject matter that was entirely different from what they had

had in the past or were likely to receive later. Every effort should be made, for instance, to prevent mere duplication of high school content, for this would only magnify the problem for the able learners and their teachers when they entered secondary education. In addition to using material that was unique, interesting, and challenging, he believed that the content should be of such a nature that ready transfer of their previous learnings might be realized.

The Kiva plan made school life richer and more exciting for the students involved. A relatively small proportion of the total school population was effected, but the effect was beneficial. For a school structured along graded lines and fairly traditionally conceived, variations of the concept of X Room can help to fill a need. One might contend that if earlier recommendations relating to school organization and grouping were employed throughout the program, X Room projects would be less necessary. This is an entirely logical contention; however, most schools are at present not so organized. Kiva students were ripe for a change and X Room provided it.

The Optional Experiences Plan

The Kiva plan was deliberately conceived for the upper 10 percent of very able learners. In marked contrast is the optional experiences plan which, theoretically, may include every child in the school. In this sense it is compatible with the broadened concept endorsed in the introductory remarks—the belief that every child has a gift and that it is the proper business of the school to give it nurture. The arrangement can be implemented within a single school, often with the resources already provided for within that school.

The plan utilizes and builds upon two concepts that were identified and interpreted in earlier discussions. One is the idea of establishing some form of priority content, and the other is the instrumentality for achieving this through the use of criteria of content selection.

If one envisions the total present content package of curriculum in a given school and then carefully screens it for its more significant elements, he has reduced the package. In this reduction the time element required to do justice to the remaining content has been correspondingly reduced. Let us assume that a minimal amount of squeezing or screening has been achieved and that the savings in time amount to only three hours a week. With this three hours a week, however, the school can implement its optional experiences plan.

One of the main elements of the plan is to inventory the unique gifts of the faculty. If every child has something that he can do better than any other child in the room, it is just as reasonable to hypothesize unique and hidden talents for each of the teachers. It is perhaps possible to have a faculty that has no unique strengths; and, if this is actually the case, then it is best to forget the whole idea. It is much more likely, however, that one is dealing here with a rather exciting set of resources that may never have been brought to the surface.

Having determined what these special faculty talents, interests, and resources are they are made available to all of the students in the school on the basis of their individual preferences. The sessions are scheduled during the three hours that have been saved by screening the content, and students may elect to attend them or not to attend them. If they do not find any of the options interesting, they will attend study halls supervised by teachers whose sessions did not fill. The optional experiences sessions are to represent an environment of special freedom and are to bear no resemblance to regular classes. There are no tests, courses of study, assignments, grades, or any of the usual paraphernalia of the program. People who have a special gift to share meet with those who want to share it, and the nature of the sessions evolves in terms of whatever is comfortable and helpful. One school which worked out a plan similar to this for their sixth grade presented to their students the offerings indicated in Figure 12.

The optional experiences approach rates very high in the degree to which it can invoke the intended philosophy and serve a very wide segment of the students in a school. It has a second advantage, similar to that of team teaching, in the sense that someone with a special gift can share it with a greater proportion of the student population. Its third advan-

Figure 12 PROPOSED "MINICOURSES," SIXTH GRADE, 1969–70

Nancy Kneale

1. Personal Grooming
   Hair care, skin care, nails, clothes, etc.

2. Interior Decorating
   (General for the children's needs)
   Color, fabrics, furniture, knickknacks

3. Plants and Indoor Gardening
   Types of plants, equipment needed, general care to insure healthy plants

4. Art Projects
   Wood projects, stitchery

Frank Tunnell

1. Sportsman's Hour
   Athletic and outdoor sports dependent upon the season—marksmanship, camping, game animals, football, baseball, etc.

2. This Wonderful World of Science
   Group projects, discussions

3. Arts and Crafts
   (Depends upon course from Jamieson this summer)

4. Newspaper Activities
   Stock market (finance), current events

5. Games
   Bridge, others to be added

Joe Weaver

1. Basic Electrical Wiring
   (Around the house)
   Small appliance repair, lamps

2. Game Room Tournaments
   Chess and checkers—how to play, then championship games

3. Indoor Sports
   Baseball and volleyball

tage is the possibility of contributing to faculty attitudes and morale by recognizing and prizing their unique strengths. In schools whose faculty strengths need to be supplemented in order to enrich the possible options, there is an excellent opportunity to reach out and involve leaders in the community.

Individualized Curricula

The Kiva plan focused upon the very able learner for a limited portion of his day, whereas the optional experiences plan

Figure 12 (*Continued*)

4. Creative Thinking and Expression
   Modern poetry, pop music, expression of thought concerning all art forms

Charlotte Binder

1. Note Script
   Alphabet shorthand, speedwriting

2. Practical Sewing

3. Beginning Journalism
   How to write for different purposes, gathering and editing news, layout, production

Roger Simpson

1. Square Dancing

2. Physical Fitness

3. Reading Club

Optional Courses (In addition to or instead of study period; varies each week)

1. Movie
   Selected from our catalogue, for general interest

2. Community Ties
   Visitors to show slides, speak, give demonstrations

3. Story Hour
   Teacher or taped

4. Junior Leaders
   Techniques of leadership, parliamentary procedure

5. Mythology
   Study of the Greek gods and their place in literature

6. Needlework
   Beginning embroidery, crocheting

NOTE: Courtesy of Barcelona School, Alhambra District, Phoenix, Arizona.

reached out to provide for special interests and talents for almost all of the children, also for a limited portion of the day. Even with all of the possible advantages emanating from enlightened organizational and grouping manipulations, the teacher faces a fascinating array of human differences in the composition of his class. Can better individual challenge be provided for all of the children within the more structured boundaries of the curriculum as it exists? Can a school effectively modify its basic offerings within a relatively typical setting?

The answer, of course, is that it can. Mary Ward did it in

1912 at San Francisco Normal School.[7] With the dynamic encouragement of the president, Dr. Frederick Burk, she prepared self-instruction materials for arithmetic in which children could move through the program at their own rate of mastery. The movement grew at San Francisco so that, from that point on, instruction in their elementary school was on an individual basis. Each child proceeded at his own natural rate without being retarded by slower children or hurried by faster ones. Burk wrote a monograph on what they were doing. One colorful paragraph was as follows:

> *The class system has been modeled upon the military system. It is constructed upon the assumption that a group of minds can be marshalled and controlled in growth in exactly the same manner that a military officer marshalls and directs the bodily movements of a company of soldiers. In solid unbreakable phalanx the class is supposed to move through the grades, keeping in locked step. This locked step is set by the "average" pupil—an algebric myth born of inanimate figures and an addled pedagogy.*[8]

This early experiment was one of the major inspirations for the leadership of Carleton Washburne in what was then the little suburban city of Winnetka, twenty miles from Chicago. Their curriculum modifications were to become famous as the Winnetka plan, although Washburne declared there was no such thing. The word "plan" had static implications which were distasteful to him. He thought of it more as a living, growing, evolving spirit of change. So long as he was present as the inspirational interpreter and leader, it was as he thought of it. In subsequent years, however, as his influence was diluted, the dynamic and revolutionary spirit was diminished. Thus, the ever-evolving design dependent upon a spirit of exploration and discovery became a plan. As Marland put

[7] Carleton W. Washburne and Sydney P. Marland, *Winnetka: The History and Significance of an Educational Experiment* (Englewood Cliffs, N.J.: Prentice-Hall, 1963), p. 7.

[8] *Ibid.*, p. 9.

it, "Those who were new to Winnetka found themselves coloring in the line drawings created by other artists." [9]

Much of what is considered new in education had its inception at Winnetka as they pioneered in self-teaching materials, individualized instruction, and programmed learning. They divided the curriculum into two parts which were designated "common essentials" and "group and creative activities." The program was arranged so that half of each forenoon and afternoon was given over to individual work in the common essentials, and the other half of each session was devoted to group and creative activities.

The emphasis upon self-instructional materials and individualized teaching tended to be placed upon subjects such as arithmetic, reading, spelling, and language which were referred to as "skill subjects" by Washburne.[10] Their early work in mathematics, for instance, was broken down into a simple step-by-step procedure such as the programming of today. Their explanations in the self-instructional materials were as clear as possible and were illustrated with model problems broken into very small steps containing just one new element of difficulty. If a child missed an example the answer sheet showed him in which step he was weak, and he would go back to the explanation. With additional supplementary problems of a similar nature and continued self-checking, he assumed a larger role in achieving eventual mastery by himself. He could work at his own pace but would have to complete a given step in the program without error. Time could vary, but there was a major effort to hold mastery or quality more constant.

With the wealth of materials available today from the fruits of technology and the active interests in education expressed by business and industry, such materials exist in greater profusion than ever before. They create an additional opportunity for segments of the curriculum to move nearer to the goal of individualized instruction. And, in so doing, *they may more adequately nurture children's gifts within the normal curricu-*

[9] *Ibid.,* p. 196.
[10] *Ibid.,* p. 81.

lar boundaries even as they stretch and extend the boundaries themselves.

Many of the possibilities for extending the boundaries and providing appropriate levels of difficulty do not even require special materials. They need only a modification of patterns of teaching. Such modifications can often be effected at no extra cost, little extra effort, and with considerable improvement in learning. The systematic enrichment technique in spelling, for instance, is an example of such a modification. This technique can be utilized in a traditional school that still teaches a pre-scribed list of words in spelling each week.

Teacher Joe Hall taught in such a school. It was very con-servative in its overall approach and required its teachers to focus each week on the prescribed list of words. The weekly list of words is one of the tribal rites in spelling and is utilized by teachers all over the nation. It may result in teaching the word "icicle" in May and the word "spring" in the fall, but what it lacks in ingenuity it makes up in its dogged pursuit of the problem.

Joe did what his school required but added an additional ingredient. Each week on the day of the final spelling he gave five extra words selected from the content of the ongoing ac-tivities. Students did not know in advance what the five words were going to be, but they did know that each of them would be selected from whatever units were currently being studied.

The five special words were called bonus words. No pupil was required to try any of them. If he wished to try any or all of them, however, it was his privilege to do so. A student who missed one of the words in the official list but successfully spelled one of the bonus words could still get 100 in spelling. He could even miss five of his regular words and get 100, if he correctly spelled all of the bonus words. This added a little zest to the spelling and gave it at least some semblance of being in consonance with the rest of the program.

Some teachers give the plan an additional kind of structure. They work cooperatively with children each week to identify some of the more important words in each area of the pro-gram. They are drawn from science, social studies, mathematics, and health and are selected because of their special significance to what is being studied. By the end of the week such a list may contain forty or fifty key words and the students know that their bonus words will be selected from this thoughtfully prepared list. The same scoring arrangement would prevail.

Such a simple and sensible modification of the approach adds a very important kind of depth and enrichment to the curriculum in spelling. So many good students are completely unchallenged by the weekly lists which in many instances they already know how to spell. This not only strengthens the program, but makes them participants in the process. There is a remarkable quality about the approach, however, which significantly increases its value as an illustrative teaching practice. Although it may have been originally conceived for the purpose of greater challenge of gifted students, it yields an additional dividend in the sense that it has a wholesome effect on the less able as well. It is thus the kind of factor which is most germane to the basic intent of nurturing the gifts and strengths that lie within all children. *When such benefits can be achieved within the normal confines of the school program, there is a corresponding reduction of the need to artificially contrive arrangements that fall outside the program.* This is the essence of the recommended approach to giftedness, and such modifications are possible throughout the curriculum to an extent that may not be adequately recognized.

The computerized education of tomorrow may simplify the process in such a way that a machine can program and guide a child through major segments of the entire program in an almost completely individualized manner. This is technologically possible now and implementation lies just over the horizon. Perhaps when that eventuality has arrived, the uniquely personal qualities of teachers can be freed to focus upon more basic human needs. Can this be done? Can people wisely harness technology and machines to best serve their ends or do they in some yet unexplained manner tend to take over and shape the character of our lives? At the moment technology has the upper hand and is rapidly destroying the environment. It is like an unrecognized form of cancer sweeping through the

entire universe, and it will be subordinated to its proper role
only by a massive concerted effort to do so. Whether this can
really be done is still an open question. The final decision on
this matter of human destiny is ours, but is not yet rendered.

A Key Concept

Every important idea that has been developed in earlier chap-
ters converges at this point and has some relevance to the nurture of giftedness. Goals, design, organization, use of personnel, management, content selection, and grouping all blend
together on a matter of this importance and complexity to
make the development of the individual possible. This is as it
should be, for it is what the curriculum is all about. Some professionals occasionally seem to lose their way; they become so
imbued with a given curriculum practice that they forget any
given approach is only a means to an end. Team teaching and
nongraded schools, for instance, are important but expendable, for each of them is part of a larger and more basic concept. That concept is exciting and central to the humanistic
school. *It is the idea of viewing the curriculum as a total fluid
laboratory of resources from which each child may draw what
he needs when he needs it without any senseless restrictions
being placed upon him because of age or grade level. That is
the school of tomorrow.*

Chapter

Nurturing
Creativity

9

Chapter

Nurturing
Creativity

9

If the attributes that are most vital to a free society were to be placed in a hierarchy of importance, creativity would rank very high. It is the growth edge of human endeavor and adds immeasurably to the enrichment of personal living. The creativity of two or three individuals may well have tipped the scales in favor of the Allies in World War II, and the actual survival of man on a dangerously polluted planet may be determined by creative reversal of his destructive forces in ways yet to be discovered. Creativity is linked, therefore, not only to the quality of living, but to a preservation of life itself.

The anomaly of the situation is that, as vital as creativity seems to be to human destiny, there is no concerted effort to sustain or nourish it. The creative child is not likely to be appreciated by his teacher and may even incur his active dislike. The creative adult finds two basically unattractive alternatives awaiting him. On the one hand, he will probably not be promoted as rapidly as his more conforming associates. On the other hand, if he is promoted he will then be expected to assume additional routine responsibilities which diminish his creative output. In general, the society as well as the schools have failed to attach sufficient importance to structuring a setting in which creativity may most advantageously flourish.

One of the interesting discoveries of modern psychology is that creativity does not appear to be positively correlated with intelligence. If one attempts to select the most creative members of a group by choosing those who score highest on common measures of intelligence, he will fail to include more than ⅔ of the most creative members.[1] The perceptive layman has suspected this for a long time, but the psychologist has only recently caught up with him and verified it. The real truth of the matter may lie not in the lack of correlation between creativity and intelligence but in the deficiencies of the evaluating instruments themselves. Measures of intelligence may simply be incapable of appraising *the most vital aspects* of what they are attempting to assess.

Creativity is not interpreted here in any special sense except to suggest that it is, perhaps, the appropriate conceptual cradle for all of the other curricular areas. Unless it is embedded within and diffused throughout the social studies, science, mathematics, and language programs, each of them will be lacking one of their essential ingredients. The essence of creativity seems to involve uniqueness of response. At a fairly common level of uniqueness of response one is dealing simply with individuality, for individuality is that aspect of behavior which is a unique expression of the self. At a higher level of expression, uniqueness of response may emerge in the form of new devices, inventions, solutions, or thoughts. Individuality nurtures higher levels of creative expression. The more that individuality exists in a given situation, the more likelihood there is that new forms and ideas will develop. Individuality may then be said to feed the creative process.

The elementary school has a very vital role to play in any kind of concerted effort to foster creativity. For, although the twig is already bent before the child comes to school, he is still in a formative stage; it is the earliest opportunity available to the school to nurture whatever creative impulses he may possess. In fact, any point beyond the elementary years may even prove to be too late. His approach to life and his manner of

[1] E. Paul Torrance, *Guiding Creative Talent* (Englewood Cliffs, N.J.: Prentice-Hall, 1962), p. 59.

thinking are rapidly being shaped, and they should be shaped in the image of a creative individual. Five factors that are believed to be important in the development of a creative personality are interpreted in the following. Each factor has reference and application to each child in the classroom rather than to a favored few. This is due to the belief that each child may have some capacity for creativity and it is the proper business of the school to encourage and develop it.

Environmental Richness

Thirty children in a fifth grade class were given a simple mathematical problem involving scores on spelling. The five scores given were 85, 90, 95, 80, and 100. Twenty-nine of the children added the scores and divided the sum by five. The remaining child simply looked at the scores and jotted down the answer. He had mentally added 15, 10, 5, and 20, divided that sum by five, and subtracted from 100 to arrive at the average. His teacher frowned at him and seemed displeased with what he had done. It was reminiscent of the fable of the animal school. In that delightful fable the eagle surpassed all of the competing animals in getting to the top of the tree but was criticized for using his own method of getting there.

Environmental richness is a sort of total thrust. Creativity is not *imprisoned in the art period,* as it may be in so many schools. It is nourished throughout the curriculum wherever the opportunities for being creative may occur. In the above incident the child had never been taught to compute an average in that manner. His prior mathematical instruction, however, had emphasized meaning and self-discovery, so his inclination toward a unique method of solving the problem was greater than it might otherwise have been. Many learning activities throughout the program may contribute to this total thrust. Thus, meaning and self-discovery as a qualitative ingredient in elementary mathematics makes a contribution to creativity. The attempt to resolve their own problems of everyday living in social studies affords children opportunity and practice in bringing creativity to bear on their own affairs. The nurture of scientific thinking in science and even the thought approach to spelling strengthen the capacity for creative response. When the many opportunities for individuality of thinking and approach are utilized throughout the program one is extending the total thrust. Without this general push a school cannot adequately develop creativity any more than it can develop adequate language usage in a "language period."

Another aspect of environmental richness is reflected by materials and media for expression. A school that limits children's creative experiences to paper and crayons is as impoverished and barren as the classroom in which the question and answer recitation is the sole method of instruction. One of the encouraging aspects of the modern school is the manner in which it has selectively extended the child's experiences with a variety of media. Children in the better schools have opportunities to work with wood, leather, clay, finger paint, puppets, poetry, dancing, and a host of other materials and media. One or more of these will surely light a spark for everyone so that each child in the classroom is more likely to find a satisfying means of bringing out his thoughts and feelings about his world.

Environmental richness is thus a general enrichment of the soil. Its purpose is to provide one of the basic conditions for stimulating creative response in each child. Even more significantly, it enlarges the arena in which creativity may occur and apply. It is a distinctive and essential mark of an excellent school.

Sensory Awareness

Creativity seems to be linked to sensory awareness. Beethoven could walk by the sea or through the forest and experience such a perceptual awareness of sound and mood that he could re-create it in his music. It may be that the more civilized man becomes, the less sensory awareness he has, for it is less essential to his survival. And also, many man-made aspects of the environment must be deliberately tuned out in order to maintain his sanity. He learns to selectively tune out certain noises, odors, and irritations as an essential aspect of adjusting to the circumstances of his existence. Thus, sensory awareness is dulled and becomes one of the casualties of modern civilization. It seems imperative at the same time, however, that one not dull his basic capacity for response.

Sensory awareness needs to be sharpened or heightened in the elementary school in order to maintain and develop the child's capacity for adequate response to his environment. This is a part of being fully alive and of being a fully developed individual. There are adults who can walk in the woods without hearing the birds sing, who can look at a setting sun as they drive home from work without seeing the sunset, or who can walk down the street after a spring rain without feeling the freshness of the earth. This dulling of the senses is neither necessary nor desirable and represents a shriveling of the organism. Such an individual is only partially alive. The humanistic teacher will not allow this partial death to take place in his room. He will keep a portion of the child's experiences in intimate contact with the natural wonders of the world, and he will actively seek to extend and heighten the senses themselves.

There are no well-marked trails for the heightening of the senses. It is an aspect of teaching in which one's own imagination and sensitivities may be the best guide. To emphasize the sense of feel, one teacher brought to her class an object buried under pieces of cut paper in the bottom of a sack. Each child was allowed to feel the mystery object briefly and to guess what it might be. No doubt the last child to feel it had a quite different sensation than the first, for the thoughtful examination by twenty-nine pairs of hands had radically altered its external characteristics. The object was an orange. A science teacher worked at the heightening of the senses by shutting off one of them temporarily. As an introduction to a unit on sight he arranged for his students to do without sight for twenty-four hours by having their eyes taped. Students who experienced this procedure felt that they could see more after the removal of the blind, in addition to having a keener appreciation for the sense of sight itself. A primary teacher worked at increasing her children's perceptions by blindfolding one child at a time and having him guess which of his classmates was speaking to him. Wide trait differences were apparent in this procedure; but, more significantly, the accuracy of perception seemed to increase with practice.

In a humanistic school the activities designed to heighten perceptual awareness would be a conscious and discernible part of the curriculum. At the present time they tend to be crowded out by verbal activities. In a verbal society, verbal activities are a significant part of an individual's development—but alone they can lead only to a maladjusted and malfunctioning man. The vigorous, alert, fully alive person has all of his antennae working. His sensory equipment is in full contact with his environment; and this, in turn, accents the degree to which he can achieve intellectual development. Creativity is enhanced by this process.

Imagination

Imagination is the magic carpet of childhood, and one of the great compensating mechanisms of life is that it is distributed rather equally between the rich and the poor. A child who has not saved the elephant herds with Tarzan, tramped the Himalayas with Hillary, or made his own contacts with the visitors from outer space is surely living too sedately for his own welfare. But imagination is not merely a child's pass to the magnificent dimension of make-believe. For the adult it is a continuing link between the present and the future. It is a bridge between the world of today and what it may eventually come to be. Many of the breathtaking advancements of today were spawned first in the imagination of creative men. First the dream, then the reality—this is the sequence exemplified by some of the most creative men and women of our generation. Henry Kaiser was a remarkable practitioner of this sequence. He would awaken at 4:00 A.M. with such a compelling idea that he leaped out of bed to start phoning his friends. His approach to life was summarized in the expression "living a dream fulfilled."

One of the most creative teachers of our times was once

asked to define imagination. He thought for a moment and then said simply that it was *the ability to think of things as they are not.* There is a considerable tendency in the elementary schools to think of things as they are, but almost no effort to think of them as they are not. This is an imbalance which frequently escapes attention in the schools as they attempt to shore up their defenses and teach more science and mathematics. Yet, imagination is vital in both science and mathematics. It is doubtful that Einstein could have even conceived his unified field theory without an active assist from his imagination and Applegate has aptly described a scientist as one "who builds a ladder in the air and then climbs it even though it isn't there."

A fourth grade teacher in the Southwest plays a game orally with her children. She will ask them to imagine that they are unusual objects and to speak as this object might speak if it had the power to communicate. For instance, she will ask them to reflect the feelings of the unwritten side of a sheet of paper, a squeaky board on a stairway, a sunken ship off Santa Barbara, the last chocolate in a box, or the clown's hat after the party.

A teacher's effort to stimulate the imagination of her children is often considered a sort of educational fluff. This is particularly true in the vast community of the uninformed. The enlightened school, however, whether it exists among the informed or the uninformed, will manage to keep imagination alive. For imagination is the great eye that sees beyond what is known, the giant searchlight that brings the unknown into focus, and the forerunner of research and hypothesis. It is, also, the indispensable ingredient of creativity.

Beauty

Until recently one could climb a small hill in Papago Park near Phoenix and look down on a vast expanse of desert beauty. To the east lay the majestic Superstition Mountains shrouded in mystery and grandeur. Between Papago and the Superstitions was mile after mile of natural desert dotted with the giant saguaro that stand like lonely sentinels on an eternal vigil. For those who were responsive to the simple charm of the desert it was an area of enchantment and loveliness.

The view is different now. As one approaches the rise of the hill, his senses are shocked by row after row of identical, reflecting rooftops standing in stark and ugly contrast to the scene below. This did not need to be. Imagination and a sensitivity to beauty could easily have varied the structures and blended them into the landscape. Perhaps the developer attended "art classes" in an elementary school where all of the children made identical tulips. If so, society has now reaped its commensurate reward and another area of natural beauty is forever lost to what is inaccurately labeled as progress.

In the main, the marks that man has made upon his environment do not reflect a sensitivity to beauty. He has destroyed much that is lovely and replaced it with very little in return. He has carved fine highways into areas of natural splendor and then punctuated the view with offensive advertising. He has developed retreats in the wilderness for those who wish to escape civilization and then littered them with beer cans and other sordid reminders of the civilization he sought to escape. He has blackened the cities, poisoned the streams, and is now tragically engaged in fouling the entire atmosphere.

Beauty is not synonymous with creativity, of course; for creativity can produce the nonbeautiful as well as the beautiful. But the intent of this discussion is to suggest that creativity *should consciously embrace beauty and project it into the man-made environment.* If, among other benefits, the world is not to be lovelier as a result of increased creativity, then something in the process has misfired. Children should learn in the elementary school to bring more beauty into their surroundings and into their lives.

As a case in point, the typical primary teacher makes an effort to have her room attractively arranged before the children arrive. One kindergarten teacher, however, rejected this idea. Her room was barren when the children arrived because she believed that the children themselves should undertake the job of making their room more beautiful. Their room, when it was finished, did not have a ready-made look and it was not arranged in terms of the standards of an adult. But the room was warm and pleasing to them, and they grew in their understanding and sensitivity to beauty. In the long view, such an approach should come much closer to producing a generation of adults possessing the sensitivities this one seems to lack. Beauty should be fused through the life of children. They should have experiences in replacing drabness with something better. Each child should develop a feeling of responsibility for adding in some way to the total store of beauty that exists in the world. Beauty should be learned as a pervading concept that embraces thoughts and gracious acts as well as more material things. And beauty should be consciously sought, consciously created, and consciously shared.

Creative Teaching

One of the schools in a large district in the Midwest was located on what is often described as the wrong side of the tracks. The children in this school enjoyed the blessing of some creative teachers, however, and had the reputation of producing creative work. One year the school served as host for a state conference; and, in preparation for the event, the children's art was attractively displayed throughout the building. Teachers from all over the state came to this conference and admired the fresh and original work of the children. Several of them then went to the principal and asked, "Where can we get the patterns for this art work?"

Fortunately, all elementary children are not in the custody of teachers who are this deficient in their concept of creativity. The first grade children in a laboratory school came to their room one morning in September and found some strange "tracks" on their papers. There was much speculation about what might have caused them, but no facts. The next morning they were there again; and, because they were very small and shaped like a human foot, the children concluded that their room may have been visited by a brownie. On the basis of this tentative conclusion they drafted a note to their nocturnal visitor asking him if he would like to live in their room. His reply was in such small print that it had to be read under a magnifying glass. He inquired cautiously about the rent. The children decided that a brownie might not have much money so they set the rent at two cents. He decided that at that figure he could stay, and a lively correspondence was established in the first few weeks of school. In the late fall their brownie visited Oak Creek one weekend and brought the children beautifully colored leaves. As Christmas drew near he had to leave for a period of time to help Santa and he rode gloriously to the North Pole on the wings of a redbird.

Although the children could only see their brownie in the "mind's eye," he was a discernible part of their curriculum. He helped bridge the gap between home and school during the first days. He caused them to want to write and to read what they had written. He added some color and incentive to their day. In conception and application this teaching was creative.[2]

Creative teaching seems to defy formulas and is rarely fostered by the implementation of specific techniques. One of the basic purposes of unit teaching was to free the teacher from the regimentation of a text and to inspire a freer and more creative approach. Yet, any close observer of the scene recognizes that unit teaching often became as compulsive and rigid as the form it sought to replace. Creative teaching is the function of creative individuals, and the teaching can only be as creative as the individual who conceives it. The creative teacher has an awareness of the common techniques of his profession, but is less dependent on them. He does not ignore the well-marked trails of other teachers, but strives to improve them. He understands the fundamental processes of given approaches to teaching, but frequently transcends them.

If a school wishes to make the assumption that creative development of children is positively affected by creative teaching, there are two basic roads to improvement. One road is to selectively recruit the most creative teachers that can be obtained. These teachers will not be revealed by grade point averages or intelligence quotients. They are more likely to be re-

[2] From an incident in the teaching of Dr. Merri Schall, Arizona State University, Tempe, Arizona.

vealed by classroom performance, interview, and candid appraisal of themselves in regard to their creative drives. The other road to improvement involves the creating of conditions that enable all teachers to be as creative as they would like to be. This involves removal of the penalties and fears of making a mistake, official encouragement to strike out with new ways, and active administrative assistance in the expediting of materials and ideas. It is reasonable to assume that there is a great reservoir of creative capacities in teachers that is largely unused. The administrator of a qualitative school will tap these unused resources and bring them into fuller play, for this is one of the significant ways in which he can contribute to increased creativity in his generation.

Chapter
Personalizing
Social
Studies
10

Chapter
Personalizing Social Studies
10

Social studies has always had some difficulty in establishing its status and identity. It does not enjoy the mystique of science. It has never achieved the respectability of mathematics. It does not, like reading, belong to the power block; and it was never a fair-haired child like the languages. What, then, can one say that it is?

In the more common and traditional sense it consists of geography, history, and civics. In a diffused and larger sense, however, social studies is every day in the school, every child in the classroom, and every personal relationship that occurs in the program. It is helping every child to hold his head high and to know that he is a worthy self. It is widening the ripples of understanding that indicates a growing awareness of one's world. It is kindness and love, tolerance and ideals, sacrifice and seasoning. It is a deeply etched story about man, his problems, his aspirations, his way of life, and how he fits into the mainstream of the world's culture. Each portion of the curriculum has a special purpose which is more uniquely its own. For social studies that purpose is the development of effective citizenship.

Social studies has no need to be apologetic about its existence. If history is the story of man, what area of the program has a more exciting story to tell? If social studies can help to enlighten man about the world in which he lives, when in all recorded history has he needed more ˙to be truly enlightened? And, if today man has a special need to be able to peer into the future for a glimpse of what tomorrow may bring, from what better torch can he be guided than the thoughtful illumination of what has already occurred? This area of study can sift from the lessons of the past the bits of truth and wisdom that help young learners to more resourcefully face an uncertain tomorrow. Skillfully and selectively employed, it can bring to the classroom situation all of the relevancy that the circumstances require. As the appropriate instrumentality for socialization and citizenship it is one of the areas that enjoys the closest natural kinship with the humanistic concepts. In the following interpretation six ideas are suggested as being characteristics that reflect a more person-oriented program.

The Classroom as a Laboratory for Social Living

It is possible that the richest and most dynamic source of content available to social studies is largely unworked and perhaps unrecognized. Good schools may build up their stores of enrichment materials in the form of excellent books and materials. They even build them carefully in terms of field experiences and environmental resources. Simultaneously, however, they may fail to identify the classroom living itself as a vital source of content in their program. This source of content is richer than anything that can be found in a book, and lies always at the disposal of the thoughtful teacher. It is unparalleled in the degree to which it is meaningful to the learners, and it has its own built-in or intrinsic motivation.

Hardly a day goes by in the classroom without some sort of misbehavior or interpersonal stress on the part of the students. A child may strike another child; he may lie about, deprive, or otherwise malign a classmate. Such conditions are widely regarded by teachers as difficult or unpleasant, but it is possible that these negative situations afford in themselves a unique opportunity for improving the classroom living. The fact that such an incident takes place in the presence of the class gives the members sufficient understanding of it to form a basis for resolving it. And the act of resolving it is the process of improving one's own social living.

The other side of the coin is equally rich and important. The classroom is also the stage for virtuous acts on the part of one or more of the children. Albert successfully mediates and stops a fight. Linda defends an unpopular view in the class discussion and calmly presents an overlooked aspect of justice. The class demonstrates suspended judgment in the face of circumstantial evidence and refuses to make a decision until it has more complete facts. The children show in their selection of class officers that they can look beyond the superficial aspects of personality and social status and recognize leadership. In every school there are positive elements of social living that deserve recognition, and the process of thoughtful recognition itself is also a positive contribution to improving the quality of social living.

The logical extension of this concept is to use the school and its environs as a laboratory for social education. The qualitative social studies program should selectively extract the richest opportunities it may have to help children experience social education in a realistic and guided setting. The accumulation of these experiences throughout the elementary years helps a child to be more understanding and informed about life. It helps to season him and quicken his grasp of the important link between freedom and responsibility. It provides him with opportunity and encouragement to become a finer person by being a contributing part of something larger than himself. The effective program will make such learnings a conscious part of its overall plan.

Developing Ideals and Social Values

Many professionals believe that schools should no longer attempt to influence the development of ideals and that this is a function more properly left to the church and the home. Such a decision rests with the parents, for they are the final arbiters on such a matter. The position taken here, however, is that the development of ideals is an essential function of the school in general and the social studies in particular. To leave it out of the program is a serious omission and a vast waste of opportunity, for the curriculum affords many advantageous moments that are not so readily available to either the church or the home. History is rich with instances of courage, fortitude, vision, sacrifice, honesty, and their negative counterparts. From what better source can a nation find opportunity to present to youth its national conscience and ideals?

In the past the teaching of values and ideals has been approached through the study of great men. Some teachers include such an emphasis throughout the year by initiating a project called the Hall of Fame. The Hall of Fame may be symbolized by a special place set aside in the room, an appropriate picture, or a three-dimensional construction. As great men come to the attention of the class in its study of history, science, or the arts, they receive thoughtful emphasis. Any child in the room may decide that one of these men merits being in the Hall of Fame. If so, he then studies the life of the person and attempts to prepare a stimulating and persuasive presentation which he gives to the class in the form of a nomination. The class itself decides who will be so honored. *Such an approach has a continuity of focus upon greatness.* In the hands of a sensitive and skillful teacher, it can have a constructive impact.

In recent times the great-man approach has received a special sort of criticism. It has been accused of misleading young people by giving them an exaggerated or even a false picture of the virtues of some of the eminent figures of the past. Some of this criticism may be valid. Obviously teaching cannot justify a deliberately dishonest portrayal. Human frailty and limitations can be a part of such study, however, and the approach can be a genuine searching process in which lack of vision and errors in judgment may take their proper place in the unfolding circumstances of a great man's life. This need not tarnish his image to children. In fact, it may even endear him and make his remarkable achievements seem more plausible. The approach today can thus reflect less of the concept of great men and more of the concept of *greatness in men.* This is a more realistic and attainable vision for children.

Role Playing. Role playing as interpreted by the Shaftels has a unique and significant contribution to make to the goal of helping children form social values and ideals.[1] Their important book is the result of twenty years of exploring practical ways of relating democratic ideals to the everyday life of children. It features a thoughtful selection of open-ended stories which children may complete by enacting the various roles in terms of their own decisions and values. Each story deals with a personal or social problem and confronts the enactors with a matter of character or morality at their own level of understanding. The reality practice is unrehearsed and strives to be a medium in which children's real feelings and values may find expression. Multiple enactments of the same role by different participants result in a variety of decisions and reflections of personal beliefs which are thoughtfully assessed in the presence of one's peers.

The teacher guiding such a process is not trying to palm off his own values upon the youngsters, but is helping them to search out and examine their own. The idea of the reality practice is one of honest searching for options and their consequences, rather than clever manipulation to a predetermined choice. It reflects a basic belief in the capacity of individuals to struggle with their dilemmas and to arrive at intelligent forms of accommodation or solutions. When errors are made, the same wholesome attitude is reflected in the assumption that they have the capacity to profit and grow from their mistakes.

Role playing is uniquely compatible with humanistic concepts also in the manner in which it draws from and builds upon students' prior experiences. In the enactment of their roles they perform in a new and attractive dimension—not from books, but out of the realities of their own living. They bring with them their own resources for response, and these

---

[1] Fannie R. and George Shaftel, *Role Playing for Social Values: Decision Making in the Social Studies* (Englewood Cliffs, N.J.: Prentice-Hall, 1967), pp. 203–425.

resources are so valued that they in effect become the central content of the experience. The exposure and examination of such life content from members of the group bring to the learning situation a meaning, a richness, and a relevance that has few parallels in curriculum and instruction.

Role playing also seems to nurture some very desirable forms of teacher behavior. The nonevaluative nature of the instructional role, the warm supportive relationship, the act of listening to the emotional as well as the intellectual content of what is transpiring—all move the curriculum somewhat nearer the goal of inner-directed individuals.

Influence of the Teacher. The potential impact of one's personal approach to matters of judgment concerning right and wrong was masterfully illustrated by a high school history teacher in New Jersey. After the reported incidents of rigged quiz shows he attempted to hold a discussion with one of his classes about the immorality of the events. He was surprised and deeply concerned to discover that most of his students seemed to feel it was all right for the quiz contestants to have accepted answers. He allowed the discussion to close without injecting his views, however, and the next day gave his class a surprise test. During the test he unobtrusively allowed some of the students to come up and look at the answers lying on his desk. They did so and made excellent scores, but the remaining members of the class flunked. The following day he revealed what he had done. Those students who had flunked the test complained bitterly about the unfairness of the situation. He listened quietly to their outpouring of strong feelings, then said simply, "All right, we will now have another discussion of rigged TV shows."

An analysis of this teaching episode is provocative. The teacher had made what seemed to be a very reasonable assumption. He thought that the TV incidents were within the students' context of right and wrong. When he discovered that he had misjudged the situation, he did not condemn, cajole, or debate the matter, but discreetly withdrew to think it over. Then he synthetically created a similar classroom situation that placed it squarely within the students' perceptions of right and wrong. This is the kind of master teacher who makes a difference not only in what his fortunate students learn, *but what they may actually become.*

The Selective Core of Information

Professional education in modern times has not generally placed a very high value on information itself. The gross national product of Brazil, the number of inches of rainfall in Ecuador, and the problem of erosion in Mesopotamia have not been regarded as extremely vital matters to young children. This is understandable and is in part a reaction against an earlier emphasis on hosts of unrelated and miscellaneous trivia. It is impossible to identify a core of information that is equally important for all children to learn. Presumably, however, there is a body of information falling within the special province of the social studies which is relatively desirable for most children to know even if one cannot prove that such information is absolutely essential.

For instance, it is desirable after six years in the elementary school for a child to be informed about the early settlement of his country, the westward movement, and the development of the United States as a nation. It is desirable that he be informed about the great men and women who have played major roles in the nation's growth, about great moments or events that were crucial in the process, and about the motivations and circumstances that blended together to mold the eventual results.

One part of this core might simply be a type of information that children in America should know. For example, they should know about the *Mayflower,* the Boston Tea Party, and the Constitutional Convention.

Another might have to do with types of information that are desirable or necessary as a groundwork for later steps in the sequence. The first grader who works with crude neighborhood maps and experiences their meaning and purpose is in a better state of readiness to understand grid systems and eventually the products of the cartographer. The child who is guided in his social perceptions through an understanding of his own expanding neighborhood may be in a better position to grapple with the concept of the expanding world community.

A third cluster might logically focus upon the local environment. Because of the variation in communities a given school should selectively build up an inventory of information that it especially wishes its own children to know. The community may have its special hazards, problems, accomplishments, strengths, or a special place in history. Such information should be inventoried and stressed.

The point is simply that schools can, by giving their best judgment to the matter, ascertain a much more selective and valuable nucleus of information than is currently being taught. The information may then be accorded a higher priority in the program. This process of selective identification is a team job. It requires the assistance of the subject matter specialist and is best accomplished when the interested parties come together and think collectively about what it is important for children to know. It is admittedly a time-consuming process; but almost everything that is really worth doing is time consuming. Even if one never achieved the degree of refinement desired, he at least brings about a more select core of information than he had at the beginning of his quest. His content is therefore qualitatively improved.

There is one additional ramification that seems worth noting. Social studies has commonly been regarded as the core of the elementary program. In this capacity content and experiences in social studies make an important contribution to the other areas of the curriculum. For instance, the social studies and language arts are interwoven with mutual benefit to each. Creativity, also, may receive impetus and a point of departure from the substance of social studies. One can paint Lincoln and capture the greatness of his spirit because he knows the greatness of the man. One can project in his creativity more imagination and color, perhaps because his mind is splashed with color from the great moments of his nation's past. No area of the curriculum is independent of the social studies. In varying degrees, it serves a contributing or feeder relationship to them all. It will serve this feeder relationship on a higher level of excellence as its content is more selectively derived.

Critical Thinking and Self-management

Some of the schools today are helping children develop an understanding and skill in what is frequently called critical thinking. Critical thinking is misnamed and is not so much critical as it is adequate. It means helping a child to look on all sides of a matter. Many adults have not learned to do this. This more objective approach to life is similar to the motivation of the philosopher who seeks to achieve total understanding of total reality. Human limitations are such that the philosopher may concede his task is futile, but he does not abandon the quest. In a sense, the social studies program is a setting for the development of the young philosopher, nourishing in him the desire to exercise increasing intelligence in living.

This is heady wine. One is tampering here with the stuff of maturity. If this can be developed in children, the school has given them a skill which can be used throughout their entire span of life. It can help them to be less naïve and shortsighted than the generations which have preceded them and it may also toughen their minds for the problems which somehow seem destined to grow more difficult as the future unfolds. How does social studies contribute to this?

Each of the factors suggested up to this point has some relationship or contribution to make to critical thinking. Use of the classroom as a laboratory for social living nourishes it daily, and use of the school and its environs as a laboratory for social education gives it greater perspective and realism. The selective core of information provides better ammunition for thinking. Helping children to develop ideals provides the essential ingredients of values and sense of direction. Even the feeder function points up the crisscross nature of relationships that are a vital part of thinking. From each of these one thoughtfully extracts the elements that will assist children to bring intelligence to bear on their living; but the school can do more than this to develop self-management.

The earlier discussion of internal organization interpreted a process of consciously increasing the incidence of classroom responsibilities and activities that could be taken over by children.[2] The suggestion was made that one of the key aspects of a teacher's self-appraisal might involve a look at the degree of self-managed activities functioning at the end of the year, as compared to the degree that were functioning at the beginning of the year. The general approach consisted of successfully organizing and initiating one self-functioning aspect of the program and then moving into another. Such a process lies most appropriately in the domain of the social studies, and it is this area of the program that should assume the responsibility for its direction and nurture. Beyond the classroom functions such as student councils are worthy endeavors but reach a very small fraction of the student body. The main source of developing self-management capacities lies in the day-by-day activities that occur within the classroom itself. If genuine pupil involvement at increasing levels of responsibility takes place there, then student government is a logical and appropriate extension of the basic goal; otherwise it is a facade and a sham. Social studies needs to take all of this under its wing and judiciously extend the degree to which all of its youngsters can increasingly assume the direction of their own school living. This is one of its most vital contributions to effective citizenship.

The Balanced Program

The range and versatility of the social studies provide an embarrassment of riches. Perhaps no one is in a position to describe what actually amounts to a balanced program; but, judging from mistakes that seem to be perpetuated in the classrooms, it may be in order to suggest four significant as-

[2] See p. 91–92.

pects of balance which merit special consideration. These are
as follows:

1. *A balance between learning from texts and learning
   from life.* The typical program is too heavily weighted in
   the direction of the printed word. Life is the master text;
   and books, valuable though they may be, are less vital. A
   teacher need not attempt to achieve equal balance in this
   sense, but he should filter through his program whatever
   elements of real life and experience are appropriate and
   possible in a given community. Use of the classroom as a
   laboratory for social living helps to achieve this aspect of
   balance, and the selective use of resource persons and
   field study provides an equally valuable assist.

2. *A balance between the present and the past.* History
   provides the perspective for which there is no substitute;
   today may be a great deal more meaningful to a child if
   he understands the yesterdays as well. The relationship is
   a reciprocal one, for the study of yesterday is vitalized
   when it is mirrored in the context of today. It is a wise
   teacher who weaves these threads together, skillfully relating the present to the past. A strong current events
   program beginning in the first year of school and continuing right on through the curriculum is helpful in
   achieving this type of balance.

3. *A balance between content and process or between the
   planned experience and the experience of planning.* In
   the discussion of the selective core of information there
   was provision for building up and maintaining a more
   valuable body of content. This is an important qualitative factor; but the learning process itself in which children can be active participants in planning, carrying out,
   and evaluating some of their own experiences is probably
   more valuable. Role playing enlarges the process emphasis and contributes to this aspect of balance.

4. *A balance between intellectual and behavioral goals.* The
   ultimate test of education lies in behavior rather than in
   mere knowing. A child might verbalize the concept of the
   equality of men and yet, in his actions, demonstrate a

racial arrogance. The essence of social studies is human relationships and the program is not a success unless the quality of living is demonstrably improved. So few programs genuinely nourish attitudes and enlightened human behavior *as an intrinsic part of the program.* Until this is done, social studies remains in the book and never becomes embedded in the behavior which is its goal.

Balance implies more than the four aspects that have been described. Balance is in a very real sense an attitude itself; and, if a school desires to have a balanced program, it is armed with the chief instrument for achieving it. Any school, however, that can provide for suitable and adequate expression of such forms of balance has done very well and merits a special praise.

The Major Factor in Evaluation

The nature of the evaluation in social studies is a particularly critical matter for it can so easily distort the program. If grading is the school policy and the child's grade is to be determined by a test of information, the effect is to ascribe to information such an exaggerated importance that it becomes the key point of the program. The factors that have been interpreted, however, indicate that information is only one of the results sought. Over and above facts and skills, one is concerned with a cluster of factors having to do with attitudes and total performance as a thinking and socialized human being.

With respect to the method of evaluating information or facts it is probably better for teachers to develop their own tests. This is because the content appropriately varies sufficiently from one program to another so that norms from standardized tests are meaningless. As a school works to refine what it regards as a selective core of more essential information, it can also develop items which will help to assess outcomes in this aspect of the program.

The evaluation of social studies skills, on the other hand,

may be more skillfully appraised by using commercially prepared instruments. Such tests can evaluate map reading and
the general type of work-study skills that are stressed, regardless of the variations in social studies content. The development of such skills is a part of the program and deserves to be
included in the total evaluation.

The constellation of factors that is the most significant part
of the evaluation, however, has to do with children's attitudes
and behavior. The focus of the program is upon effective citizenship and this should be the central concern of the evaluation. Whatever was initially identified as the kind of behavior
that constituted effective citizenship is the continued object of
appraisal. Thus, one is taking a closer look at progress in matters such as involvement, cooperation, respect of others, self-
management, and critical thinking.

Personal behaviors are widely believed to be less tangible
and more difficult to evaluate, but this is a questionable point
of view. Any of the types indicated above is subject to intelligent observation throughout the year. Surely a perceptive
teacher can observe whether or not students are involved, co-
operating, showing respect for classmates, and growing in self-
management and critical thinking. In the final analysis it depends upon whether or not such matters are really valued as
the essence of the program and whether or not, in consequence, one is teaching toward them and continuously appraising his success in the undertaking.

The critical aspect of the matter is that if such an emphasis
is left out of the evaluation, it tends also to filter out of the
program. Then the tail wags the animal and the more trivial
aspects of the program become its main substance. If facts and
skills in social studies are to be the main thrust of the evaluation, it should be so stated in the philosophy of the program.
If effective citizenship is claimed as the goal, then the evaluation must ascribe to the qualities of the effective citizen the
prominence that is their due. Any other course is hypocritical
and lacking in integrity.

One of the mistakes that continues to be made in evaluating
learning within different areas of the program is the failure to
fit the evaluation to the intrinsic nature of the area concerned.

The same children may keep coming to the top in different parts of the program because there is a tendency to keep measuring the same intellectual factors. *Social studies properly gives primacy to human relationships.* How then should one evaluate a gifted child who performs splendidly in the facts and skills part of the assessment, but fails to show any perceptible growth in the personal qualities that are most desired? In most schools that give grades he would be likely to receive one of the highest marks. And, in those same schools, a child who gave a great deal of himself and consistently reflected the superior qualities of the good citizen would probably receive an average mark if he had an undistinguished performance on facts and skills. School marks are completely inappropriate for such evaluation; but, if they are to be given, are they in the above instance properly assigned? Is it too much to suggest that they have been reversed? It is not too much to suggest this in a humanistic school.

Chapter

Adjusting
the
Focus
in
Science

11

Chapter

Adjusting
the
Focus
in
Science

11

Science has emerged today as a respected and powerful aspect of the school program. For many years its status was that of a leaf-pressing, rock-collecting, insect-gathering adjunct to the school day. During this arrested state of development it was interpreted as nature study and was tolerated and even regarded as a nicety, but few people other than nature lovers thought it was of any fundamental importance. Blough and Blackwood were trying to break through this attitude as far back as 1948 when they spoke as follows:

> *It's not a series of object lessons about a piece of granite, an old wasp's nest, an acorn or tulip. . . . It's not learning the names of the parts of a grasshopper or of a trillium. It's not learning to identify 20 trees, 20 insects, 20 flowers, or 20 anything else.*[1]

Attitudes toward science in the curriculum have undergone a drastic change and today in most informed schools it is likely to enjoy the same attention and esteem that has tradi-

[1] Glenn O. Blough and Paul E. Blackwood, *Teaching Elementary Science,* Bulletin No. 4, Federal Security Agency (Washington, D.C.: U.S. Government Printing Office, 1948), p. 2.

tionally been reserved for the three Rs. There need be no regret attached to this transition, for science is deserving of a more favored role than it has enjoyed in the past. It has served its time on the bench and belongs now on the varsity. Anyone who has seen the excitement on children's faces in the excellent science class knows how they reach out for understanding about their world and what an impetus this can give to the entire tone of the program.

Perhaps much of the science program for elementary grades will continue to be based on the immediate environment: Trees, insects, stars, clouds, rain, flowers, rocks, and machines are part of the lives of children. They are sources of wonder and beauty and satisfaction. They can contribute richly to childhood—and they should do so, for there is a time when such important matters need to take place as one grows up. Science, however, is not just stars and clouds and rocks and flowers. It is not even rockets, fuel cells, and interplanetary travel. Science is a way of thinking.

The relationship between elementary science and social studies is an overlapping one. One such overlap is the core function which has traditionally been assigned to the social studies. Science has an equally pervasive quality and a similar inherent capacity to provide content and inspiration to other areas of the program. In some schools this overlap is recognized by allowing double time for the science unit and following it with double time for the social studies unit. Thus, the units are taught alternately rather than concurrently, with additional benefit to the core factor.

There is a great deal of folklore surrounding the science area of the curriculum. The chief bit of nonsense which has wide currency among elementary teachers is that science is hopelessly complicated and difficult. In fact, however, elementary science can be less complicated and difficult than the teaching of either reading or language. Certainly it functions in terms of more orderly and logical principles. Anyone who can master the disorderly array of contradictions that comprise an understanding of the language should find the mastery of basic scientific principles comparatively easy. It is the lack of adequate preparation in science, rather than its inherent difficulty, that seems to create the problem. Most of the following factors should be manageable within the context of the present resources of the school.

Focus on Scientific Thinking

The chief element of quality in science lies in its capacity to develop scientific thinking in children. This forms part of the intent of the science program in most schools, *but lacks the degree of emphasis which it requires in order to be effective.* It tends to become interwoven with other purposes and loses some of its strength in the process. The stating of multiple purposes for elementary science, however, tends to obscure the unique and central role to be played by this aspect of the curriculum, thereby weakening its contribution. Its central purpose needs to be clarified, and the position taken here is that the focus is properly and logically placed on scientific thinking itself.

Some professional people believe that this is too restricted a role for science to play. Actually, it would seem to be both a pervading and vital function. To contribute substantially to a child's ability to think scientifically is an accomplishment of the greatest consequence and can exert a beneficial influence on his personal life as well as being beneficial to the national destiny. The objective can even embrace morality, for truth is one of the respected approaches to morality. Socrates, one of the greatest philosophers produced by western civilization, believed that if one knew (had knowledge) he could not do wrong. Scientific thinking has weakened prejudice and intolerance and may be one of the chief hopes for a higher level of world morality.

A goal of scientific thinking has reference to mental processes such as observing, comparing, analyzing, generalizing, and problem-solving—all within the reach of children. Such processes have a common denominator. They are all *ways of getting at truth, appropriate to different situations and with different degrees of reliability.* Scientific thinking is thus regarded as the kind of thinking that may be utilized in the search for truth. Children are keen observers and are quite capable of detecting likenesses and differences. They are able to perform rudimentary analysis and to generalize after a number of experiences with the same kind of a problem. Their first efforts at problem-solving are scattered and ineffectual but show remarkable improvement by the end of the sixth grade. *An excellent groundwork in scientific inquiry can be made in the elementary school if the goal is directed to that end.*

This focus is one of the more significant aspects of the modern school and affects the entire program. The teacher who is so guided works with children in such a way as to awaken and sustain their curiosity. He will listen more than he talks, and stimulate more than he answers. He will build interesting phenomena into his program and sharpen powers of observation and analysis. He will provide time and resources for pursuing answers to questions asked by the children. He will show respect for truth as well as truth seeking and will help each child to mature in his ability to approach problems as the true scientist approaches them.

Inquiry Learning

There is no substantial agreement on the subject matter of science in the program. Agreement is less necessary, however, in view of the basic goal of developing scientific thinking. The basic goal is best advanced by processes that strengthen and refine thinking itself; to some extent any particular content is relatively expendable. There is no reason to believe, for instance, that leaving out any given segment of content such as magnetism and electricity would seriously impair the development of scientific thinking itself. Neither is there any substantial basis for believing that any given segment of the program must be taught at a specific grade or age level. In other words, science as an area of the curriculum is such that *content is subordinate to process.*

This is a vital opportunity which is not enjoyed by many aspects of the program. Teachers in most schools still observe grade level boundaries and sequences in the teaching of reading, mathematics, and even social studies. In science, however, there is more of an opportunity to try out and explore different types of content with considerable freedom. Thus creative teachers may enjoy the special luxury of pursuing with children the real interests they have about their world, with attention devoted primarily to improving the processes of their thought.

If an approach to teaching was ever ideally suited to the intrinsic nature of the program it is inquiry method in science. The purpose of the method is to help students learn to formulate and test their own theories and to become aware of their own role in learning. In the approach formulated by Suchman, middle grade children are shown short films of a scientific episode that pose problems of causality.[2] They are then asked to construct a possible explanation of why a given phenomenon occurred. This requires information that was not shown in the film. They can acquire this information only through their own efforts in asking questions to elicit the missing data, and the questions must be asked in a form that can be answered by yes or no.

The idea behind this is to keep the inquiry as empirical and inductive as possible without resorting to the physical manipulation of materials. If a child is exploring a piece of apparatus the teacher has little access to his reasoning processes. Requiring the child to talk, however, provides a clearer picture of how he is thinking. Restriction of the questions to a yes-or-no format eliminates open-ended questions and teacher-structured answers. This helps to assure that the direction and flow of the data are controlled by the child.

There are three stages to the approach. The first is called episode analysis which focuses upon verification of facts in the filmed demonstration. In the second stage the inquiry is directed at determining what conditions are necessary in order for the phenomenon to occur, and the third is a search for hypotheses that might explain why it occurred. The level and quality of thinking required in stage three is obviously far

_____

[2] J. Richard Suchman, "Learning Through Inquiry," *NEA Journal*, March 1963, pp. 31–32.

greater than in the earlier stages, for here the learner is engaged in putting the pieces together and testing to see if the hypothesis is tenable. Thinking at this stage may move into the kind that is intuitive and creative. The entire process is one which may enthuse and inspire all children as well as extend to the limit the most gifted ones.

An additional characteristic of the practice sessions is the manner in which the demonstration films are organized and presented for maximal conceptual growth. Most of the films involve some principles that have played a role in previous films with the addition of a new principle or a new application of one previously used. This *pyramiding of principles* promotes subject mastery and generates motivation for further discovery learning.

The sessions are taped and played back to the group in order to evaluate the questions and the heuristic process. Out of this comes an additional sophistication and understanding of inquiry strategies.

Inquiry methods throw the responsibility for thinking right into the laps of the learners and, like role playing, reflect faith in the capacity of the persons involved. It decreases teacher talk and directiveness and structures a setting in which pupil responses are freer and less threatened.

Bruner is probably the most eloquent defender of learning by discovery. He has long been concerned with the development of intelligent behavior and has researched in education-oriented situations to a much greater extent than most of his contemporaries. He identifies four principal advantages of discovery learning and each of them is of central importance to the kind of a school under discussion.[3]

One of the many advantages is that it appears to increase the learner's intellectual power or potency. If one identifies the major purpose of education as being the development of the power to learn, then this advantage lies at the heart of the process.

The second advantage is that it utilizes intrinsic motivation, or the enjoyment of learning for its own sake. This is in

[3] J. S. Bruner, "The Act of Discovery," *Harvard Educational Review,* XXXI (1961): 21–32.

marked and healthy contrast to the practice of giving children extrinsic rewards in the form of trinkets, candy, or grades for completing a given task.

A third benefit is that the learner gains an understanding of the heuristics of discovery or the processes used to arrive at facts. Such a vital end product as *learning how to learn* can emerge only through the individual's interaction with problems in actual problem-solving situations.

And the fourth advantage is in the conservation of memory. The greatest problem in human memory is not one of storage, but of locating and retrieving information. Having personally organized and appropriated his learning, the individual has easier and more ready access to it when he needs it.

These advantages constitute an impressive set of credentials for a particular form of methodology. Have they been overstated? Perhaps so, but one should remember that they are highly endorsed here, in part because they are so well suited to the central purpose which was identified for science as an area of the program. If one identifies a different role for science, then perhaps expository methods would be more helpful in reaching that goal than discovery methods. For the goal as it has been identified, however, some form of discovery approach such as Suchman's seems more on target.

One science educator in a midwestern university said that if the elementary teacher could develop the strategies of inquiry in children, all else in the science program could afford to be forgotten. This will be too much for many to accept, even though it represents an attainment that is far greater than children in traditional programs have experienced. Of all the factors having to do with excellence in the science program the emphasis upon discovery learning may prove to have the greatest single importance. It is open, flexible, evaluative, challenging, and creative. It enables the learner to go beyond sensory data to achieve additional insights. This going beyond the environmental data is generic learning which may even provide special benefits to youngsters from disadvantaged or deprived environments, for it is not so much what is "out there," but what is in their own heads. In so many ways it embodies the nature and intent of a humanistic school.

Functional Extension of Learnings

The fact that an area of the curriculum accepts the major responsibility for developing scientific thinking gives it an additional function. The process is nurtured and receives special direction in a basic set of experiences provided within the program; but it must be extended and applied additionally throughout the curriculum if it is to be effective. In other words, if scientific thinking were to receive emphasis in the science class and then remain suspended until the next science period, the goal would be seriously compromised and the program crippled. Growth in the kind of thinking sought in science is a part of one's mental processes. It cannot be turned on and off like an electric current, for if it is effective it becomes embedded in the personality of the individual. Thus, the habits of curiosity and truth seeking require a freer and more meaningful expression and must be able to function throughout the school day.

There are some interesting and challenging ramifications to this extension. The same truth-seeking process that probes into rainbows, humming birds, and chlorophyl will probe into other aspects of the curriculum as well. School personnel must be oriented to live with this curiosity, to direct it as best they can, and to search with children for the most reliable sources of information that can be found.

Sometimes the questions will move into an area that is believed to be the exclusive domain of adults. "Why do we do our arithmetic with laborious hand and mental methods when the real world of business and industry uses machines?" "Why do we claim that certain types of food are necessary for a balanced diet and health when some of the healthiest specimens on the globe do not eat them?" "Why do we write spelling words in lists when the real use of spelling is in the expression of thoughts?" Such questions should be answered. If there are no good answers the practices should be revised. This is tremendously important—for anything less does not show a respect for truth. Some of the questions children ask are perceptive as well as amusing. One fifth grade boy asked why people spoke of dressing a chicken when they were in fact undressing it. The same boy called attention to the unusual logic displayed by women in wearing their fur coats with the fur outside.

Asking questions and searching together for the best possible answers stimulates and realistically extends the kind of thinking that is the primary goal of the science program. So long as science is regarded as a way of thinking, it must also be regarded as a way of life. It cannot be achieved within the science period alone. The excellent teacher develops a special sensitivity or awareness of opportunities to extend the science learnings throughout the classroom. This functional extension is an essential one and is one of the important characteristics of an achieving school.

Science-Oriented Teachers

At this point it might be well to bring to the surface a rather candid question. Can a nonscience-oriented teacher produce science-oriented children? Perhaps he can, but it does not seem to be a very realistic assumption.

Suppose that a teacher is somewhat slovenly in his thought patterns, that he uses language loosely rather than precisely, that he depends too much on his textbooks, that he is complacent about what he knows, and has no real desire to extend his present horizons. Suppose that he reasons in stereotypes, clichés, and prejudices which he is unwilling to examine; that he is intolerant of questions which contain a hint of challenge or disbelief; and he feels that the thinking has already been done and it is the job of children to memorize it. Can such a man teach science as a way of thinking? Can he by any stretch of the imagination demonstrate through his own behavior the extension of scientific thinking throughout other portions of the school day?

The question may involve the kind of academic background possessed by the teacher, but also goes beyond it to the kind of person he happens to be. It is perhaps primarily a personality factor, for there are many rigid, inflexible, nonscientific "scientists" as well as many open-minded, flexible, scientifically oriented laymen. The matter seems to be of considerable importance, for this is obviously an age in which science learnings must be refined and intensified; the entire process could be defeated by failing to provide the right kind of classroom leadership. The point is equally valid and critical in the social studies, but was not discussed in order to avoid repetition. Obviously, the characteristics of excellence sought in the social studies could not find expression under the custody of an intolerant and narrow-minded teacher. Not a single one of the selective factors could flourish in such a setting.

The problem is compounded by the fact that money alone will not solve it. Higher salaries are just as attractive to the dull as to the thinkers. For the individual school the problem is at least partially subject to control. The values of the culture are such that good classroom teachers are much less in demand than a successful coach; and so it is apparent that the school that knows what it wants can generally go out and find it. The writer is acquainted with schools that consistently reach out and attract the best teachers, even though they may not pay the highest salaries. They wisely devote extra effort to this, for the school that wishes to provide the best possible environment for its children will make a major effort to get the very finest teachers. A brilliant football coach once said that he won more games between December and September than he did between September and December. The same devoted search for talent is vital to the classroom as well.

Science and Personality

Science has an important relationship and contribution to make to the developing personality of children. Haan has called attention to the manner in which the teaching of science could diminish a child's sense of trust:

> *We can teach day and night in a way to show precision*
> *and certainty of the earth's turning in space; we can also*

*teach that we are hurtling through space in a nameless
void at incredible speeds with unknown dangers at every
turn.*[4]

It is doubtful that many of us are sufficiently imaginative
and articulate to produce the sophisticated interpretation
above, but the point that many aspects of science can be
taught in such a way as to arouse either fear or trust is well
made.

A second aspect of science and personality has to do with a
child's drive toward it. Most adults can recognize a teacher
whose relationship to children is too sticky. Sometimes such a
teacher is unconsciously exploiting children as a result of his
own unfulfilled emotional needs. A somewhat similar condition may also prevail between science and an individual child.
Kubie has called attention to this in outlining the process
through which a young scientist may have selected his voca-
tion.[5] A gifted child develops some neurotic tendencies that
inhibit his normal psychosexual development. He is intellectually stimulated by some esteemed adult and turns to books.
Finding that success follows these efforts he may restrict himself to intellectual activity during adolescence. The physical
and emotional drain of laboratory time can also result in one's
putting all his emotional eggs in the intellectual basket. His
sense of security and self-esteem come to stand on one leg.
When original research finally begins, it is charged with many
irrelevant and unfulfilled emotional needs.

It would seem that the school has a guidance function to exercise in cases of this kind, even if in the process the world
stands to lose a scientist. Sometimes science seems to overobjec-
tify a person and to factor out basic qualities of human
warmth. This is more than a personal tragedy, for today the
world needs compassion and maturity from its scientists even
more than it needs their remarkable achievements.

In a more general personality sense, an excellent science

[4] Aubrey Haan, *Elementary Curriculum: Theory and Research* (Boston:
Allyn and Bacon, 1961), p. 215.

[5] Lawrence S. Kubie, "Some Unsolved Problems of the Scientific Career,
Part I," *American Scientist*, XLI, no. 4 (1953).

program can help children to become more resourceful, more creative, and even more humane. This potential seems inadequately explored. If a given experience in science can contribute to the major goal and also be presented in such a way as to exert a constructive and wholesome influence on children's lives, it is desirable that it be done.

The Primacy of Health Science

Health is a part of the curriculum in most elementary schools. It may be combined with safety to comprise one of the six major segments of the program or both may be merged with science. The inclusion of each of them here as a part of the excellent science program is in no sense an attempt to minimize their importance. In fact, in the immediate future this may well be the central concern of the science program. The relationship is a natural and logical one. Health is dependent upon science and in many respects is one of its products as well. Science has eradicated some of the major diseases that have plagued mankind and is the chief beacon of hope for eradicating those that remain. From science has come also the most reliable principles that man has for building and maintaining his health.

Now, however, by an understandable pyramiding of events, the existence of all life is threatened by much of what science and technology have achieved. The seriousness of the threat to planetary life still can only be estimated, but each new finding fits into a general pattern that seems increasingly ominous.

Thermal pollution of streams has killed lower forms of life upon which higher forms were dependent. The result is that life cycles gradually evolved by nature have been disrupted and destroyed, with many forms threatened with extinction. Lakes are dying. When the attorney general of Illinois sent a team to find out why Lake Michigan beaches were being closed, the first man to check the water supply passed out and the next one threw up. The North Shore Sanitary District was pouring raw sewage right into the lake where children swam.

The pollution of air may be even worse. Air is finite and in many metropolitan and industrial centers it is being contaminated faster than it can cleanse itself. The amount of toxic gas and particulate matter that is spewed into the atmosphere by utilities, mines, and industry almost surpasses belief. For instance, as this is written the smelters in a single state throw out 5500 tons of sulphur dioxides daily; each automobile on the highway contributes an additional seven pounds of deadly carbon monoxide a day; and a single jet is believed to emit an exhaust equal to one thousand cars. The effect on human life is incalculable.

The list of hazards grows as the facts become clearer. Noise pollution is only now being recognized as one of nature's cruel enemies and seems to have been vastly underestimated in terms of its deleterious effects. The Supersonic transport will magnify this problem in a manner for which there is no present solution. Even garbage looms as a threat that must be resolved before it buries us. Almost all containers are presently of the nonreturnable type and are virtually indestructible. By 1976 it is estimated that the nation will be faced with getting rid of 61 billion units of used packaging materials that will not burn, break, crush, degrade, dissolve, or disappear. Even the underground nuclear blasting may be seriously underestimated with respect to its danger to the earth's crust. Knowledge of the nature and extent of man's destructive activities must be painfully assembled and those activities must at all costs be reversed and controlled.

In the recent past school health programs have attempted to teach and promote sound principles of living. Now an entire new set of dangers must be recognized and the priorities reordered. It is a minimal achievement to radically reduce smoking of young people if they are to be systematically poisoned in the normal process of breathing. It is a hollow victory to achieve balanced diets in a society that has allowed many of its most basic and nourishing foods to be contaminated by additives and pesticides. The drug menace is still a legitimate concern of tragic proportions, but it may soon be dwarfed by some of the problems that are now emerging.

What greater gift can man bequeath to his children than a heritage of clean air and water, of green meadows and forests, and the unspoiled miracle of the chain of life. Scientists have predicted that in the eighties it may be necessary to wear oxygen masks and that by the following decade man may even need to live in domed cities. It is unthinkable to bequeath such an existence to our children. The fight must be won.

The hope for survival depends upon mounting a massive determination to halt the suicidal activities and reverse the process. This can be done only if people know what is occurring and apply their genius to counteractive measures. All segments of society must be mobilized to meet the threat. Science, government, industry, business, education, and individuals are all needed to wage man's most momentous war—the war against his own destructive way of life. Even though it deals with children, the elementary science program must also become involved and contribute its mite. Health science comes front and center. At stake is survival.

The Science of Safety. The rationale for including the science of health applies equally well to the science of safety.

One classroom approaches this problem in the following way: The teacher and the class study their school environment for potential accident situations. They carefully observe these situations, thoughtfully discuss and analyze them, and then propose what seem to be the most promising means of eliminating or guarding against them. This procedure parallels the approach of the scientist and directs thinking at a realistic and vital problem that is of genuine concern to the participants.

Each time a major accident occurs the routine machinery of the classroom comes to a halt and the accident comes to the top of the agenda. The class may go out to the scene of the accident for firsthand investigation and then come back to their room where the sequence and conditions are reenacted. The children attempt to analyze the cause and to make suitable recommendations. The process is calm, objective, and analytical. It is scientific thinking in action directed at a meaningful situation in the children's own lives.

The same class engages in a somewhat comparable approach that has strong appeal to the children. An identification is made of the chief causes of death and accidents to children, for instance, as a situation where a child is running from behind a parked car into the path of an oncoming automobile. This situation is portrayed in the classroom with actual materials which show the playground, the parked car, the children playing, and the approaching automobile. A child sets up the arrangement, which contains a potentially dangerous situation, and the children think through and discuss it. Later, they may invite in a class of younger children and portray it for them. The careful identification of the kinds of accidents which are real hazards to children is an important part of the approach, and helps to maintain a vital type of content in the program.

Evaluation Factors

In keeping with the primary focus of science, the evaluation is directed at the children themselves and how they think. Observation is probably the most valuable guide to this process. One evaluates what he has been trying to achieve; and, in the case of any given child, the evaluation might reasonably be concerned with matters such as the following:

1. Is he more interested and curious?
2. Is he more open minded?
3. Is he more observing and analytical?
4. Is he more able to generalize?
5. Is he more sensitive to causality?
6. Is he more resourceful in his attack of problems?
7. Is he more careful about the sources of his information and more tentative in his conclusions?
8. Is he more scientific in his pursuit of learning beyond the science class itself?

An especially rich evaluative practice is that of having children evaluate themselves on questions such as those above. It is particularly effective when the class has cooperatively determined what they are striving for and have pinned it down in terms that are meaningful to them. A group form of this type of evaluation is also possible. It takes place when the teacher has set up a problem which is carefully interpreted. The teacher then steps aside while the children, entirely on their own, advance, discuss, and interpret their hypotheses. The teacher then returns to more active participation and all of them thoughtfully assess what they have done.

Another rich possibility for special observation occurs when a class puts on a demonstration or experiment for another group. Following such an activity they will then evaluate the strengths and weaknesses of their presentation. The teacher's function here is best carried out when he carefully hears out the children themselves before advancing any of his own evaluative remarks.

Such activities have a special inherent strength. Critical thinking is present in each, the children are significantly involved in the process, and evaluation remains an integral part of the program.

Chapter

Making
Mathematics
Sensible

12

Chapter
Making
Mathematics
Sensible
12

A substantial portion of the revolution in elementary mathematics has now occurred, leaving some happy, some gasping, some alienated, and some merely bewildered. Was this radical curriculum change wise and well conceived, or did it take a wrong and unfortunate turn? In general the movement seems to be regarded as acceptable, and it causes one to wonder whether the widespread acceptance is based upon solid convictions that the changes were in fact good, or whether the situation reflects instead a general condition of confusion, apathy and mass capitulation.

Many of the remarks which follow will be highly inflammatory, but this is not their intent. If modern programs are really good for children they will not be hurt by critical analysis; if they do represent unsound concepts and practices, they roundly deserve whatever damage occurs.

A bit of background may be necessary for this discussion. From 1900 to 1935 the arithmetic program was admittedly traditional with an emphasis upon such matters as rote learning and intensive drill for speed and accuracy in computation. The period may be characterized as *traditional mathematics taught traditionally*. No enlightened person defends that period and it was a dark hour for professional education.

After 1935 leaders such as Morton, Wheat, Spitzer, and Brownell were successful in shifting the emphasis to meaning and understanding. It was argued that meaningful learning would result in better skills and stimulate children to further mathematical learning. Curriculums were then revised to make *why* as important as *how*. Great strides were made during this stage and the period may be described as *traditional mathematics taught meaningfully*.

The present emphasis began in the fifties and again shifts the concern back to the content or structure of mathematics. It was initially directed at high school programs, but then found its way into the junior high, and has now filtered down to the first grade. Changes and refinement of content are necessary and should be supported; but it is also necessary to beware of extremes. Rappaport says that the new emphasis is bringing sophisticated mathematics to children at too early an age and that logic has often become predominant over psychology at the expense of learning.[1] He is not alone in his concern.

One of the first to sound the alarm during the fifties and challenge the present movement was the eminent mathematician Morris Kline. After joining the New York University faculty he had sought—with widely acclaimed success—to humanize the teaching of mathematics and to transmit to his students the larger significance of the great mathematical creations. As chairman of the Washington Square College mathematics department and director of electromagnetic research in the university's Institute of Mathematical Sciences, he had impressive credentials for the challenge. In an unqualified indictment of the recent curriculum changes in mathematics, he said that the direction of reform was almost wholly misguided and that it would undoubtedly result in far less successful teaching of mathematics, as well as injury to the mathematical and scientific development of the country. One of the most significant of his remarks, published in the *New York University Alumni News,* was the charge that the reformers were from the less scientifically motivated domains of mathematics and neither

[1] David Rappaport, "Does Modern Math Ignore Learning Theory?" *Phi Delta Kappan,* June 1963, p. 445.

knew what should be taught in the high schools nor even how young people think. A number of mathematics professors of varying competency, however, then jumped on the bandwagon. Professors of mathematics education, believing they were hearing from those who knew what they were talking about, abdicated their professional roles, according to Kline, and supported a mathematics which in his view was entirely unsuitable for young people.[2]

Kline did not believe there was anything wrong with traditional mathematics that could not be resolved by better teaching. Modernists were advocating that material currently being taught be replaced by topics such as symbolic logic, Boolean algebra, set theory, some portions of abstract algebra such as groups and fields, topology, and postulational systems. In examining the value of those topics from the standpoint of their application and importance to the central body of mathematics, he thought that one could hardly select more peripheral material.

For instance, in regard to symbolic logic he said that no mathematician except a specialist in the problems of mathematical logic uses symbolic logic.

First of all, every mathematician thinks intuitively and then presents his arguments in a deductive form, using words, familiar mathematical symbols, and common logic. This is true of 99.9 per cent of all the mathematics that has been created.[3]

Kline brilliantly took the new math to task for being too trivial and sterile, too obsessed and confused about rigor, too isolated from the physical and social sciences, too abstract too soon, and too unconcerned with student interest in the subject. "The fact is," he said, "that we have been guided in our choice of material not by the effort to arouse interest, but to teach the mathematics that will be needed in the subsequent

[2] Morris Kline, "Math Teaching Reforms Assailed as Peril to U.S. Scientific Progress," *New York University Alumni News.*

[3] Morris Kline, "The Ancients Versus the Moderns: A New Battle of the Books," *Mathematics Teacher,* October 1958, p. 419.

study of the subject." [4] It does not seem to be well known among educators that his views were also widely endorsed by some of the leading mathematicians in prestigious institutions all over the country.

In a more recent expression of equally candid and informed dissent, Howard Fehr, former chairman of the department of mathematics education at Teachers College of Columbia University, makes a very perceptive analysis of sense and nonsense in a modern mathematics program as applied to the elementary schools.[5] He points out that modern mathematics, as exemplified by such topics as modern and linear algebra, point set topology, finite mathematical systems, set theory and the like, is properly pursued by students majoring in mathematics and science in the universities. He indicates that these *subjects have no place in elementary school mathematics.* "To do any of them in the elementary school would amount to more than nonsense— . . . it would be insanity."

Fehr finds many evidences of nonsense in the newer programs and attributes it, as did Kline, to the fact that some of the mathematicians who have taken a major role in writing the programs have a tremendous lack of understanding about how children learn and what they need to learn. The following points represent an attempt to accurately interpret some of his beliefs.

1. In many programs today sets are introduced through the use of letters and brace notation. Children struggle to make the so-called curlicue braces when they should be learning to write symbols for numbers such as three (3). Later Venn diagrams appear along with the symbols for union ($\cup$), intersection ($\cap$), is an element of ($\in$), and is a subset of ($\subset$). At the elementary school level this is nonsense. *Set notation and symbolism and any theory of operations on sets have no genuine significance for the learning of elementary school mathematics.*

---

[4] *Ibid.,* p. 425.

[5] Howard F. Fehr, "Sense and Nonsense in a Modern School Mathematics Program," *Arithmetic Teacher,* February 1966, pp. 83–90.

2. *The introduction of formal logic into elementary school mathematics is also nonsense.* Truth tables, truth value, logical connectives such as "and," "or," and "not" are totally unnecessary for the acquisition of correct concepts and usages of arithmetic and physical geometry. In fact, individuals need to experience and understand number, number relations, and geometrical configurations a great deal before they see the need for reasoning about this acquired knowledge and sense how it may be arranged in formal structures. The emphasis should be upon understanding, use, and skill, not on abstract patterns. Why? Because all past and present research on human learning indicates that until the human mind has acquired a vast reservoir of experimental knowledge and matured to a mental age of ten or eleven years, the ability to do two-way reflective thinking is absent and it is impossible to understand formal logic.

3. The teaching of place systems of numeration in bases other than the decimal and the computational algorisms in these other bases is also nonsense. All over the world, in every nation and in every type of communication (social, business, scientific, professional, etc.), the one system that is used is the decimal system. This is the only system that 95 percent of the population will use the rest of their lives and they will probably use it every day of their lives. Of course, other systems are used in digital computers and special scientific studies, but to educate elementary children as though this applied to all of them is the sheerest of nonsense. That learning place systems in other bases such as four, five, or seven will increase understanding of the decimal system is an interesting hypothesis, but one which has never been tested. Such generalizations on scales of notation can well be deferred to high school study where the use of algebra makes them simple and easy to understand.

4. In this connection, too, it is nonsense to stress the distinction between numeral and number. Of course numbers are abstract and numerals are names or symbols for the abstract, but in general no misconception arises in using

the two words synonymously. If a person says he writes numbers on a blackboard, everybody knows what he is talking about. Even some of the mathematicians who started this nonsense are now recanting.

There is a story that one experimental group in writing its elementary books used a chapter heading "Learning to Read and Write Large Numbers." When someone called their attention to the fact that this was impossible they changed the word "numbers" to "numerals." Then, because this implied that the numerals were to be large, or written in enormous size, they finally changed the title to "Learning to Read and Write Numerals for Large Numbers." By this time, says Fehr, no one understood what was meant.

5. While there are other minor innovations that are useless but harmless, Fehr mentions one other major piece of nonsense as follows:

*This is the attempt to formalize the structure of arithmetic
—that is, to enunciate formal laws and attempt to build
and extend arithmetic through the use of these laws.
Now it is essential to understanding that we recognize
the principles involved in operations on numbers. But to
enumerate explicitly the commutative, associative, and
distributive laws in a formal (algebraic) form, to spell
out every algorism into a flow chart in terms of these laws,
to stress the identity laws of zero and one, and to use a
product set to define multiplication is utter nonsense.
The books that are doing this are really substituting a
new rote formalism for the old rote learning of so-called
facts of arithmetic, and this does not spell progress.*[6]

Near the end of his penetrating and provocative article, Fehr makes the following highly significant statement:

*If at the end of the sixth grade almost all of the children
know the decimal system of notation; can read and
write the numerals for whole or fractional numbers; can*

[6] *Ibid.,* p. 85.

at an adult level of performance do all four computational operations on whole numbers and on fractions, both in common and in decimal notation; have an intuitive understanding of the rationale and structure underlying these computations; can apply this knowledge meaningfully to solution of problems involving measure and per cents; and know and recognize common geometrical figures and relations among them; we shall have achieved an outstanding and notable advance in elementary school mathematics education.[7]

The author would add to this only the notion that *the newer math programs are unnecessary to do any of the above;* and, as indicated by Kline, all of it could be achieved in stage two which was characterized as traditional mathematics taught meaningfully.

Even some of the original advocates of the newer programs are having second thoughts. In a dateline from Montreal, one of the original leaders in the "New Math" movement is reported as saying that we are in danger of raising a generation of children who cannot do computational arithmetic.[8] He attributed the danger to excessive and unskilled emphasis upon esoteric mathematics at the expense of fundamentals. Kline predicted as much in the beginning of the movement, but too many influential advocates pushed for the hastily conceived and disruptive changes. Under the old system parents could help the child at home even if the teacher did a poor job. Now parents cannot help because of the marked difference in content and approach as well as the forbidding symbolism.

One does not have to be a curriculum expert to conclude that the newer programs were guilty of excesses and were, in fact, not sensible in many ways. Irrespective of whether or not the change was wisely conceived in the first place, *the manner of change was deplorable.* Programs in too many instances were hastily conceived and implemented with teachers wholly unprepared for coping with what had been tossed precipi-

[7] *Ibid.*, p. 89.

[8] Max Beberman, "Math Expert Says Changes Too Hasty," *New York Times Service,* reprinted in the Phoenix *Arizona Republic,* January 4, 1964.

tately in their laps. Out of this chaos came frightened teachers, bewildered parents, and youngsters who had one foot in both programs without understanding either of them. It was practically a model of *how not to initiate curriculum change.*

With respect to the substance of the change and whether it was wisely conceived, it seems reasonable to suggest that there is considerable room for doubt. Figure 13 indicates four stages of curriculum development in mathematics, the first two of which were mentioned earlier in the discussion. Because of lack of insight on the part of teachers who were plunged overnight into the new programs there was much *mechanical* teaching of mathematical concepts which resulted in stage three described as newer math taught traditionally. Propo-

Figure 13 STAGES IN MATHEMATICS CURRICULUM CHANGE

1	2	3	4
Traditional Math Taught Traditionally	Traditional Math Taught Meaningfully	"New Math" Taught Traditionally	"New Math" Taught Meaningfully

nents of the change no doubt hoped for stage four which is newer math taught meaningfully.

In restrospect, more solid improvement might have been generated by a thoughtful and more moderate approach to the refinement and extension of stage two. A great deal of progress had been effected within this period, and the profession could rather easily have consolidated its gains and moved forward on the basis of some substantial progress already achieved. This would have been more of an *evolutionary type of change with which schools are prepared to cope.* Revolutionary change seems justifiable only under moments of crisis *that did not exist, or in the light of hard evidence of the need and superiority of the proposed change that also did not exist.* Some of the more radical changes could then have been more carefully analyzed with respect to (1) whether they were really desirable rather than merely possible, (2) for what ages they might be desirable, and (3) with what kinds of students they might be most effective. With respect to the latter, it is quite possible that some of the newer content, such as computing in bases other than ten, might have been found to be an excellent type of enrichment program for gifted learners. Regarding the first two questions, careful curriculum probes might have revealed that much of the material was too sterile, trivial and pointless and that the content which remained was more appropriate for youngsters in the upper elementary grades. The important observations and criticisms of Kline, Rappaport, and Fehr raise grave doubts about whether or not the programs as conceived were sensible and conceptually sound for children.

So far as the humanistic school is concerned the door is always open for mathematical change that is genuinely oriented for the benefit of the learners rather than the professional mathematicians. The events of the past decade, however, seem to indicate that many of the changes were not so oriented. The early emphasis upon theory of sets, formal logic, and ex-aggerated notation and symbolism may all be premature, incompatible with the nature and needs of the child, and in effect self-defeating. Youngsters still need much firsthand experience with reality and concrete materials before they are prepared to handle abstractions intelligently. Many of the practices developed during the period of teaching mathematics meaningfully provided for such experiences and should be retained in present programs until something really better is envisioned. A few illustrative practices which still seem to reflect a desirable and sensible program are presented in the remaining discussion.

Emphasis upon Meaning and Self-discovery

An enlightened primary teacher took a job in a very backward school where children had learned to manipulate numbers without understanding what they were doing. One day she went to the board and wrote the following subtraction problem:

$$37$$
$$-18$$

Out of her thirty children twenty of them could get the correct answer but not a single one of them could explain it. So she walked over to a device known as a place-value pocket, and in the tens pocket placed three bundles of popsicle sticks with ten in each bundle. In the units pocket she placed seven individual sticks to represent the seven ones. Then she asked the children if they could prove that their answer was correct. One of the newly enrolled children came up timidly and performed the proof. He took one of the bundles of ten from the tens group, removed the rubber band to transform it into ten additional ones, and demonstrated to the class that the problem involved regrouping three tens and seven ones into two tens and seventeen ones in order to be able to proceed with the subtraction. There are a number of adults in today's society who could not rationalize the problem as clearly as the above child because they learned arithmetic mechanically rather than meaningfully.

Since the early texts on pedagogy teachers have been admonished to teach arithmetic meaningfully, but for many years the problem seemed bogged down in implementation. Now in the schools there is more sophistication to the movement, and teachers have a better grasp of what it is all about. Thus, an upper grade teacher may distribute three-dimensional cardboard models around his room several days before he plans to take up linear surface area with his class. The students may unfold the models and examine them at their leisure. Many of them will discover for themselves how to compute the area before it is ever brought up in class.

In a seventh grade the writer observed students in the process of discovering the relationship between the diameter and circumference of circles. They were using a device called a Circlometer [9] which consisted of a grooved measuring device and four wooden circles each of which was a different diameter. Placing a handle on the smallest of the circles a student

[9] Distributed by the Winston Company, 1010 Arch Street, Philadelphia, Pennsylvania.

rolled it carefully down the grooved measuring device to determine the circumference. Each circle was measured and the circumference was determined and recorded. Then the students were invited to take their recorded data and generalize: "Is there a definite relationship between the diameter and the circumference of a circle?" The students' efforts roughly approximated 3.14 and they were informed that 3.1416 was considered accurate enough for all practical requirements. The understanding of students who work through such a process is surely superior to the understanding of students who deal only with the abstract concepts.

In the recent past the stress upon a meaningful arithmetic was the dominant theme running through the professional literature. A good start was made in the actual implementation of the idea in the classroom, and changes contemplated for the schools of tomorrow should hold and consolidate the gains that were made. Building into the program additional opportunities for children to understand and discover mathematical principles for themselves is one of the rich veins of curriculum development. It gives a laboratory quality to the program of mathematics. It calls for a higher and more stimulating level of mental activity from teachers and students alike, and it promises a more realistic and exciting program. It should be a continuing dominant note in the programs of the seventies.

Use of Conceptual and Manipulative Devices

In the past a teacher might have taught a lesson on measures such as pints, quarts, and gallons without having any in the room for children to see and to handle. A child in such a class may have memorized the units without having any real conception of what they were actually like. The sensible classroom does not perpetuate this mistake. *It attempts to follow the principle of moving in a sequence from the concrete, to the semiconcrete, to the abstraction.* For example, the concept of area in early grades may be introduced by going out and measuring the school garden preliminary to deciding what can be planted. The dimensions of the garden can be reduced to a cardboard model in the classroom where the deliberations are continued. From these experiences the child can be taught the area formula, which is an abstraction. An effective school regards conceptual devices and materials as an indispensable part of its mathematics program and systematically builds them up in each room just as it would build up its printed materials.

One of the most versatile and inexpensive of the valuable aids that are used in a modern classroom is the string of one hundred spools. This device costs practically nothing. It consists of one hundred spools on a string or wire and is placed in the room where it can be easily seen and manipulated by the children. The thirteenth, thirty-eighth, sixty-third, and eighty-eighth spools are cut in half to concretely portray $\frac{1}{8}$, $\frac{3}{8}$, $\frac{5}{8}$, and $\frac{7}{8}$. Additionally, the thirty-fourth and sixty-seventh spools are cut into thirds to show $\frac{1}{3}$ and $\frac{2}{3}$. At the primary level, this device is useful for simple counting, for crossing the tens as in the example of ten plus three, and for seeing numbers that are less than one hundred in relation to the total number of one hundred. At the middle and upper grades the device is still useful for fractions, decimals, and percents. This simple aid is one of the most versatile the school can provide.

A second interesting type of material is the Stern Structural Arithmetic materials.[10] Developed by Catherine Stern, the beginning set is used for the last half of kindergarten and the first half of first grade. The Stern materials strive to achieve all of the properties of abstract numbers. An example of their application and value is indicated by one portion which is called the number frames. These frames resemble a nest of square trays which, for convenience in storing, fit inside one another. A teacher can take the nine tray and sit down with the children as she might sit down with a small reading group and teach them the story of nine. The story of nine unfolds as the children proceed to fill the nine tray. The nine block just fits into the tray, so it is placed in the tray first. Then all the possible combinations of nine are also placed into the tray. When the tray is filled it holds the eight and the one block as well as the one and the eight, the seven and two and the two and seven, the five and four and the four and five, and the six and

[10] Distributed by Houghton Mifflin, 777 California Avenue, Palo Alto, California.

three along with the three and six. This is the story of nine—learned by the actual manipulation and placement of attractive, scientifically designed materials into all of the possible combinations of nine. When the child has learned the stories of nine, eight, seven, six, five, etc., he has moved a good portion of the way toward mastering his fundamental addition combinations. More important, it has been accomplished through understanding rather than memorization.

A spot check of classrooms in an excellent elementary school indicated that the following conceptual devices were being used in grades one through eight:

1. Stern Structural Materials
2. One Hundred Spools
3. Giant Ruler and Thermometer
4. Place-Value Pocket
5. Abacus
6. Fraction Board
7. Wooden Area Models
8. Three-dimensional Cardboard Models
9. Circlometer
10. Cuisenaire Rods [11]

The above materials are typical of what has been used in some of the schools. If a mathematics program doesn't have such conceptual devices in active use, it probably has made no substantial effort to build up its *library of concrete aids.* Building them up, refining their use, and making them a vital part of the day-by-day operation is an essential aspect of a meaning or discovery approach.

Increase of Functional Mathematics

Functional arithmetic is the arithmetic that is a normal and natural aspect of the child's existence. A primary teacher writes on the board the following:

[11] Distributed by Cuisenaire Company of America, Inc., 235 East 50th Street, New York, New York.

*On Friday we will have our Valentine party. Six
children in our class will bring the cookies for the party.
How many cookies should each child bring if there are to
be thirty-six people at the party and each person is to have
two cookies apiece?*

One child instantly says each child should bring six cookies.
He is asked to explain. Another child says, "I think each of
them will need to bring twelve cookies." He is invited to explain. A third child says that he agrees the answer is twelve
but worked the problem in a different way. He wants to show
how he did it. Is this just wheelspinning and wasted time? Is
not the nature of mathematics such that it requires systematic,
sequential instruction rather than this kind of a haphazard approach?

The arithmetic program does need to be systematic and sequential; almost all the mathematics authorities agree on this
point. But arithmetic also needs to be a vital and meaningful
part of one's existence. The two ideas are not basically incompatible, although they have been presented as incompatible in
some of the earlier discussions of incidental teaching. The
hard core of the program is the portion dealing with the basic
nucleus of mathematical understanding. It is sequentially and
systematically presented in text or workbook series. What the
text or workbook cannot possibly do, however, is satisfactorily
relate to the experiences of a given classroom. The experiences
of a particular classroom are unique elements that can never
be satisfactorily mirrored in commercial materials.

The Valentine incident supplies a missing ingredient; it
draws from the real setting of the situation the opportunities
for arithmetic to function in the normal processes of classroom
life. This allows mathematics to have a more vital role and
provides graphic representation of how and why mathematics
is a functional part of one's existence. The mathematics from
the book alone cannot do this. There is nothing haphazard
about this practice when it is intelligently conducted, for it
may either precede or follow through on the sequential aspect
which has been or will be developed. It is, therefore, motiva-
tional and reinforcing. Additionally, it is one of the primary

contributors to the basic intent of creating a meaningful program.

Functional arithmetic involves a minor element of rescheduling. Instead of having a formal period of mathematics forty minutes a day for five days a week, a teacher might have his time arranged for forty minutes a day three days a week, or thirty minutes a day five days a week. In those periods he moves ahead on his systematic sequential instruction. He has, however, picked up in this manner from fifty to eighty minutes a week which may legitimately be devoted to functional arithmetic as the opportunities arise. He looks for *the teachable moment* and attempts to develop a sensitivity to natural openings or opportunities. Some teachers do this remarkably well. Under such an arrangement the formal periods are somewhat more streamlined, but this streamlining may be advantageous rather than detrimental. Furthermore, the combination of *formal plus applied mathematics is a much stronger thrust.* This factor is a vital one, and it should continue to be a characteristic of the newer programs.

Extending Skills in Problem-Solving

If an 8-ounce can of sauerkraut costs sixteen cents and a 16-ounce can costs twenty-nine cents, which is the better buy? In the old days, students would have been inclined to say that the 16-ounce can was the better buy; and, divorced from reality, that was the logical answer. Placed within the framework of real circumstances, however, it may not be the answer at all. For the fact of the matter is that it depends on whether or not one likes sauerkraut.

Problem-solving in modern times needs to strive for practicality. Old textbooks in arithmetic were full of highly improbable situations which were of limited value. Problem-solving in good programs stays closer to life as children know it and is not only more practical but more significant as well.

A basic purpose of mathematics in the curriculum may be identified as the development of children's abilities to think quantitatively. This refers to all thinking which involves numbers and number relationships. Problem-solving, thus, is right at the heart of the curricular role. It is a reflection of the child's ability to come to grips with real problems of living, utilizing what he has learned in one situation, and applying it to another. It involves careful assessment of the facts and circumstances and logical, sometimes even creative, application of reasoning to the desired end. This is a highly prized aspect of the development of modern man and deserves the school's best effort to achieve it. What elements in the program will highlight and nourish this vital factor?

In terms of what has been recommended as desirable elements thus far, the stage is already set for such achievement. Promoting the self-discovery approach, building up conceptual materials, and stressing functional applications to the day-by-day operation all contribute to problem-solving.

One factor which has traditionally stood in the way of better problem-solving is the ability of the child to read. The ability to read critically and with understanding is interlocked with problem-solving at this point. The reading lessons might properly draw from the mathematics texts for specific focus on the thought problems in order to improve understanding and skills of this nature.

Another way to achieve a degree of improvement is to concentrate on fewer, more selectively chosen problems. All adults can recall being assigned one or more pages of written problems that were chores to do and seemingly unimportant. Five carefully selected problems might provide the desired types to be focused upon in a given period and also allow ample time to dwell upon the intrinsic nature of each. There should be time for children both to interpret different ways of arriving at their solutions and to thoughtfully compare and weigh approaches. Much of the arithmetic instruction of the past has been too hurried. Mathematics is a thoughtful process and must be so conducted without someone breathing down the child's neck with a stopwatch. Five problems might even provide challenge for the more gifted by choosing them in terms of increasing difficulty. The number assigned should be chosen with the idea of doing each of them thoroughly and right. The number would obviously vary with the nature of the content and should be flexible. In some instances even one problem might suffice.

Whatever form mathematics takes in the elementary school in years to come, problem-solving will still be of major importance. It now is and will continue to be one of the major factors in the quality of a program.

Making Mathematics Fun

A seventh grade teacher in the Southwest has a worthwhile practice which he uses two or three times a week with his class just before he dismisses them for the day. He gives them problems that are "just for fun." The following is an example of one of the problems he gave his class:

> *A primary teacher had in her first grade a very bright boy who was always finishing his work before the other children and coming up to ask what he could do next. It was difficult for the teacher to keep him busy, but she was usually able to provide something constructive for him to do. One day, however, she was particularly pressed and was caught unprepared. Therefore, she gave the child a piece of busywork which she tried ordinarily to avoid. She asked the boy to go back to his seat and write the numbers from one to one hundred, then to add them and bring her the correct sum. The child went to his seat and was busy for about sixty seconds. Then he came happily back and handed her the correct answer. How did the child work the problem?*

The students in this particular class have a high degree of interest in mathematics and they particularly look forward to the occasional problems. It adds zest to their mathematical diet and provides an additional stimulus to thought. It even constitutes an example of a type of homework which is completely palatable to students. The teacher of this class is a scholarly, well-rounded young man who can have a wholesome and lasting influence on his students' lives. He has selectively through the years developed a very interesting collection of stimulating problems and keeps adding to them as he goes along. *He is not a mathematician, but he is developing mathematical interests in his students.*

Mathematics is an area of the program which in recent times has been afflicted with "rigor-itis," and there is a danger that it may become a stolid and muscle-bound segment of the program. The nature of the beefing-up process will make the difference. The fun factor is a safeguard against such a potential danger. It is also an incentive to creativity, for many of the fun problems such as the one above offer several possible answers.

There is an additional reason, however, for suggesting that this element be deliberately built into the program. In what other way can mathematics become a part of people's lives to the degree that a modern technical society demands? It is not enough for a society to have an elite corps of well-trained mathematicians who carry on its highly specialized processes while the rest of the population retreats in fear and frustration to a state of mathematical pauperism. Too much attention to rigor and too little attention to interesting the learners can cause this. The nation must have a better mathematical posture than this and the factor under discussion is one of the ways of achieving it. Giving sensible emphasis to mathematics for fun opens up the situation and makes it inviting enough for more children to become involved. Such widespread interest and involvement is essential to the success of the program.

Chapter
"Childrenizing"
the
Language
Arts
13

Chapter
"Childrenizing"
the
Language
Arts

13

The language arts are at a very critical juncture in their stage of curriculum development. For many years the schools have wasted their substance by persisting in the myth that the teaching of formal grammar would make an important contribution to more effective speaking and writing. Now the mood for revolutionary change is such that it is possible to emancipate the program from the burden of this misconception and move it boldly into a simple, naturalistic, and person-oriented kind of approach. *Will this occur or will educators now allow themselves to be enslaved by a new grammar so that the effect is to substitute one set of rigidities for another?*

Moffett says that in the schools' uncertainties about how to teach an extremely difficult subject they too readily drag university disciplines into elementary and secondary schools and that the mystique of grammar tends to be equated with a "good basic education."

Besides Noam Chomsky's transformational grammar, we want to teach Francis Christensen's rhetorical analysis of the sentence and the paragraph, or Northrop Frye's mythic theory of literature. For the teacher, these are all important things to learn about. They may increase enormously his understanding of what he is trying to teach. . . . But to teach them directly to his students, or to base exercises on them in the discovery manner is misguided. . . . This effort to transmit in one way or another the generalities of scholarship almost always ends by forcing on students an arbitrary and therefore unwelcome knowledge, and by forcing out of the curriculum much more powerful learning activities.[1]

In British schools the strongest trend is away from teaching grammar, marking papers, and using textbooks; the trend is now toward more creative approaches. Their educators do not share this country's compulsive drive to scientize the teaching of English, and they are appalled by the programming in minute steps reinforced by right answers, the highly structured literature presentations, the technical grammar programs for all ages, and the inhibited composition assignments that are loaded with rhetorical analysis.

Moffett is an unusually keen observer of the current scene and offers the following perceptive observations concerning the false rationale for teaching the science of language:

Linguistics filled the bill to dispel the last wisps of progressivism and to establish the post-Sputnik age of intellectual rigor. By a deft switch of rationale we could now go on teaching grammar, not as an aid to speaking and writing—for massive evidence forbade that—but as a humanity for its own sake, or as an intellectual discipline (like Latin) to develop the mind. A student who is told to learn the different kinds of determiners, or to transform one arbitrary sentence into another, might well ask, if it's a humanity why is it so inhumane? It can only be a symptom of hysteria in the profession to swallow the argument that any modern grammar is a humanity, or that the study of it has some special virtue for developing thinking. A study of the uniquely human ability to pro-

---

[1] James Moffett, *A Student-Centered Language Arts Program* (Boston: Houghton Mifflin, 1968), p. 15.

*duce language and organize life symbolically is indeed a
humanity, but that study is conducted by paying attention
to everyday verbal behavior, and, in later years, by becoming acquainted with psychology, sociology, and anthropology, subjects which are hardly even touched upon in
the overall college curriculum. Yes, language is central
to human life, but grammar is a drastically small and
specialized subject, limited essentially to nothing broader
than syntax, that is, the relations and patterns of words
in a sentence.*[2]

Moffett looms on the horizon as a most refreshing harbinger
of the kind of curriculum change that should occur in language
arts. His student-centered approach is highly compatible with
the framework of ideas that has been developed for the humanistic school and the following is an attempt to summarize some
of his thinking.[3]

1. In its most profound sense, a course of language learning
   is a course in thinking, for conceiving and verbalizing
   must be intertwined.
2. The stuff to be conceived and verbalized, however, is the
   raw stuff of life. The real business of the school is to ren-
   der experience into words, not linguistic analysis, or literary analysis, or rhetorical analysis which are proper subjects only for college.
3. The student will be aided by very practical perceptions
   about what he is doing when he speaks or writes, rather
   than with generalizations or formulated advice about
   what others regularly do or ought to do. What he needs
   most of all is to perceive how he *is* using language and
   how he *might* use it. *This requires awareness rather than
   information.*
4. The most effective process is trial and error, which is
   roughly sequenced to provide a student cumulative experience in (a) acting verbally and (b) receiving an enlightened reaction to what he has done.

[2] *Ibid.*, p. 14.
[3] *Ibid.*, pp. 11–13.

5. The only way to provide children with enough of this language experience and reaction is through small group interaction. The teacher, therefore, must teach students to teach one another.

6. The large goal is to expand the students' cognitive and verbal repertories so that they become capable of receiving and producing an increasingly broad range of kinds of discourse, compositional forms, points of view, ways of thinking, styles, vocabulary, and sentence structure.

7. The essential path to this goal is a progression from the personal to the impersonal, from low to high abstraction, and from undifferentiated to finely discriminated modes of discourse.

Moffett's point of view indicates the kind of natural and wholesome approach to language arts that is needed in humanistic schools. The interpretations that follow do not constitute an attempt to elaborate upon his recommendations, but the ideas are highly compatible and may at least reflect a sympathetic and kindred view.

Selected Factors in Language Usage

Across the length and breadth of the land an articulate chorus of voices complains that today's youth are grossly deficient in their ability to use language effectively. Even if one assumes that much of the current criticism is exaggerated and uninformed, it is still apparent that schools have not yet turned in their best effort to develop good usage. Most people learn only one language in a lifetime, and it seems reasonable to expect that they should learn it well. The ideas which follow are believed to be in the spirit of both a humanistic and productive approach to this complex and vital goal.

The Enlightened Setting. Perhaps everyone at some time in his life has been in a classroom where he did not dare to express an idea—for if he did it would be chopped off. It does not take much chopping to create a psychological wasteland with a conspicuous absence of ideas.

Perhaps everyone at some time in his life has been in a group where one of the members, in a moment of spontaneity, beautifully captured the spirit of an idea and someone else took the fun out of it by correcting his English.

Perhaps everyone in his lifetime has seen a child groping for just the right way to express something when a precipitate adult supplied it for him, effectively shutting off any further thought.

Perhaps everyone has read or written a theme full of feeling, imagination, and color that was red-penciled all over by an adult who long ago had lost his capacity for feeling, imagination, and color.

And then perhaps everyone has wondered why at age six the child is so full of ideas and the desire to express them and at sixteen he seems so dehydrated.

An enlightened setting is simple and unpretentious. It is a place where interesting things happen that are worth writing and talking about. It is a place where one is encouraged to express his ideas and then is made to feel that what he has to say is worth listening to. It is a place where the tables are turned and the children talk a little more and the teacher talks a little less. It is a place where a good dose of freedom is the sunshine; thoughtfulness is the rich, black earth; and responsiveness is the rain.

There is a comfortable feeling in such a classroom. One does not have to convey all of his thoughts as though he were addressing a joint session of Congress. He does not have to speak like a stuffed shirt in a manner which is unnatural to his way of life and alien to his peer group. This is one of the refreshing differences of the modern school. In the old days there was a stilted twist to correct usage that restricted its development. The modern teacher recognizes the psychology of a situation and its relationship to correctness of speech. Thus, the circumstances determine whether it is more appropriate to say "Beat it!" or "Please go." Obviously, it is improper to wear one's fatigues to a ball; but it is equally improper to overdress for a track meet. It is the latter concept that the old style grammarian has been so reluctant to concede. Some have been so pristine and sterile in their approach that they have almost destroyed the demand for their product. It is no wonder that many young people rejected a concept of language so separated from life. The adaptation of language to the circumstances in which it is used adds to the sensitivity and richness of expression and gives it a greater range. It is somewhat like the adjustment of music to mood. A significant segment of realism has been added and the language is improved. It is more virile and attractive to young learners and more worthy of their efforts to achieve. No one but a fool would announce that he was going to bed by saying, "I shall withdraw to seek repose."

Such elements of comfort and realism, however, are not to be construed as a license to leave things as they are. It is more of a license to be enlightened about what is appropriate and the kinds of improvements that should be sought. Tension and anxiety are reduced but thinking is increased, and thinking is directed at responding to and improving the language used. The enlightened setting then is a comfortable one, a realistic one, and an interesting one—but one with a growing edge.

Realistic Goals. *Stuart Little* is the title of a delightful book which has been enjoyed by thousands of children and adults. In one passage Stuart has asked a bird, appropriately named Margalo, where she is from. Then comes this splendid line: "I come from fields once tall with wheat, from pastures deep in fern and thistle. I come from vales of meadowsweet, and I love to whistle." [4]

Margalo, a mere bird, has spoken at a very high level of literary expression. Her words are simple and expressive and they fall together in such a way as to create beauty and imagery. Few adults ever achieve this level of expression. What are the goals which one might realistically expect of children?

Grammarians have recognized five levels of usage which merge together in such a way that they cannot be clearly sepa-

[4] E. B. White, *Stuart Little* (New York: Harper & Row, 1945), p. 51.

rated. One is known as the illiterate level and is outside the boundaries of acceptability. This level is reflected by expressions such as "you is," "I seed," "he knowed," etc. The language program of a cultivated society will strive to eliminate this level entirely.

A notch or so above the illiterate level is one which is called the homely level. It may be characterized by such expressions as "whip cream," "light-complected girl," "I reckon," and "Mary, she." This one is sensitive because some element of it is a part of the speech patterns of many worthy men and women, and most children are likely to hear such usages in their own homes. The language program of the elementary school seeks to eliminate this level also, but must do so with great kindness and tact.

The third and fourth levels constitute that broad range of acceptable usage known as standard English. Its lower extremity, called informal standard, should be the normal usage of the elementary classroom and the goal set for most pupils to attain. It is a comfortable type of usage of the kind that might characterize the relaxed and informal conversation of cultured persons. It is not satisfactory, however, for more formal talks and written work. The upper level of this range, known as formal standard, is the goal for carefully prepared written work, prepared talks, and formal correspondence. A formal standard level is more selective in choice of words, more attentive to word order, and more careful about such matters as case and number agreement.

At the top of the mountain is the highest level of all. It is called the literary level, and it beckons many but is attained by only a few. It is a form of writing or speaking that goes beyond mere communication to achieve beauty. Lincoln's Gettysburg Address is a classic example of this level of language. Those who achieve it are exceptionally gifted in their vocabulary, are likely to have an unusual sensitivity to how words fit together to create a desired effect, and are able to transcend utility to achieve beauty, as did Margalo in her reply to Stuart. Children cannot be expected to achieve the literary level of language, nor, indeed, can most of their teachers.

No aspect of the curriculum is more in need of realistic

goals than language usage. The child who comes to the doors of the school with six years of illiterate or homely usage ringing in his ears has a great struggle ahead of him to achieve even the lower rungs of acceptance and respectability. He needs massive doses of patience, incentive, and encouragement. His goal must be set where he can reach it. It is all right to make him stretch a bit, but having stretched and tried, the goal must be within his reach. He must never be made to feel awkward and unworthy because of his language and, when he has tried his very best, his best must be regarded as good enough. Any other approach to such a child is morally and professionally wrong.

At the other end of the continuum is the child who is twice blessed. He comes to school with six years of good usage patterns woven through his language. His parents have listened to him attentively and given him all possible encouragement. He is confident and poised. In the first two years of elementary school he moves perceptibly into the informal standard level at the early age of eight. The goal must be different for him; there is no other sensible way.

For the child at either end and for all those in between, the goal must fit like an expertly tailored suit. Choose the size and the color and the fabric with care. Don't hang a thirty-eight jacket on a skinny little guy. Don't put a bulky tweed on a child who is already too fat. Don't put faded color on a hollow-cheeked little girl. Make it fit every child in the room. That's the realistic note in goals.

Using Action-Response Groups. The skilled athlete practices his specialty over and over again. He may, in fact, practice it ten thousand times. Some of this endeavor takes place under the observation of the coaching staff and a great deal more is carried on alone or with his peers. The end result is almost a miracle of improvement, and the blossoming of superbly developed athletes all over the country. Why are the schools not getting this kind of improvement in the use of language?

Would the athletes achieve the level of development that occurs if they spent a fourth of their time diagraming moves, another fourth in workbooks and text materials, and most of the remaining time answering questions and problems posed by the teacher? Under such a scheme, athletics would either die or go underground and the relentless educators would then make it compulsory.

The simple fact is that in order to develop language power one must use language over and over again in situations conducive to *directly influencing its growth and potency.* The framework for stepping up usage and peer reaction to that usage is through realistic activity in small groups ranging in size from two to four or five.

In discussing social studies the first humanistic suggestion was that of using the classroom itself as a laboratory for social living. In so doing, one takes actual happenings that are transpiring in the day-by-day scene and takes a closer look at them with a view toward enlarging understandings and improving behavior. Many of these events lend themselves to small group reaction prior to their consideration by the class as a whole. Any problems or topics about which the children have strong feelings or thoughts are appropriate for such deliberations. Language is then focused upon things that are important to the students in a context which they can see may benefit them. Their thoughts and feelings can be externalized, and this is therapeutic even if nothing more significant occurs. Something more important, however, should occur, for their ideas are worthy of the kinds of consideration that makes for the changing of school policies and classroom activities. They thus see their thinking and language influencing their lives.

Within these sessions peer reaction feeds into their thoughts and expressions so that the original thought or expression of the child may undergo a qualitative improvement. A minimum of ground rules apply to the small group discussions, but among them would likely be the simple obligation for all members to contribute relevantly to the discussion and to help summarize it for consideration by the class as a whole.

Some of the inquiry sessions in science in which an interesting episode has been presented may offer excellent points of departure for group talk. In mathematics the handling and use of some of the conceptual devices may offer rich opportunities for meaningful talk sessions. The point is that talk in the school should be *cultivated rather than discouraged,* and the teacher should be relieved of the feeling that he must personally hear and react to everything that is produced. The same format can be used for many aspects of written expression, and children may read and react to one another's writing with more responsibility placed upon the children themselves than has traditionally prevailed.

Such a procedure may vastly increase the *amount of language activity as well as the amount of reaction and response to that activity.* It is a way to bring it out and look it over in a setting that is conducive to developing more sensitivity, more proficiency, and more respect for the language itself. Even for the teacher it is an easier and more stimulating approach.

Cooperative Analysis and Improvement. Out of the observations made by the teacher there may emerge a small and very selective list of common and important errors made by the class. Some of these are more unacceptable than others and deserve a more concerted attempt at improvement. Care must be exercised in identifying these errors so that the matter is kept in perspective, and there is deliberate avoidance of some of the mistakes made in language teaching of the past. Those mistakes included attempting to change too many errors, attempting to change usages that were actually acceptable forms of expression, and drilling on items that were in the workbook whether or not they were errors made by the class.

Out of this select list that is to be focused upon it may be advisable to choose only *one* as the primary target. The initial emphasis is upon an effort to develop as fully as possible an understanding of why a given form of usage is desired. This may be followed by opportunities to select the right over the wrong form in specific paired choices. The third phase is the follow-through of thoughtful attention to the correct usage of this single item throughout the school day. It enjoys no privileged sanctuary and may receive attention in any part of the program in which it may occur.

After target number one has received the amount and kind of attention that is desired, the procedure may be repeated with the second item on the priority list. The entire process needs to be kept under close surveillance for its effect. If the effect with a given class tends to be inhibiting or negative, it should be curtailed; for this suggestion is not of the same degree of importance as the preceding one in which the emphasis was placed upon producing and reacting to language. If it is limited to really important forms of usage, however, and worked at one at a time over a leisurely period of time, it should be manageable and constructive. At some stage in the development of proficiency in any skill there is a time for kindly correction of performance and form. A single error may significantly affect the quality of individual performance in a variety of activities, ranging from diving and swimming to handwriting. Professionals should emphasize the positive, but they should never allow themselves to become so overwhelmed by their human relations function that they are rendered incapable of gentle remediation.

Developing a Love for Language. It does not seem to be generally recognized that one might remove all the errors from expression and still not have good language. Freed from all of its undesirable forms it might still be sterile and unimaginative, lacking in color and warmth, and essentially uninviting. To shift into a forward gear and build into usage the positive elements it should possess is discussed by some as the development of language appreciation. The writer does not care for the term "appreciation." One may appreciate the refuse department without feeling any particular warmth for it. The young learner should have more of a "crush" on language, this mysterious lady who serves us all so well. He should reach out to her, embrace her, and love her.

This state of loving requires a quality of vibrant living which helps language to come alive. It conveys sensitivity, inspiration, pouring out, and giving of oneself. Less than that is simply not enough. How does one promote such a relationship?

One thing that a teacher can do is to show his own feeling for language in thought and deed. When something is said by a child in a child's way and it is said just right—he holds it up for all to see and enjoy. When in their reading the chil-

dren come across a delightful passage that says just what everyone would like to say in just the way they might have liked to
say it—they display it for all to see and enjoy. The hurry and
the bustle and the driving machinery of ongoingness is all
temporarily suspended for the sake of enjoyment, just as one
would stop to marvel at a rainbow or a flash of lightning in
the sky. The teacher shows by his personal example that he
places a premium on these things. He helps children to sense
the beauty of language and to be responsive to it when it appears.

He teaches them to be proud of their thoughts and to want
to clothe them adequately and appropriately with words. He
teaches them to bring color into their language and to express
their thoughts in such a way that people really want to hear
what they have to say. Then he shows them how to do this by
speaking to them in such a way that they want to hear him.
Day by day he reacts sensitively to the bits of color and the
kind of weave that create a comfortable and lovely garment
that one is proud to wear. This is the forward gear, the positive element, the development of a *love for language;* and it is
a vital element in a strong program.

Vocabulary Development. Many of the products of learning
do not seem to have any direct relationship either to one's success in life or to his personal happiness. It would be difficult
for instance to demonstrate that skill in spelling or computation has any marked effect on one's salary or social position.
This is not true, however, of vocabulary development. An excellent vocabulary is one of the educated man's most prized
possessions. It has a personal value in making and keeping
friends, in successfully meeting the hurdles of college and university standards of excellence, and in getting a job and win-
ning promotions. There are few important aspects of modern
life that are not in some measure affected by this achievement.

The relationship between intelligence and vocabulary is a
positive one. Individuals with high intelligence are likely also
to have large vocabularies and in some psychological tests the
vocabulary section often has the highest correlation with the
total score. There is also an interesting relationship between

vocabulary and the level of one's position. Some of the highest scores on tests of vocabulary are made by the top level executives of business and industry. Top executives outscore junior executives and even outrank college and university professors. Top executives seem, also, to make the high scores whether or not they have had a college education.

The elementary school has so many responsibilities that it is certainly understandable when some of its larger tasks tend to be put aside for more expedient matters. Thus, vocabulary development in many schools may not be receiving the degree of emphasis that it deserves. Somehow the alert school must manage to keep this factor near the top of its agenda, for the dividends are high and nothing influences language usage as much as the right word in the right place at the right time.

In the primary grades, the emphasis on vocabulary continues to be through direct experience. A child in first grade probably has a speaking vocabulary of several thousand words when he enters school. He developed this vocabulary through the direct experiences of seeing, hearing, feeling, tasting, and smelling. His teachers build upon this and extend it by providing additional firsthand experiences which are used for further language growth. For instance, in an enlightened primary room the firsthand experience is carefully discussed and then recorded. First graders will dictate to the teacher what they wish to record about the experience and these stories may be used as a basis for some of their reading. The language is at the linguistic level of maturity of the children, for it is their language. It is of course richer and more advanced than the language of their basic reading series, which has a very carefully controlled vocabulary. Words from the recorded experiences are studied and the total vocabulary is strengthened more than it could be strengthened by basal readers alone.

With older children the approach can be more structured. Structural analysis teaches children the root words and their derivations. The child begins to develop some independence in increasing his store of words. He may keep a record of new words which he finds attractive and wishes to add to those which he already knows. Teachers deliberately use colorful and effective new words to add to their store of meanings. The value and function of the dictionary is taught as an additional tool for developing independence.

Language activity in the classroom constantly reflects the importance of words and their essential role in the adequate expression of one's thoughts. When nature or circumstances have created a special mood it is used to add to the richness of language. Thus, a gentle rain or a new fallen snow may precipitate talking or writing about the feelings that it inspires and there is an effort to describe feelings with sensitivity and beauty. Words that are overused are replaced with others that are better and more meaningful. Words that ascribe meanings too loosely are replaced with others that are more concise. The child's language is enlarged. He is taught in such a way as to add new meanings to old words as well as to add new words.

In vocabulary development there is no substitute for wide reading. Wide reading alone will expand the child's vocabulary, but wide reading plus the kinds of assistance that have been described will add to the gains that are made. The expansion of vocabulary is accomplished in part by deliberately invoked procedures in the school. If the school can also develop in the child *the desire to add to his store of words on his own, then he would seem to be on his way.* He will find for the remainder of his life that this achievement can serve him well. His language usage will have more strength, it will be more stimulating and colorful, and he will be more capable of doing justice to his thoughts.

Selected Factors in Language Tools

In the "good old days" the spelling bee was a fairly substantial segment of the social life of a community and handwriting was regarded as one of the distinctive characteristics of a cultivated person. Their status is lower today. The best of handwriting appears somewhat crude in comparison with a beautifully typed letter, and the spelling bees which remain are somewhat artificially contrived. They have passed away like the old-fashioned box suppers which offered to the lucky buyer the additional fringe benefits of the companionship of the lady who had prepared it. Another of the simple, wholesome aspects of an earlier day has disappeared and one cannot help feeling a twinge of nostalgia at the loss.

Spelling and handwriting are skills which are brought into play for expressing ideas in written form; they are tools of communication. Although they no longer enjoy the esteem and place in the program that they once held, they are still important even though they are, admittedly, a minor part of the curriculum.

Spelling may possibly function at the same intellectual level as language usage, but handwriting is more of a mechanical skill. One invokes his brain in spelling, but his handwriting is a habituated form of motor activity. Perhaps this is one of the reasons why handwriting seems to deteriorate with advanced levels of education or achievement. An early study indicated that the illegibilities of high school students exceeded the illegibilities of elementary students by 136 percent. The illegibilities of adults, however, rose additionally to 350 percent.[5] An interesting journal item graphically portrayed the point that the higher one rises in status the less legible his signature becomes.[6] As a young naval officer, the signature that was reproduced was quite legible. As a United States senator the signature of the same young man was less legible. As President of the United States, however, the signature was almost unrecognizable. The signature was that of John F. Kennedy. The journal noted that a Harvard well wisher had spent $3 to enroll President Kennedy (without his knowledge) in a handwriting correspondence school.

The current criticism of young people's spelling is understandable and the schools can do a better job than has been done. What may be overlooked, however, is that no adequate data is readily available to reveal precisely how the spelling of people today compares with the achievements of years past. Perhaps the spotlight of attention focuses more brightly on the errors made today than on yesterday. Certainly some very distin-

---

[5] T. Ernest Newland, "An Analytical Study of the Development of Illegibilities in Handwriting from the Lower Grades to Adulthood," *Journal of Educational Research*, XXVI (December 1962): 249–258.

[6] *Reader's Digest*, October 1961, p. 186.

guished men of the past made overt errors in spelling. The writing of Lincoln revealed common misspellings even though this great man achieved such a remarkable level of literary usage.

Spelling is a more intriguing topic than handwriting because of the higher intellectual level at which it may function. With so many more vital matters at stake it is unrealistic to become preoccupied with handwriting. One should write legibly and there are well-established procedures for doing so. It poses no great challenge. The biggest obstacle today to its highest potential achievement is misguided parents, as will be interpreted in later remarks having to do with the special factors.

The Core Vocabulary of Spelling. Spelling is one of the few aspects of the curriculum for which research can provide a reasonably specific picture of what should be taught. The many studies that have been made on word usage indicate that some words appear more frequently in the written expression of both children and adults. Thus, a relatively small number of words may constitute a relatively high proportion of the total number used. This important discovery is the key to one of the qualitative factors that can be identified for spelling. Its value is revealed by findings such as the following:

1. The one hundred most frequently used words constitute approximately 60 percent of all normal usage.
2. The five hundred most frequently used words constitute approximately 82 percent of all normal usage.
3. The one thousand most frequently used words constitute approximately 90 percent of all normal usage.
4. The two thousand most frequently used words comprise about 95 percent of all normal usage.[7]

Beyond the first two thousand words, usage tends to be influenced by special vocabularies having to do with particular vocations or areas of special interest and the thread of commonality tends to disappear. Thus, a total of three thousand

[7] Ernest Horn, *A Basic Writing Vocabulary*, Monograph No. 4 (Iowa City: University of Iowa, 1926).

words increases the percentage to only 97.66 and four thousand raises it to only 98.73.

There are two major implications for the spelling program in the evidence derived from the word studies. One is that, up to the point of two thousand words, the school is dealing with a type of content that has considerable importance for every child in the school; beyond that point one is moving into a zone where individualization of the content seems more desirable and necessary. Thus, the first two thousand words comprise what may logically be regarded as the basic or core content of the program. It is by no means the total content of the curriculum in spelling but it is certainly an excellent start.

Although almost all elementary schools use spelling texts, they are relatively unnecessary. A school needs to know which words are more frequently used and more basic, but this information is readily available from several studies and could easily be provided in the form of a list at considerable savings to the schools. Furthermore, the book may actually become a hindrance by introducing a rigidity into the sequence and presentation of the words that is absurd and even detrimental. A wise teacher with a basic list of assigned words can weave them into the curriculum as they are needed and used in the natural course of events. Each word can be checked off as it is mastered so that there is a record of what has been done, and the haphazard aspect of incidental teaching is removed. Some of the modern schools have approached the job of teaching basic spelling words in this way, for it is systematic in addition to being a more natural and meaningful approach. Regardless of whether the words are presented in a manner that is natural or contrived, the school should identify and stress a basic core of words. The core spelling vocabulary pays a handsome 95 percent return and is one of the important characteristics of a sound program.

Spelling's Giant Booster Mechanism. It seems reasonable to assume that if the elementary school could achieve the teaching of two thousand words comprising 95 percent of normal usage this would be very desirable indeed. Elementary schools, however, can do better than this.

Dolch, in an old but useful pamphlet on the teaching of spelling, identified the chief issue in spelling as the "list versus the learner" approach.[8] In this discussion of the issue he points out a very important matter that is not commonly known. Whereas two thousand words can and do provide for a substantial *percentage* of words used by an individual, the number necessary to meet what he calls "one's life spelling needs" is nearer to ten thousand words. Obviously, the elementary school cannot specifically teach ten thousand words —such a task would be physically and mentally impossible. What then should be done?

What seems to be needed is some sort of giant booster mechanism. The step from two to ten thousand words is a phenomenal one and requires some kind of an auxiliary device. The booster is to be found in a change of lens. The school must shift the focus from the spelling content itself to the child. It must face up to the fact that teaching the words assigned to any given grade level is for each teacher involved the lesser part of the task. It is of even greater importance to help each child develop and perfect *a way in which he can master new words*. This is the power factor which makes it possible for the child to reach out independently on his own and take up where the school program left off.

The Dolch pamphlet contains some excellent suggestions on this matter. It identifies five approaches to the learning of spelling which are described in lay rather than technical terms. Briefly interpreted, *lip spelling* is a mere habit of the speaking apparatus and is an inferior way of learning to spell. *Eye spelling* stresses visualization of the word in the "mind's eye"; it is probably the method most widely used in the schools and may be particularly helpful with the common words or with words that are somewhat unusual or tricky. *Ear spelling* means spelling by sounds and is more helpful in spelling some of the longer words, like Mississippi, that tend to be spelled more like they sound. Ear spelling, in contrast to eye spelling, is not very valuable for the common words, since they are often the most unphonetic of the language. *Hand spelling* is

[8] Edward W. Dolch, *The Modern Teaching of Spelling* (Champaign, Illinois: Garrard Press, 1950).

exemplified by the child who actually moves his finger over letters to trace the physical outline of the word and is ordinarily used only in cases where other methods do not seem to get results. *Thought spelling* has reference to developing the habits of the good speller and is regarded by Dolch as the best solution to poor spelling no matter what the cause. It involves asking—and answering—three important questions:

1. What is the correct pronunciation?
2. Does the sound tell the spelling?
3. How can I remember the hard part?

The word "subtle" provides an example of this technique. Having established the correct pronunciation and having determined that the sound does not reveal the correct spelling, one comes to the question of how to remember the hard part. One college student pointed out that "sub" comes from the Latin, meaning "under," and that "subtle" has an underhanded sort of connotation. This association helped him to establish in his mind the pattern of the spelling. Presumably, in a technique of this kind a pupil links the idea to be learned with one or more ideas that he has already learned. It is what has been known as an association technique. An association technique would seem to place some tax on the imagination and power of thinking of a pupil in order to make the necessary links. This, however, could be construed as being beneficial in the sense that it makes the learning a more thoughtful process.

The point is that each child needs to be helped to develop a way that is effective for him. It seems advisable to give primary emphasis to the thought method and to add to that whatever additional elements from the sensory approaches are helpful in creating a smoothly working attack for each child. It is worth whatever time it takes to accomplish this. The child who perfects an approach or combination of approaches that enables him to unlock or master new words, is well on his way to a higher level of independence, which is the only reasoned hope for attaining mastery of the ten thousand words necessary to meet his life's spelling needs. This factor of independence in attack is spelling's giant booster mechanism.

Personally Appropriated Spelling. In addition to the core content of spelling, there is a personal content which provides an individualization ingredient in the program. This individualization ingredient may dip into the core material or go considerably beyond it in terms of the maturity of the pupil. The following example illustrates one such approach and at the same time weaves it appropriately into the total language arts program.

A primary teacher took her children to the top of a small hill overlooking the village to prime them for a creative writing lesson. The little community was very picturesque. Some of the children had never seen their village "from the top side" before and were impressed by the difference in the view. Later, they returned to the classroom to write about what they had seen. At this point their teacher used a rather novel mechanical procedure.

On the board she had written each letter of the alphabet in both small and capital letters. When a child asked how to spell a word he wished to use in his writing she supplied it for him and wrote it on the board under the correct letter. For instance, if a child asked for the spelling of "beautiful" she wrote it for him on the board under the letter "b." She freely supplied the spellings because she felt that if she did not the child might substitute a word like "pretty" which he could spell instead of looking up the word he wanted in the dictionary. The net result of such substitutions would be to impoverish and detract from the quality of the writing.

Having asked and received help, the child would then record that particular word in his personalized dictionary. This dictionary was kept by the child and contained two pages for each letter of the alphabet. It was neatly stapled together and had an attractive cover which each child had designed and made for himself. The dictionary hung from his desk by a colored string so that it was always readily accessible. Words were added to the dictionaries throughout the year.

The value of such a procedure is that *it adds to the spelling content of the curriculum an element that is individualized and personal.* It is unlikely that the lists of any two children in a room would be the same. This is in sharp contrast to the core list which is exactly alike for everyone. Both types of content, however, are vital. One provides a big boost forward on the common words everyone needs to know; the other helps a child come closer to reaching his own life spelling needs. The excellent program in spelling is not complete without such personally appropriated content.

Spelling's Secret Weapon. In 1947 Thomas Horn reported his study on the effect of the corrected test.[9] One group in the experiment followed a weekly plan that is typical of many traditional classrooms. Such a plan involves introduction of the words, attention to pronunciation, formal study, pretest, and final test at the end of the week. An experimental group followed a quite different procedure. This group simply took a test over words which they had not studied, corrected their own papers, studied any errors they had made, and then repeated the same test. The purpose of the study was to determine the effect of allowing children to grade their own spelling.

The results were startling. The experimental group achieved almost as much as the group which formally studied spelling throughout the week. When attention to pronunciation was added to the experimental approach, achievement was approximately 95 percent of the achievement of the group using the traditional plan. Horn concluded that allowing children to correct their own papers was the most important single factor contributing to achievement in spelling. Although the study was conducted with students in the sixth grade, primary teachers who have tried it have reported excellent results even with children in the first grade.

There are several significant aspects to this unusual study. One is simply that *it constitutes one of those rare innovations in which the teacher works less and the children learn more.* Most teaching ideas seem always to result in extra time and effort on the part of the teacher. It is probably true that most conscientious teachers spend too much time grading papers for children at considerable expense in terms of their own personal lives. Too much of this can drain their vitality and

[9] Thomas D. Horn, "The Effect of the Corrected Test on Learning to Spell," *Elementary School Journal*, XLVII (January 1947): 277–285.

thereby rob them of the greatest gift they can take to a classroom. The self-corrected test technique offers a sort of respite. One might even conclude that the teacher who corrects the papers himself is actually denying children a rich learning opportunity.

A second significant aspect has to do with cheating. Probably a great deal of the cheating which is done in spelling is generated by the pressure children feel to get 100. This approach would seem to remove some of the incentive to cheat, for the purpose is so completely different. The test is used as *a way to learn*. It does not carry the usual warhead. It does, however, carry a bigger payload in that it is a more wholesome and hygienic approach. The ultraconservative teacher who might hold the fear that "things would get out of hand" can weave in a periodic review lesson in which he grades the papers himself as a precautionary measure and as a check. The self-corrected session itself, however, should be carefully preserved as a way to learn.

There is a third significant aspect of this approach that is difficult to put into words. It is that the spirit of the approach seems to reflect learning in its finest sense—a sort of reaching out process instead of a pouring in. Learning is freed from its usual adult restrictions and becomes more self-active and alive. This quality is especially prized in a humanistic school.

Spelling in Context. In 1927 McKee made a study to determine the relative efficiency of column versus context forms in the teaching of spelling.[10] As a result of his investigation, he concluded that the teaching of spelling in context was less efficient and was an impractical procedure. More recently Horn has stated in the NEA pamphlet in spelling that:

> *Research has consistently shown that it is more efficient to study words in lists than in context. Words studied in lists are learned more quickly, remembered longer, and transferred more readily to new context.*[11]

[10] Paul McKee, "Teaching Spelling by Column and Context Forms," *Journal of Educational Research*, XV (April 1927): 246–255.

[11] Ernest Horn, *Teaching Spelling* (Washington, D.C.: NEA, 1954), p. 16.

Such a statement may be true in a highly specific sense, but seems questionable in a much larger one. The element of truth in the assertion is that, naturally, one learns to spell a given word more efficiently by studying that specific word rather than a more loosely construed target. Thus, the word should be temporarily isolated for a sharp close look and attempted mastery. Spelling it correctly in a list after this good hard look, however, *is not a test of mastery*. Life, fortunately, is such that one does not go around spelling words in lists. Spelling is, instead, a completely functional part of the process of expressing a thought. Words are used in context in the expression of a thought and are properly tested in the same manner. Anything short of this constitutes an inadequate evaluation of the child's mastery of the words.

The point becomes more significant when observations are made of the occasions in which children spell a word correctly in their weekly list, but misspell the same word on other occasions when they are expressing ideas in written form. The classic example of this was the child who was required to practice the word "written" fifty times before going home. He did so and correctly wrote the word. He then penned the following note to his teacher: "I have writen the word fifty times and gone home."

It is not known to what extent words spelled correctly in lists are later spelled incorrectly in context. Teachers can provide an extra boost or reinforcement, however, by dictating the words in sentences or complete paragraphs in order to appraise mastery in more realistic terms. Spelling words today are ordinarily introduced in context as a regular classroom procedure, which is a sound and logical practice. They should be checked for mastery in the same manner.

Maintaining Manuscript. Thoughts that are adequately expressed and words that are correctly spelled deserve a handwriting which pleases the eye. Above all the writing should be legible and legibility is the logical goal. This is a sensible and wholesome change from the writing of an earlier day which was characterized by flourish and affectation. Although the handwriting of the past was an inextricable part of its own life and times, it does not serve the purposes of the present. The writing sought in the schools today is more simple, more clean-cut, and more crisply a part of today and tomorrow.

The type of handwriting that best serves present purposes is manuscript. Manuscript is superior to cursive writing on practically every count. It is easier for children to learn in their initial writing, for the simplicity of the circles and strokes is more compatible with their degree of motor control and can be learned with less strain. In addition, the child needs to learn only a single letter form of the alphabet for both reading and writing since manuscript closely resembles the print he is beginning to read. The above reasons are largely responsible for the fact that almost all schools begin writing by teaching manuscript. The decision is a sound one.

The mistake made by schools is in shifting to cursive writing in the later grades. Some make the transition in the second grade but most of them change sometime during the third. It is an error in judgment to change at all, for it involves shifting from a superior to an inferior style. Many schools will privately admit this, but claim that the parents insist on the change. Parents, for instance, are reported as believing that manuscript is "baby writing." This attitude is completely unfounded, for architects, surveyors, and engineers all use manuscript writing. If parents actually have the attitude that is attributed to them, they are simply not well informed about what is going on in the world.

Occasionally, the reason given for changing to cursive is the need for a legal signature. In view of the fact that one is dealing here with elementary children, this becomes even more preposterous but indicates the mental level at which some curriculum decisions are made. So far as the need for a legal signature is concerned, the one in manuscript is entirely satisfactory. One's habitual signature is his legal signature, whether it is in manuscript or in cursive.

A third reason given for the change is the claim that cursive writing is faster. This claim is probably not even true. Washburne and Morphett demonstrated many years ago that when children used nothing but manuscript on through high school their speed was greater than with cursive.[12] Even if cursive were faster it would not be of any particular importance, for legibility rather than speed is the imperative goal. And, where legibility is concerned, manuscript is the undisputed champion. Schools need to reaffirm their leadership on this matter and lead their respective communities. In an enlightened school manuscript skills will be strengthened and extended throughout the program.

Handedness. The teacher of handwriting has a personal obligation to get the beginner off to the right kind of a start, but this does not mean that a left-hander should be made into a right-hander. In the past, and even today, many left-handed children have been required by their teachers to write with their right hand. This curriculum practice seems completely unjustified.

The human organism is such that the motor activity of the left-handed person is linked with the right hemisphere of the brain. For the right-handed person, the link is with the left hemisphere of the brain. By the time the child enters first grade these patterns are well established. Forcing the child to alter the pattern by writing with his right hand instead of the left creates a disruption in the process. It is not known to what extent this is detrimental. What is known, however, is that if one takes at random one hundred children who stutter, the group contains an abnormally high incidence of children who have been changed from left-handed to right-handed writing. This does not prove that making such a change causes stuttering; it does, however, flash a danger signal and casts the practice of such changes under a shadow of doubt.

Why is it important to take such a chance? Is this particular aspect of individuality somehow out of bounds? Is the world so right-handed that all its inhabitants must be right-handed also? Is the left-handed person at any real disadvantage? It would seem that the burden of proof of any real disadvantage

---

[12] Carlton Washburne and M. V. Morphett, "Manuscript Writing—Some Recent Investigations," *Elementary School Journal*, XXXVII (1937): 517–529.

of left-handedness should be placed on those who advocate the change.

Some of the nation's most prominent authorities on education seem to believe that it is all right for the child to be changed if he is changed early enough and if the transition can be made without strain on the part of the child. This belief should be challenged!

In the first place, the school does not get the child early enough; his habit associations have already been established. He is oriented to a left-handed existence and is off to a running start. In the second place, who knows whether a child who is being changed is under any strain? It is unrealistic and dangerous to place this much reliance on a teacher's perception, for inner strain may often take place without its outward disclosure.

Left-handedness should be regarded as another form of rich individuality. It has an attractiveness and grace all its own. Left-handed children who write like cripples with their hand twisted down from the top do so because their teachers were uninformed and placed their paper at a slant that was correct for the right-handed writer but not for the left. There is no reason for the left-handed child to be required to write in such a ludicrous fashion. All the fuss and furor over changing children from left to right should be channeled into more constructive pursuits. The humanistic school allows left-handed children to remain left-handed, and it nourishes their handwriting skills in the ways that are most beneficial to them.

Selected Factors in Teaching Reading

One August afternoon in Miami a seven-year-old boy who had completed first grade went over to his old classroom with his former teacher. They were accompanied by another boy who was six and would enter first grade in the fall. In the room, the older boy pulled out one of his preprimers and proceeded to show the younger child how to read. In a few minutes the six-year old was reading from the second of the preprimers. The process was something like popping corn. His thrill at his accomplishment was exceeded only by the pride of his parents when he read the book later to them.

Many children learn to read as simply and as easily as the child in Miami. They are the children who are perhaps predestined to read and would do so even without teachers. Others will learn with the help of intelligent teaching; and, for still others, the process may become enormously complicated. Schools are constantly searching for better ways to facilitate mastery for a greater number of children and to prevent the piling up of disorders on the part of those who experience difficulties.

Parents are very concerned about the manner in which the schools teach reading. They realize how important it is to the personal happiness of their children as well as to their academic success and they press the schools for quicker and better results. As Cabell Greet expressed it so delightfully in his foreword to Dr. Gray's book:

> Isn't there a wonderful modern short cut? Phonemes, semantemes, morphemes, intimes, word counts, meaning counts, nose counts, no-counts. These are new? Surely there is an easier way to teach reading now, even though I can't seem to get my television to work right.[13]

There are a number of interesting experiments and innovations in the teaching of reading, but none of them are shortcuts. Each of them requires patience, time, effort, and skillful teaching. Success is rarely due to a single factor; it is more likely to be the result of a constellation of factors. Reading as much as any other aspect of the curriculum reflects the need for a multiple offense and a versatile approach to the problem. Three illustrative considerations that are believed to be particularly relevant to the kind of school that is sought are interpreted in the concluding remarks.

Building Sensibly upon Prior Experiences. One aspect of humanism and excellence in a reading program is the degree to which it can relate itself to the rich stream of experiences chil-

[13] William S. Gray, *On Their Own in Reading* (Chicago: Scott, Foresman, 1960), p. 12.

dren have had before they come to school. This is significant in several ways. One is in the sense of establishing a natural, person-oriented induction into the reading process; another is in making reading a more meaningful activity; and a third has to do with the possibility of ameliorating the influence of disadvantaged backgrounds.

With respect to the latter it was pointed out in the earlier discussion of life content that the child entering school may have known loneliness, thirst, and vast reaches of space; or he may have known crowding, littered streets, and patrol cars moving ominously through his neighborhood. Whatever he has known, however, he brings to school. To disregard his prior experiences as though they were unimportant is tragically unreal and may produce an artificial schism in his life that later becomes very difficult to bridge. The disregarding of prior experiences represents a failure also to capitalize upon a splendid opening for teaching-learning, for what the child knows best is a base and transition point for further learning.

The approach which seems to best fulfill the conditions indicated above is the language experience approach. Van Allen makes some very pertinent points in raising what he calls some soul-searching questions about reading instruction. One is that he wonders whether the use of a predetermined and controlled vocabulary is as significant as it was once believed to be. Might there not be enough control in the daily natural language of the child to guide early word recognition without systematic control from outside sources? Another is whether or not the choppy, unnatural sentences of primers and preprimers are really easier to read than more natural sentences composed by the children themselves. Might not the greater meaning and motivation of the natural sentences outweigh the factor of greater concept difficulty? If a child really understands what he is doing is there not a possibility of higher levels of development? And is it not of vital importance to develop in children a feeling that their own ideas are worthy of expression, and their own language is a respected and prized vehicle of communication? [14]

[14] R. van Allen, "More Ways Than One," in *Readings in Reading Instruction*, Albert J. Harris, ed. (New York: David McKay, 1963), p. 97.

All of the above lies well within the concept of a humanistic school. In addition, however, such an approach to reading *seems to be productive.* Studies such as the one at San Diego have indicated that no important words used in the basal readers are neglected when beginning reading is based upon the children's own creative writing. The vocabulary that is used may be three or four times as great as that which is used in a standard series of preprimers and children who wrote and read from their own experiences prior to reading from basal readers could then read the textbooks with ease. In fact, they were able to read from fifteen to twenty preprimers in a single month.[15]

The method avoids putting external pressure upon the child. For instance, it may be carried out as the San Diego teachers did by having a child make a picture expressing an idea that has meaning to him. Putting what he is saying with his picture into words may be the beginning of his reading; each day he is provided with an opportunity *to come to the threshold of reading without forcing an entrance.* It is a highly individualized approach and opens the door to a program that is limited only by the language and experience level of the children concerned. It reflects a basic conviction that no preplanned materials can equal the resources that lie within the children themselves and, as in the case of using the classroom itself as a laboratory for social living in social studies, it contains its own intrinsic or built-in motivation.

Such a plan helps youngsters to get off to a good start by capitalizing upon their prior experiences and moving naturally from that point onward. It weaves the language arts together realistically into their proper sequencing as exemplified by R. van Allen's widely quoted rationale:

What I can think about, I can talk about.
What I can say, I can write—or someone can write for me.
What I can write, I can read.

[15] R. van Allen, "Initiating Reading Through Creative Writing," *Twenty-Second Yearbook of the Claremont College Reading Conference* (Claremont, California, 1957), pp. 109–116.

> *I can read what I can write, and what other people can*
> *write for me to read.*[16]

The process functions at the linguistic level of the children involved. It is interesting, challenging, creative, and individualized. It should be regarded as one of the highly significant approaches to the teaching of reading.

Developing Early Independence and Word Perception Skills.
Regardless of the approach used in the teaching of reading, one common element which must be present in a program is some kind of instruction in word perception skills. These can be an accompanying part of the language experience approach and help the youngster advance more rapidly to an early independence in his ability to attack new words and content. The aspect over which there has been the greatest confusion and controversy is the one relating to instruction in phonics.

Jeanne Chall's extensive study of reading is one of the most carefully conducted inquiries available.[17] Her investigation indicated that children do learn better with an early code emphasis and that children of low socioeconomic background profit more than those from middle and high socioeconomic groups. She did not find evidence, however, that seemed to justify endorsing one code emphasis over another. In addition, she recommended a code emphasis only as a beginning method. Once the pupil has learned to recognize in print the words that he knows (because they are a part of his speaking and listening vocabulary), she felt that additional work on decoding would be a waste of time.[18]

The swing back to more intensive phonics that occurred during the sixties may pose a possible hazard of overemphasis. One program, for instance, presents almost one hundred phonic generalizations. Clymer's study of the utility of phonic

---

[16] R. van Allen, "More Ways Than One," *op. cit.*, p. 99.

[17] Jeanne Chall, *Learning to Read: The Great Debate* (New York: McGraw-Hill, 1967).

[18] *Ibid.*, p. 307.

generalizations, however, indicated that only eighteen of the forty-five generalizations he analyzed had a 75 percent utility level (or were applicable in three out of four cases).[19] In a more recent study of the same forty-five generalizations used by Clymer, Bailey applied them to words taken from the vocabularies of eight basal reading series running from grades one through six.[20] Only six generalizations were found to be simple to understand and use, to be applicable to a large number of words, and to have few exceptions. It seems fairly clear that many commonly taught phonics principles are confusing, contradictory, and relatively useless. Reading programs should reflect a continuing effort to keep this portion of the program sensible and balanced.

The broader goal sought in an excellent program is advancing maturity in word perception. This is a larger factor than phonics and refers to competency in *multiple forms of word attack*. The sounding out of words is balanced and strengthened by the concomitant use of context clues, structural analysis, skill in using the dictionary, and a quick, smooth assimilation of the image or configuration of a rapidly growing stock of words. These skills are in a sense the muscle of the program, and in the highly skilled reader they are as effortlessly invoked as the actions of a superb athlete in his chosen endeavor. This maturity, based as it is upon a more versatile approach to word mastery, is a balancing factor which protects children against splinter movements and elements of faddism which tend to emerge in any given era of program development.

Word perception skills are extremely vital and relate primarily to the intellectual goal of *developing the power to learn*. The language experience approach may contribute more to *the spirit of desiring to learn* and to the child's sense of *why it is important to learn*. Sensitively and sensibly interwoven they combine effectively to increase the general potency

[19] Theodore Clymer, "The Utility of Phonic Generalizations in the Primary Grades," *Reading Teacher*, January 1963, p. 252.

[20] M. H. Bailey, "The Utility of Phonic Generalizations in Grades One Through Six," *Reading Teacher*, February 1967, pp. 413–418.

of this aspect of a child's development and help to speed him on his way.

Individualized Reading. Individualized reading is one of the refreshing innovations that has moved into current practices. Teachers have always attempted to have some degree of individualization in their program, but the approach bearing this label represents a bolder and more clear-cut break with traditional methods. One of the conspicuous requirements for success of the method is a belief on the part of the teacher in the importance of developing in children a larger measure of personal responsibility for their own success in reading. A teacher who has this personal conviction regarding the importance of self-direction is more oriented to the kind of teaching style that is essential for making the program a success.

Pupils should be developed to the point where they can read independently for short periods without constant supervision before the program is put into effect. This would have been adequately achieved by the language-experience approach previously discussed and by the initial attention to word recognition. The method may be used effectively with children having a range of reading ability extending from low second grade level up to and including an adult level. General procedures are likely to entail the following:

1. A large number of suitable books and materials are assembled. This would feature creative writing that the students have produced themselves. In addition, it would ordinarily include a few copies of several different basal readers as well as a rich selection of fiction, travel, history, biography, adventure, science, and poetry. The range of the material at any given time would extend from what the lowest reader in the class can read independently up to the appropriate level of difficulty for the best readers in the class.
2. The children must be functionally oriented to the new procedures. This means that they must be taught how to select books for themselves and how to get the book

which they have read properly checked if this is required. In addition, the children must understand the importance of their own efforts to the success of the program.

3. After orientation and the beginning of the program, the child keeps in his possession at all times a book of his own choice. As he reads he may keep a vocabulary list of the words which cause him difficulty in his independent reading.

4. The teacher will have a personal conference with each child at least once a week, during which he concentrates on a single portion of the child's reading which the child himself has selected and prepared for presentation. The conference is very important and no one is neglected, not even the gifted youngsters. It is a vital personal moment between the instructor and the student that generates a higher level of understanding and individualization. It is conceived as an opportunity to appraise strengths, difficulties, and next steps for the child. It is constructive and supportive of the youngsters' efforts and gains and provides essential clues for later instruction.

5. Reading instruction parallels the other aspect of the program and is generally handled in small groups. This instruction systematically extends reading skills rather than leaving them to chance.

6. Children who have read the same book may meet with one another in small groups to discuss it and may share what they have read with the entire class. This avoids the false audience situation which exists when a child reads to other children all of whom have the same book.

7. In order to avoid a bottleneck resulting from the necessity for the teacher to personally check each book, the system makes use of pupil checkers. The first child to complete a book is checked by the teacher and becomes the pupil checker of that book. The name of the pupil checker is recorded in the book file.

The individualized reading program aids considerably in moving the program away from the lock-step character of older forms of instruction. It makes reading a more personal act, for the choice of material is an expression of the self. When a pupil commits himself to a piece of material there is more incentive and opportunity for optimal growth, and the love of books and reading is best nurtured when loved books are read.[21] Attitudes toward the program are more favorable, for everything is not only more individualized but is also more fun. And perhaps of even greater importance is the fact that the assumption by the child of more personal responsibility for his own success is a distinctive contribution to the development of maturity and self-direction.

Reducing the Task to Size. In recent years the reading teacher has begun to reach out and assume responsibility for a longer and longer list of mental functions. Recalling, comprehending, relating facts, making inferences, drawing conclusions, interpreting, and predicting outcomes have all been appropriated and, as Moffett says, tucked under the skirts of reading.[22] These mental activities are general properties of thinking that apply to many areas of human endeavor and have no more necessary connection with reading than with other aspects of intelligent living. Vocabulary building and concept formation are also placed in the domain of the reading teacher, although neither of them has any necessary connection either. Even subject matter reading, as in the social studies and science, is interpreted as requiring additional skills that fall under its responsibility, when in reality what is difficult for the young reader are the vocabulary, the concepts, and the experiential background, all of which can be learned without ever opening a book. Moffett contends that if a reader can translate print into speech with normal intonation and still fails to key in and grasp the idea, then he has no reading problem—he has a thinking problem.[23]

The situation is comparable to what took place in the social studies when curriculum guides began to proliferate with an

[21] Jeanette Veatch, *Reading in the Elementary School* (New York: Ronald Press, 1966), p. 5.

[22] Moffett, *A Student-Centered Language Arts Program*, pp. 16–17.

[23] Moffett, *op. cit.*, p. 16.

expanding list of objectives. Ernest Horn reported in 1937 that one junior high school course of study began with forty-seven mimeographed pages of objectives and American history teachers claimed fourteen hundred different objectives. With tongue in cheek he suggested for the social studies a single objective cast in the form of a biblical injunction:

> *Finally, brethren, whatsoever things are true, whatsoever things are honest, whatsoever things are just, whatsoever things are lovely, whatsoever things are of good report, if there be any virtue, and if there be any praise, think on these things.*

The development of reading as an aspect of the program can continue its omnivorous process of assuming the complex responsibilities of other areas of intelligent living until it reaches the point that the entire curriculum is reading. On the other hand, it may suspend its process of appropriation long enough to take a sober look at itself, and attempt to reduce its responsibilities to something that is more realistically conceived. It is the latter which seems to represent a more reasonable path, and the movement is overdue.

Chapter

Evaluating
and
Reporting
Progress

14

Evaluating
and
Reporting
Progress

This aspect of the curriculum is a very powerful determinant in what children learn as well as how they feel about what they learn. In class after class a sensitive student who cares about his school marks will try to key in upon what he thinks will be asked upon a test. The more he cares, *the more he will tend to exclude what he really needs and wants to know in favor of what he thinks he will be required to give back later.* The net result is that learning environments which emphasize tests and grades tragically circumscribe the quality of his education. One can hardly imagine a more devastating way to distort and limit the freedom to learn and to corrupt the general process of becoming the unique self that one wishes to become.

Some intelligent students choose to beat the system and superficially learn many banalities which they will later produce upon cue. Other intelligent students reject the entire mindless process and, as a consequence, acquire a poor school record. Such students are often more capable and promising than their teachers. Still others struggle desperately to survive the system. They suffer damage to the self-image and are frequently driven to cheating and other forms of subterfuge. The remaining students may see it as such a stacked deck or monu-

mental farce that they chuck their education and become drop-
outs. There is no other aspect of the curriculum in which
inhumanity to youngsters is so institutionalized and condoned.
Is this what America wants for its children?

The essential purpose of a system of evaluating and reporting progress is to provide information and a process that will
be helpful in furthering the development of the child. The
key criterion to apply to any given form of marking and reporting, then, is whether or not it facilitates this purpose. The
chief approaches to evaluating and reporting seem to be em-
bodied in a relatively small number of types and a cursory examination of each of them may be helpful in providing
perspective on this vital matter. Such a review may also be
useful in pointing up clues to some of the more beneficial factors.

The Percentage Method. This method graded a child on the
basis of 100 being a possible and perfect score. Thus, a child
might get 85 in arithmetic, 90 in geography and 99 in health.
Relatively few schools use this method today. Some felt it an
act of hypocrisy to pretend that they could appraise with such
accuracy that there was a discernible difference, for example,
between a 74 and a 75. Others felt that it was impossible to
compare and equate a score in one area of the curriculum
with that of another. For instance, is an 85 in mathematics
comparable to an 85 in art? Some pointed out that the act of
quantification was in itself out of line with major purposes of
the curriculum. That is to say that the curriculum was seeking
to further personal development and many forms of desired
growth could not presently be quantified even if it could be
established as desirable to do so. The criticism and objections
were sufficiently strong to give rise to a different technique,
and many schools seemed to move toward the five-point scale.

The Scale Technique. In this technique, there was a tendency
to use grades such as A, B, C, D, E. The grades were competitively derived and were to be based on what was known as the
normal curve. The largest number of students (approximately
⅔ of a given group) were to receive the C, or average grade.

The grade B represented work that was definitely above average. Approximately the same number of students that received a B were also to receive a D, which was the grade representing work definitely below average. The distinctly superior grade was A and the failing grade was E, with again an approximately equal number of students to receive the highest and the lowest grade.

A major criticism of the scale method centered around the obscurities upon which it was based. What did the grade mean? Was it, for instance, based upon achievement, or effort, or attitude, or growth, or some combination thereof? This controversy was never adequately resolved. Therefore, the A did not mean the same thing from school to school nor from teacher to teacher. There is even considerable reason to believe that A's given by the same person do not have similar meanings. This weakness is an inherent aspect of the technique, for the letter grade is simply a symbol of the multiple aspects of achievement which it hopes to represent but cannot adequately convey. Too much meaning has been packed into the symbols. Grouping multiple meanings and attempting to interpret them by symbols causes a loss of identities. The meanings are thus jumbled together, blurred, averaged, and obscured. The symbol is glorified and meanings as they relate to any specific or significant aspects of the child's personality and growth are lost in the process. No one knows when he looks at a letter grade what it tells about a particular child that will be valuable in furthering his development; but more curiously, so few seem to care. One of the anomalies of the current educational scene is the degree to which parents uncritically accept a reporting device which fails to report. One can only conclude that this is an area of the curriculum in which a substantial number of people are uninformed.

The Modified Scale. Some of the schools that abandoned the five-point scale changed to a modified version in the form of plus ($+$), check ($\sqrt{}$), and minus ($-$). A plus ordinarily indicated very satisfactory work, a check meant that the work was passing but needed to be improved, and a minus was given for work that was unsatisfactory. There were many variations of the plan. One variation that was commonly used was the S, I, and U. S indicated work that was satisfactory, I indicated the need for improvement, and U meant unsatisfactory or failing work.

The modified scale represented a big point of departure from the scale *in the sense that the grades were not competitively derived.* Under this plan, children tended to be graded in terms of their ability to perform. Thus, no matter how little a child learned he was given a satisfactory mark if he had done as well as he could do. On the other hand, a child whose ability was greater and who was not achieving as much as he could, might receive an I or U.

This was difficult for parents to understand, for under such a system in a graded school it was possible for a slow child working up to ability to receive S for each marking period throughout the year and still fail the grade. Conversely, it was possible for a bright child working beneath his level of ability to receive unsatisfactory marks each grading period and still be promoted. Something was obviously wrong with the communication. The evaluative symbols did not mean what the recipients thought they meant. The reporting device was again failing to report.

The Narrative Report. One of the more recent forms of reporting to parents is the narrative report. With this method, the teacher has an opportunity to write an intimate and personalized account of the child's growth. He is free to select and interpret any information which would be constructive and helpful in furthering the education of the child. Both positive and negative factors may be woven into the account. Items of information appearing in the report are chosen by virtue of being true, being important or significant with respect to interpreting the stage of development of a particular child, and being useful to the parents in increasing their understanding of the child's progress as well as their own role in facilitating the process. The report usually begins and ends on a positive note. It attempts, within the bounds of professional discretion, to provide the *kinds of information parents want to know.* It may indicate specific ways in which the child can improve and specific ways in which the parents may assist in the undertaking. The method is directly keyed to the factor of child growth and to the basic function which marking and reporting as an aspect of the curriculum should serve. It is dynamic enough as a practice to be as effective as the person using it. Its potentiality is limited only by the understanding and skill of teachers themselves. In the hands of a person who has a deep understanding of his children and the power to communicate his thoughts, it can be a highly personalized and extremely effective reporting device.

Some critics say of the narrative report that it is too time-consuming to be practical. This claim has no merit. Anyone who can organize and write down his thoughts can develop the report as quickly and easily as he can average out and arrive at letter grades. Even if it required more time, however, it would be considerably better to have one good report each semester than two or three which have little to communicate. Others say that teachers cannot write well enough to use the narrative report. This statement is too incredible to dignify with an answer. Still others say that the teacher does not know enough about his individual children to write a report about them as individuals. It is true that if one has no information to convey, then a method of communication is unnecessary. Any teacher whose thoughts are that barren should be excused not only from writing the report, but from masquerading as a teacher as well.

The Planned Parent Conference. The planned parent conference is similar in philosophy and intent to the narrative report, but sets out to do the job in a face-to-face relationship rather than by note-writing. Such a conference is usually scheduled in advance so that the parent as well as the teacher may plan for it. Half an hour is ordinarily set aside in order that it may proceed in an unhurried atmosphere, and classes may be dismissed in order that the job can be given priority attention. The teacher has actual specimens of the child's work to be discussed with the parents, and the well-handled conference becomes a reciprocal process, with the teacher receiving as well as giving valuable information relative to the child.

The planned parent conference has certain inherent advantages over the narrative report. A face-to-face relationship makes possible a spirit and degree of cooperation that can hardly be engendered in any other way. *Furthermore, the understandings can go beyond what were held by either party prior to the conference, for the discussion may provide new clues and stimulate ideas and insights that did not exist before the conference was held.* In addition, there is a communication advantage. Concrete evidence of the child's work offers one communication advantage. Another is afforded by the give and take of discussion which enables a perceptive teacher to reinterpret and reemphasize an idea that may not be clearly understood, to answer questions stimulated by the information, and to otherwise more nearly create the exact shades of understanding desired.

The Concept of Essential Functions. This concept is similar to the approach used in identifying significant elements in grouping. It seeks to rise above the debate of a specific issue such as competitive grading and to delineate the major functions to be performed by this aspect of the program. Seven essential functions are interpreted as being necessary in order to perform the role that evaluating and reporting should serve. These seven essential functions constitute a powerful set of criteria. If the system used by a given school is adequately performing each of the seven, it has achieved a marked degree of excellence in its approach. Each of the functions will be described and interpreted in the discussion which follows.

The Information Function

The system, whatever its form, should stress the kinds of information about children that parents want to know. Obviously the information should be within the bounds of professional discretion and should be selected so as to be helpful rather than harmful. The parent, however, needs and deserves to be informed about many aspects of his child's work. Being informed means being in a position to help the school maximize its influence and makes the essential relationship between

schools and parents a more effective partnership. The reporting system might reasonably include information such as the
following:

1. The child's feeling and attitude toward school
2. His relationships with others
3. His personal strengths and gifts
4. His work habits
5. His specific progress
6. His present deficiencies
7. The reasons for his deficiencies
8. The degree to which he can be expected to improve
9. The ways in which the parents can help

This aspect of the reporting system would be strengthened
by working directly with parents to determine what they wish
to know. Such information is not conveyed in reporting systems
which use the percentage method, the scale method, or the
modified scale. *Any information desired, however, can be
reflected in either the narrative report or the planned parent
conference.*

The Individualization Function

The system, whatever its form, should lend itself to the description and interpretation of a unique human being. The uniqueness of human personality is largely an unchallenged concept.
Almost everyone accepts the fact that this child who is being
reported upon is like no other person in the world. A report
on the child, therefore, should reflect his uniqueness. It should
direct itself specifically and personally to his individuality and
portray it as it is revealed in his school. *It should strive to be
genuine and present the truth.* It should portray weaknesses
as well as strengths. It should present growth as well as barriers to growth—and all of this should be developed in an
individual setting *so that it is about this child that the report
speaks and no other.* Consider the following descriptive report
on a fifth grade girl:

Nancy is one of the best students I have ever had. On her recent achievement tests she scored at the eighth grade level. One of the unusual aspects of her achievement is that it is so well-rounded. She is performing well above grade level in all of her subjects, and yet, she has time to enter and enjoy all of our extra class activities. She seems well-organized in her study time. She has strong powers of concentration on whatever she undertakes. She thinks unusually well for a ten-year-old girl, and her ideas are likely to be original and imaginative.

She is extremely well-liked by her classmates. This is partially because she is thoughtful and considerate of others, and partially because she has won their respect. She never pushes herself forward. She seems to have a very wholesome and positive attitude toward school and toward life. She is a cooperative child and a tremendous asset to our room.

The school could use a report card that informed Nancy's parents she had made A's in all of her subjects and an A in conduct, but the personal qualities of Nancy as a unique and distinctive child would be lost in the process.

The Self-evaluation Function

A reporting system, whatever its form, should make some provision for each child's evaluation of himself. Some teachers handle this by holding personal conferences with each child prior to the teacher's conference with the parents. This conference is planned with the children in advance so that they may consciously work toward it and prepare for it. As a result of such planning, they may keep samples of their own work and records of their progress. They may even keep a notebook in which they jot down ideas they want to remember for use in the conference.

Each child may have a time to talk privately with his teacher about his own work. He suggests ideas which he feels should be brought to the attention of his parents at the time of their conference. He tells what progress he feels he has made since the last report. He makes suggestions about specimens of his work which can be shown to his parents, and he may suggest also his plans for further improvement.

This can be a very rich experience for a child and a powerful means of motivation. It encourages pupil responsibility and heightens his awareness of the purposes of school and his progress and shortcomings in relation to those purposes. Often it produces a desire in children to make better use of their school time. It is also a rich source of information to the teacher. She has a golden opportunity to look inside the child at such moments and to better understand his standards, his anxieties, and his concept of himself. In addition, it tends to draw a child and his teacher closer together in the undertaking of a common task.

The Communication Function

The system, whatever its form, should be able to *communicate* the desired information to the parents concerned. This means that the information must actually *be conveyed*. Such information cannot be conveyed by percentages or by letter grades. A few parents may actually want to know *only* how their child has performed in competition with other children and may think that the percentage or letter grade method can do the job. This, however, is rarely the case, for very few teachers grade alike. Strang has indicated this marking variance in her reference to a study conducted by the NEA.[1] In this study the same arithmetic paper was given to 111 different teachers to grade. The scores given to the paper, however, ranged all the way from 21 to 88. Even on such a narrow and limited responsibility as stating the relative standing of a child, percentages and letter grades are inadequate. Most parents want to know more than that, and a descriptive report or a conference approach *can interpret whatever it is desirable and possible for them to know.* If a fourth grade child is the poorest reader in

[1] Ruth Strang, *How to Report Pupil Progress* (Chicago: Science Research Associates, 1955), p. 4.

her class, information such as the following may need to be given to the parents:

> *Sharon is reading at second grade level. She cannot yet independently master new words and seems tense and overanxious in the reading lessons. At the present time we are giving her a rather simple and interesting type of story content and are attempting to build up her word attack skills. She is just now beginning to relax and show some confidence in her work. It is extremely important to avoid pressuring her or criticizing her about her reading at this time.*

The above information needs to be communicated, for it may make an important difference in what happens to the child. Such information can be *transmitted,* however, only in a school which uses one of the more personalized types of report.

The Cooperative-Action Function

The results of the evaluation and reporting of progress should lead to additional constructive action. Out of the conference with the child and the subsequent session with his parents there should be ideas which can be used to improve the quality of a child's experiences. Some leads will come from the child himself in his preconference. These ideas should be honored if at all possible. They are the seeds of a developing sense of self-direction to which the curriculum should give a constant priority emphasis. Some of the leads will also grow out of the parent conference. As indicated earlier, one of the unique strengths of the parent conference is that it may generate ideas and insights which neither the parent nor the teacher had before the conference was held. The teacher is then in a position to put the pieces together and to coordinate the efforts of all concerned. The proposed action may be quite simple, such as the temporary removal of pressure; or more involved, such as the change of teachers and rooms. Simple or complex, however, the action is keyed to the basic notion of improving for a given child the personal quality of his learning environment.

The Fair-Play Function

The reporting system should be one in which every child has an approximately equal chance to succeed. Children are captives in the elementary school. They have no choice as to whether or not they come to school; they are forced to attend. Even though they do not go by choice, many of them have a fine attitude toward school and do their very best to succeed. There are still many schools, however, that fail children who do their very best because their best is not good enough. This is very unjust. If children are forced to attend a school which sets standards they cannot possibly reach, it is morally wrong to fail them because they did not succeed. If in a professional school of medicine or law the instructors wish to set standards which many students cannot reach, that is a different matter. No one is required to be a physician or a lawyer. Such students are there by choice and can leave in the same manner. The elementary child, however, has no such choice. His environment is by necessity a specially designed and protected environment. The society which forces him to spend his formative years in such an environment has an obligation to create the environment in such a way that his efforts can produce success. *His best should always be good enough, and it is a mark of ignorance and brutality to have it otherwise.* Both the percentage method and the scale method permit such brutality; neither the narrative report or the planned parent conference allow it to occur.

Perhaps much of the cruelty that takes place in this regard is thoughtless rather than deliberate. The American citizen has an almost innate passion for justice. He is quick to sense unfairness and is always rooting for the underdog regardless of how mangy and undeserving it may be. Yet, he is likely not only to accept but to approve letter grades which reward the "haves" and degrade the "have-nots." He would not tolerate a track event in which the swiftest runners were moved up closer to the tape, and the slower runners were moved farther back. This he would recognize as a grotesque injustice. *Yet he tolerates it every day in the schools, for the informed teacher knows that some children are at the A level of achievement in a subject before the instruction even begins.* Others are so far back in achievement in the subject that even though they progress faster than their more favored friends they will still get a poorer grade. Fair play can be reflected in the report only by being sensitive to such facts as (1) background, (2) starting point, (3) native endowment, and (4) achievement in relation to ability to achieve. The older systems of evaluating and reporting are not designed to make allowance for such considerations. Only in the narrative or conference approach is there sufficient latitude to exercise the function of fair play.

Some will say that the idea under discussion is too soft and unrealistic. Many believe that failure is good for children and that it helps mature them so that they may grow into seasoned adults. This is partially true. Failure *can be a seasoning or maturing experience* and should not be eliminated from the elementary school. The nature of the elementary school is such, however, that failure should occur *only under circumstances over which it is possible for the child to exercise control.* If he can do it and does not, then failure may properly and justly apply. To fail a child, however, for not achieving a task which is impossible for him to achieve is senseless and cruel. Such failure is not realistic, and instead of maturing a child it causes him to harden and withdraw. He learns to dislike learning, and a mortal blow has been struck at his desire as well as his capacity to grow. That is why the fair-play function must find expression in any system striving to achieve an excellent approach.

The Standards Function

A system of marking and reporting should reflect and maintain the high standards of the school. Many sincere patrons of the school would be disturbed about the philosophy that was enunciated about fair play in the preceding discussion. They feel that accepting achievement which is relatively low, simply because it is the best one can do, will lower standards and detract from the quality of the program. This is a thoughtful observation and a legitimate concern. Standards are levels of expectation or achievement indicating degrees of acceptability or excellence. Will they be harmed or strengthened by the fair-play concept?

The essential meaning of the fair-play concept is that no one should be expected or required to do something that he cannot do. Conversely, it is legitimate within the fair-play concept to expect and require students to do as well as they can. This is precisely the point at which the concept of standards moves in. If the children in a given school are doing as well as they can, then standards are as high as they can go. How can standards be higher than this? The only way to raise them beyond such a level would require reselecting (perhaps from brighter parents) the children who will attend school. Expecting children to do only as well as they can and reflecting this in the system of evaluating and reporting would seem to be a method of strengthening rather than weakening standards. It establishes a wholesome climate for achievement. It more adequately challenges the gifted as well as the slow. It is realistic as well as humane and would seem to be in the best interests of all concerned.

Point of View. The curricular purpose of a system of evaluating and reporting progress has been interpreted as the providing of information and a process which is beneficial to the continued development of the child. In something of a chronological sequence, elementary schools have tried the percentage method, the scale method, the modified scale, the narrative report, and the planned parent conference.

This search for desirable practices in evaluating and reporting has attempted to rise above a more restricted issue such as competitive grading and has identified *functions to be performed* by this aspect of the curriculum. Seven such essential functions have been described and interpreted. If one applies these functions to the older methods which tend to be favored by parents, he finds that *those methods are incapable of adequately performing a single one of the essential functions.* This is one of the interesting anomalies of the current scene. For people who sincerely seek excellence in their schools will, in this aspect of the curriculum, uncritically accept a reporting system which fails to report.

Humaneness and excellence is reflected in schools which develop a system that can adequately perform the full scope of the task. A qualitative approach, therefore, is indicated by the degree to which the system:

1. Provides the kinds of information parents should know
2. Describes and interprets a unique human being
3. Makes provision for each child's evaluation of himself
4. Communicates accurately what it seeks to convey
5. Points up desirable forms of cooperative action
6. Reflects the concept of fair play to all the children concerned
7. Maintains the high standards of the school

The skillfully conducted parent conference can adequately provide for *all of the above functions.* Such a conference can convey in an open and friendly setting a great deal of useful information about this unique child who is the focus of the deliberations. The information is highly personalized, highly relevant, and sensitively selected for its total beneficial impact. All interested parties can cooperatively converge at this moment in their mutual goal of understanding the circumstances of this child's school living and improving the quality of his experiences. It is, at its best, a uniquely effective and humanistic process.

Chapter

Evaluative
Reflections

15

Chapter
Evaluative
Reflections

15

This is a moment to look back and engage in sensitive speculation about whether the thoughts have led where they sought to go. The remarks are evaluative in nature, but the term is used with some reluctance for so many people think of evaluation as an impressive array of tests and measuring devices. Somewhere along the way they have developed a feeling that they cannot trust their own perceptions and that the most reliable resources lie *outside themselves*.

Harry Broudy tells an interesting fable about two rather uneducated brothers who owned horses and thought that they had a problem in knowing which horse belonged to which brother.[1] To solve their problem they decided to knick the ear of one horse, but some predatory creature knicked the ear of the other so that this no longer set them apart. Therefore they docked the tail of one and this worked until the other backed into a buzz saw. In desperation they agreed to settle the matter once and for all by measuring their steeds. This they did and discovered that the white horse was two inches taller than the black one. One wonders how much of the research and testing of the past has told us that the white horse was taller

[1] Harry S. Broudy, "Remarks at the Twenty-Sixth Biennial Convocation," *Kappa Delta Pi Record*, October 1968, p. 1.

than the black horse or that "further research needs to be done in this area."

The late and beloved Kimball Wiles once said that he could simply walk through a school and tell a great deal about what kind of an environment it was. Indeed he could and his perceptions were probably more important than those of the individuals who had tested it. Most sensitive and informed educators can do this, but they are unlikely to discuss it for they have been conditioned to feel that their subjective impressions and views are not quite respectable. Let us say right here and now at the beginning of this discussion that such views are not only respectable—they are indispensable. How can one create a more humane environment without giving primacy to the perceptions, the feelings, and the views of those who most intimately experience it?

Subjective evaluation has an additional appeal in the sense that those involved use, and consequently place value upon, their own capacities for sensitive assessment. This not only enhances the individual but strengthens him as well. In his involvement he may decide that any given curriculum practice which may have been highly endorsed as a humanistic factor is simply failing to make the intended contribution. If so, the practice is expendable and gives way to a more promising approach conceived by the participants. This is very important and should contribute to a goal of *more personal and creative implementation*. The affected parties may also decide that the stated goals themselves are off target and need redefining or new direction. The process of doing this heightens the awareness of those who are so engaged and is a positive element in moving toward a more person-oriented program.

Looking Back

Although the expression has become almost painfully trite, one does evaluate in terms of the goals sought. The personal-social goals tentatively identified in Chapter 1 were broad overarching concepts that were thought to be highly important in creating a more humanistic school. Each of them was believed to be highly relevant to the larger task, compatible with one another, specific enough to provide concerted emphasis toward the school desired, and globular enough to avoid prescription and rigidity. Each is briefly examined here in an effort to look back and determine whether or not the proposals that have been made seem to adequately provide for their expression and nurture. It should be recalled at this time that no given curriculum practice was required to contribute to all of the goals, but was appropriately expected to make a discernible contribution to at least one of them. Some do better than that and make a multiple contribution. This is due to the general desirability of the practice, as well as to the interlocking nature of the goals.

Achieving Intellectuality. Many significant provisions for the development of intellectuality have been made in the overall framework sketched out for a humanistic program. The multiage model of the nongraded school was interpreted as offering a more natural opportunity for children to work at their ability levels without some of the emotional penalties and difficulties associated with crossing grade lines. Approaches to giftedness were presented in terms of a basic concept of developing the giftedness within all children, rather than a chosen few bearing the label "gifted child." The difference here is almost incalculable in terms of the total benefit to the individual as well as to society as a whole.

Within the areas of curriculum and instruction there was a consistent effort to open up the teaching-learning situation for the functioning of higher levels of intellectual activity. Bloom's taxonomy of educational objectives in the cognitive domain lists those intellectual functions in the following order of descending importance: (1) evaluation, (2) synthesis, (3) analysis, (4) application, (5) comprehension, (6) knowledge.[2]

Many of the illustrative suggestions were focused upon the higher rungs of Bloom's cognitive ladder. In mathematics conceptual devices were endorsed because of their potentiality for developing greater understanding or comprehension. Func-

[2] Benjamin S. Bloom, ed., *Taxonomy of Educational Objectives: Handbook I: Cognitive Domain* (New York: David McKay, 1956), p. 18.

tional application of mathematical concepts was stressed in the technique of using practical problems related to school and personal living. Inquiry strategies in science constituted an excellent example of the kind of curriculum practice that makes an outstanding contribution to higher levels of intellectual development. *Knowledge* is an important part of the process in observing and studying the science episode. *Comprehension* and *analysis* are stressed through the personal involvement and responsibility of the learners in selectively eliciting additional essential information. *Synthesis* is reflected in formulating a tenable hypothesis and *evaluation* is stressed throughout the process as well as being further enhanced by playing back a recording of the inquiry sessions so that students may rethink their role in the undertaking.

Throughout the instructional areas there was a deliberate but sensible stress upon intellectual potency in the context of *providing the incentive to learn* as well as *developing the power to learn*. In spelling, for instance, the basic core was interpreted and recommended, but greater emphasis was placed upon helping each child master a way to learn new words on his own. The teaching of reading was endorsed in the sense of building upon and relating to what he already knew so that it was natural and attractive to move from that point forward; but, within that approach, initial steps to develop early independence in word perception skills was recognized as the road to a more complete development.

There were many additional intellectually focused suggestions, but the central idea is that the curriculum as envisioned and projected was hospitable to the full play of intellectual development of the learner *in a manner which is appropriate to children*. The intent was to create a setting in which the intellectual powers of young learners might have outlet and nurture in an interesting and nonthreatening environment. The school of tomorrow was interpreted as a total fluid bundle of resources from which each child could draw what he needed, when he needed it, without any senseless restrictions being placed upon him because of age or grade level. All of this, however, was provided in a natural and sensible way without the application of misguided adult concepts of rigor. For the development of intellectuality in the child was conceived as more of a gentle than a rigorous process, more of a quest than a race, more a loosening than a tamping of the soil, and more an opening of the doors of the mind than the pages of an encyclopedia.

Nurturing Creativity. This was one of the central characteristics of the point of view throughout the interpretation. In earlier days this vital aspect of personal development was too narrowly construed. A more productive approach requires that it be nourished throughout the program whenever and wherever the opportunities for being creative may occur. Weaving it appropriately through an expanded portion of school endeavor makes it more of an approach to life and enables it to serve as a conceptual cradle for the rest of the program.

Contributions to its general nurture seem possible in a number of significant ways. One is through a deliberate attempt to achieve what was described as environmental richness. This is influenced by the quality and variety of materials and media and, even more importantly, by a psychological climate that encourages a wide range of ideas and approaches from both children and teachers. This is an example of a general condition or factor which applies to all areas of the curriculum.

Seeking in many areas of school living to heighten the senses themselves is another provocative form of general beneficial influence. A technological society tends to blunt the senses and detract from the quality of being fully alive. It is a personal tragedy for one to suffer such biological erosion that he can walk in the woods without hearing the birds sing, or drive home and look at a setting sun without seeing the sunset, or take a walk after a spring rain without feeling the freshness of the earth. Such a shriveling of the organism is antithetical to a humanistic school. The curriculum must actively counteract this and help to preserve this vital aspect of being a person. For the vigorous, alert, vibrantly alive individual has all of his antennae working. His full sensory equipment is in contact with the wonders of the world, and this enhances the degree to which he can be creative as well as achieve intellectual development.

The desired program was conceived as one which places a very special value upon imagination. It encourages such responses from children, teaches them that this mysterious quality of the mind is a precious gift, and helps them to understand its relationship to the hope for a better tomorrow.

All such general factors were beamed at the areas of the curriculum to enrich them and provide greater personal satisfaction and depth. Social studies then becomes a process of more gracious and creative living, science a way of personally searching out and appropriating some of life's basic meanings, and all aspects of the program reflect an effort to achieve a more creative interaction of the self with the manner in which one can best develop his powers to learn.

Helping to Forge Character. A beneficial impact upon character was interpreted as one of the special obligations of the envisioned school. Several of the recommended curriculum practices were thought to be beneficial in aiding students to grow in the desire and ability to apply morality to their living. One of the major approaches that was believed to be appropriate was role playing. This approach focused upon practical situations confronting youngsters in which it was necessary for them to make moral decisions. The reality practice skillfully provided for a shifting of roles and enactees in order to bring out a rich array of the children's own thoughts and feelings. Out of such dimensions of their own living students have an opportunity to weigh their views and those of their peers. Adult manipulation is scrupulously avoided and the learners themselves explore the options, consider the probable consequences, and make their decisions. It is a learner-centered process which again reflects a high measure of faith in the capacities and developing wisdom of the young.

The understandings that emerge from this activity have a practical outlet in the concept of using the classroom itself as a laboratory for social living. Here the students can focus upon the realities of their own situation and strive to improve it.

They have a chance to try their wings and attempt to make their own social microcosm a more worthy and ennobling experience. The approach may utilize rich moments from the nation's past, the influence by example of the teacher, and the positive moral influences of the culture itself. But the child's self-active role in it all is prized and encouraged. He grows in a setting in which he is allowed to think, to act, to make some inevitable mistakes, and to emerge from the piling up of such experiences as a more seasoned and wiser person.

Creating a Humane Environment. The entire thrust of this book has been one of moving toward a more authentic and humane environment. A cold and impersonal school may be condoned in some societies, but it is not acceptable for the children of America. The school as envisioned is not one of sentimental slush. It may be firm with its children, discipline them, and hold them accountable for their acts. But beneath it all it will love them, gently guide them, and free them to fulfill their destiny.

This paramount consideration of being humane was conspicuous in the proposals relating to grouping children in such a manner as to expand their opportunities for development and yet protect the self-image. It was equally conspicuous in formulating sensitively construed guides to an effective system of evaluating and reporting progress. The overall proposals for curriculum design, flexible organization, and faculty utilization were all conceived with the humanistic factor being accorded primary consideration.

In retrospect, therefore, the thoughts seemed to faithfully pursue the ends sought. A considerable array of conceptually organized ideas were brought together for consideration as a tentative formulation of a humanistic program. Some of those ideas will work and some may not, but the participants who embark upon such a noble undertaking will build upon and improve the suggestions so that whatever emerges can better serve those who are most intimately involved. The image presented here was intended to reflect a spirit of gentleness along with its muscle and a quality of the heart as well as the mind. If the concepts are thoughtfully and creatively implemented they will help transform the learning environment into a more humanistic school.

A Look Ahead

Man stands poised upon the planet earth preparing for one of his grandest adventures—moving out into space to explore his galaxy. He looks at the stars and knows now that it is possible for him to reach out and go where no man has gone before. And he will surely find other life forms, some of which are more highly developed than him, and some that are not as far along the way. It is an overwhelmingly exciting chapter in his life and part of his unfolding destiny. But the undertaking, splendid as it may be, is basically flawed; for his grievous destruction of his own mother earth and his inhumanities to his fellow men do not constitute a state of civilization which he should dare to export.

Along with his preparations for this great adventure, he must make corresponding efforts for an even more splendid achievement—that of improving the quality of his own existence. He must restore the purity of his environment, and he must work in such harmony with nature that she can continue the miracle of life. He must deal more understandingly, effectively, and lovingly with all men and somehow conquer war, poverty, human bondage, and other destructive forces. If he can more nearly achieve the basic virtues of truth, justice, wisdom, and love then he can move out among the stars with the pride and confidence of taking into the galaxy a positive life force.

Can he do such things? Perhaps, but one should not underestimate the enormity of the task. The hour is later than he knew and the difficulties compound even as he now shows a belated recognition of his peril. An ecological disaster draws ever nearer, and the distorted furies from accumulated brutalizations of the human spirit smoulder ominously throughout the land. Difficult though it may be to contemplate, man would not be the first major species to become extinct—only the first to fashion his own destruction. There is still hope that all that is most treasured in life and human values can survive if men accord them their rightful priority and mount their best efforts to that end. And if this deepening crisis is successfully resolved, humanistic schools as they are eventually conceived will play a significant role in the achievement.

Index

Accomplishment, criterion of, daily programming, 92-93

Action-response groups, using, language usage, 247-249

Action programs, curriculum design, 41-42

Activity designs, 22-25

Administration, flexible and enlightened, 5-7

Admissions, flexible, multidimensional grouping, 135-137

Aides, teacher, 80-82, 84

Analysis, 295

Anderson, Robert, 71

Appropriateness, criterion of, content selection, 123-124

Areas level, teacher's professional role, 116

Articulation, curriculum design, 42-43

Assistants, academic or technical, 78-79

Authority, discipline factor, 106-108

Bailey, M. H., 270

Balance, criterion of, daily programming, 90-91

Balanced internal grouping, 138-140

Barnard, Barney, 125-126

Bay City Program, 80

Beauty, creativity nurtured by, 180-182

Beberman, Max, 226

Blackwood, Paul E., 202

Bloom, Benjamin S., 294

Blough, Glenn O., 202

Bossard, James H., 141

Broudy, Harry S., 292

Bruner, J. S., 207

Burk, Frederick, 168

California Test of Mental Maturity, 153

Chall, Jeanne, 269

Character, developing, 11-13, 297-298

Character education, 12

Children, concern for, continuing, 3-4

Chronological age, admission by, 136-137

Circlometer, 229, 232

Classroom, laboratory for social living, 187-188; self-contained, 66, 67-71

Clymer, Theodore, 269-270

Collins, Michael, 121

Columbia University Council for Research in the Social Sciences, 100

Communication function, evaluating and reporting progress, 284-285

Comprehension, 295

Conceptual devices, use of, in mathematics, 230-232

Conduct, rules of, discipline factor, 110-111

Cone of experience, concept of, 129

Content, improving, 114-132; life, 128-131; priority, in curriculum design, 35-36; selection of, see Content selection; simulation, 131-132; teacher's professional role, 115-116

Content selection, criteria of, 116-127; appropriateness, 123-124; difficulty, 121-122; interest, 125-127; maximum return, 118-120; quality, 124-125; shortage, 120-121; survival, 122-123; universality, 118; utility, 117-118

70 71 72 73 74   7 6 5 4 3 2 1